The chief administrative officer? A legal adviser? A mere keeper of the records? What is the true role of the English Town Clerk who for centuries has been the leading official in the country's great towns and cities. Here, for the first time, is a volume which surveys in detail his duties, and the problems and opportunities facing him in this day and age.

The Town Clerk is the council's leading spokesman in their contacts with the outside world—the public, Members of Parliament, and government departments. The Town Clerk is also the co-ordinator who harmonizes the work of the various departments and helps the council to ensure that their activities are combined in a consistent whole.

Good relations between the Town Clerk and the council and its committees are essential to efficient administration. The book discusses the Town Clerk's contribution from the preparation of committee agenda to his role in council meetings. Equally important are his relations with the council's leading members—the mayor, the committee chairmen, and the party leaders, and these, too, are vividly portrayed. These are the vital aspects of the practical daily functioning of the system on which the textbooks so seldom throw much light.

The author, T. E. Headrick, an American scholar, brings a fresh and detached view to the English local government scene with this illuminating study of the local council's chief officer.

THE TOWN CLERK
IN ENGLISH LOCAL GOVERNMENT

THE TOWN CLERK

IN ENGLISH
LOCAL GOVERNMENT

by

T. E. HEADRICK

Published for the
Royal Institute of Public Administration

GEORGE ALLEN & UNWIN LTD

LONDON

PRINTED IN GREAT BRITAIN
in 11 point Baskerville type
BY SIMSON SHAND LTD
LONDON, HERTFORD AND HARLOW

PREFACE

THE Town Clerk—to the ordinary foreign visitor he arouses a vision of a town scribe, an elderly gentleman who keeps the council minute book up-to-date; to the foreign student of government he inspires thoughts of a city manager, the energetic executive who has six buttons and the city's administration at his five fingertips. Both are wrong. The Town Clerk finds his place somewhere in the vast area between these two vague visions. Very simply, this book is an attempt to describe that place.

This book grew from a rather adventitious set of circumstances. From 1956 to 1958 I was a very fortunate beneficiary of a Fulbright scholarship to Oxford. My purpose for coming was to study British local government, to see how it worked, and to learn about those who ran it. After several months' study, the office of Town Clerk began to intrigue me, in part because I had been beset with the above misconceptions and in part because to me the proper blending of elected and professional people is the crucial issue facing democratic government today and at the local level this problem is posed in a most poignant form. The result was I undertook the preparation of a B.Litt. thesis on the Town Clerk. This book is a revision of that thesis.

This book is a broad survey. It attempts to encompass all Town Clerks, all 431 of them: Town Clerks in small towns, large cities, market towns, mill towns, seaside resorts, spas, metropolitan slums, metropolitan suburbs. Consequently it is a purely introductory study in which the broad generalization with all its inherent deficiencies is more frequent than the intimate detail.

The material was collected from a wide reading of published materials on local government and Town Clerks; a questionnaire which was distributed to all Town Clerks with the generous help of the Society of Town Clerks; personal interviews with Town Clerks, their chief officer colleagues, members of their staffs, councillors and ordinary citizens; and personal observation of Councils and their officers in their day-to-day and month-to-month operations.

No claim to exhaustive use of these sources is laid. For the

7

aim has been to portray a total impression—like the painter with his brush, not the photographer with his lens—without getting every wrinkle on the face, every hair in its place. To satisfy this aim the thoughtfully chosen sample has been a necessity.

On the other hand, I recognize some problems posed by confining this study to Town Clerks. For one, it has forced me to ignore their counterparts, the clerks of the county, urban district and rural district councils. This was largely a matter of convenience. Yet I do find the government of urban settlements more fascinating to study, more interesting examples of the interplay of government, groups and individuals.

But more importantly, there is the problem of placing this study in proper perspective. Town Clerks are local government officers. They are employed by councils to do their bidding and, at least according to law, may be dismissed if they fail to do it. Town Clerks are as well only one of a number of equal or nearly equal chief officers, and each of these chief officers has his own particular and exclusive responsibility to the council which employs him. As a result, to study the Town Clerk is to study only one wheel in what often is a large machine.

At the same time this is intended to be an exposition of the Town Clerk in English local government, not a study of English local government with the Town Clerk in it, nor a study of local government officers with the Town Clerk among them. Quite obviously a balance should be struck which permits an accurate description of the Town Clerk and his work but also does justice to the rest of the machine which must necessarily be left largely undescribed. The best I can do now is offer this as a warning and hope the reader finds a proper balance or remembers this warning.

I now turn to a very pleasant task. Very few people are able to produce a book without help from someone. At the same time very few owe as many debts as I. In preparation of this book information, advice and assistance came to me from many wonderful people.

People in local government—councillors and officials—were without exception most gracious and helpful and long-suffering. To single any from this fine group would be vastly unfair to those not mentioned, so my only course is to offer my sincerest appreciation to them collectively.

But there were people much closer to my work whom it would be unfair not to mention. There was my supervisor at Oxford—D. N. Chester, the Warden of Nuffield College—from whose acute criticism and perceptive mind I learned and benefited much. There was my tutor, Bryan Keith-Lucas, who introduced me to local government in England and to Town Clerks and who was ever ready to share with me his great academic and practical knowledge. There were Messrs F. M. G. Willson, J. F. Garner, R. J. Roddis and Raymond Nottage, all of whom read and criticized the manuscript in part or entirety. Their counsel was, and still is, deeply appreciated. At the same time this is not an attempt to shift the burden of error. The mistakes which remain are mine—wholly and exclusively mine.

I record my thanks to the Society of Town Clerks and to their Hon. Secretary, J. Waring Sainsbury, for their help with the preparation and distribution of the questionnaire. And I greatly appreciate the permission extended by the Hon. Editor of *Public Administration* to re-publish the portions of this book which first appeared in that journal.

To the managers of the Fulbright scholarships—in England, the United States Educational Commission in the United Kingdom and its Executive Director, Dr William Gaines—I owe a debt of gratitude I shall never be able to repay. They arranged for me to come to England and to Oxford and so amply provided the wherewithal for enjoying two most delightful and valuable years. Whatever may be the merit or usefulness of this book to others, if any, or of this study to me, it will never compare with the benefits of studying in a foreign country. Only then can one appreciate what unites and divides men of different nations. I richly applaud the farsighted people who conceived this programme and the diligent people who are now working to make it successful.

Both of my typists, Mrs Donna Stavig and Mrs Etha Westman, performed excellent jobs under difficult conditions. But for their fine work, this would still be some illegible scratchings upon a pile of foolscap sheets.

And finally, I must register my deep-felt thanks to my wife

who has endured all the trials of research and writing and experienced few of the joys. Her interest and enthusiasm have been a never-ending source of encouragement.

T. E. H.
San Francisco, California
Thanksgiving Day, 1961

CONTENTS

CHAPTER I

THE TOWN CLERK:
A BRIEF LOOK AT HIS PAST

THE office of Town Clerk, it is said, is an ancient and honourable one. To probe deeply into this antiquity is neither within the purpose nor competence of the writer. On the other hand, to dismiss the work and activities of the early Town Clerks without mention would be to ignore a great deal which still has relevance today. Indeed the Town Clerk, like so many British political institutions, is the product of a gentle evolution, a gradual transformation to meet the needs and demands of each period of history. This being so, to compare the fifteenth or eighteenth or nineteenth century Town Clerk with his counterpart of the twentieth century would be a gross mistake. To examine, however, these officials of bygone centuries in order to ascertain what they have contributed to this evolutionary process, what characteristics of the office and what duties have been carried along into the twentieth century, should prove more fruitful.

Evidence of the Town Clerk as a paid official, drawing his remuneration from the revenues of corporate property, the fees for the market and the like, dates from the thirteenth century.[1] Concerning his origin, at least three theories have been advanced. According to one theory, the burgesses in the early municipal corporations, influenced by the foreign commune, symbolized their unity of administration by establishing the office of mayor.[2] The mayor, as head of the corporation, became responsible for much of the administrative work.[3] As this work increased it often became necessary to devolve some of his duties upon a clerk, as the Mayor of Nottingham appears to have done by 1354.[4] In time the

[1] L. Hill, *The Local Government Officer* (London, 1938), p. 11.
[2] J. Tait, *The Medieval English Borough* (Manchester, 1936), p. 234.
[3] S. and B. Webb, *English Local Government: The Manor and The Borough* (London 1908), p. 324. The Mayor of Leeds, down to 1764, paid the salaries of the Recorder, the Town Clerk and all other officers (p. 416).
[4] D. Gray, *Nottingham Through Five Hundred Years* (Nottingham, 1949), p. 19.

Mayor's clerk was transformed into an officer of more general duties and wider powers, the Common or Town Clerk. Another, but similar, theory establishes one more step to the process. In the manorial boroughs and many of the early municipal corporations, the Mayor's or Lord's functions, particularly those concerned with the various local courts, were delegated to a Steward or Steward of the Manor. Gradually the Steward's duties became more onerous, and a deputy steward or clerk was appointed and his duties came to be differentiated from those of the Steward.[1] The third theory concerns itself with the small class of municipal corporations which based their membership upon the local guilds or trade companies. It is altogether possible that some of the officers of these corporations were carried over from the guild organization; and among these was the Common or Town Clerk.[2]

Each of these theories must be given some currency, and no doubt other theories could be advanced of equal validity, but perhaps less general application. With the growth of urban life, the duties acquired by the local government, no matter what its institutional pattern, increased. The greater the number of functions, the greater the number of officers needed to perform them. As a result at some time in this expansion certain duties were placed upon an officer titled the Town Clerk, or the Common Clerk, as he was called in many places. It was usual that the only authority for his appointment was a resolution of the governing body, or simply immemorial custom.[3] In general it was not until the later part of the sixteenth and early part of the seventeenth centuries that the Town Clerk appeared in the borough charters.[4]

DUTIES OF EARLY TOWN CLERKS

The duties which these early Town Clerks performed varied, even as they do today, from place to place. Even so, although

[1] Webb, op. cit., pp. 325–6. In a few boroughs even now the offices of Town Clerk and Steward are still combined.

[2] Ibid., pp. 296–7.

[3] Ibid., p. 273.

[4] M. Weinbaum, *British Borough Charters 1307–1660* (Cambridge, 1943). Only fourteen boroughs could be found whose charters made specific reference to the Town or Common Clerk prior to 1600. Of these the earliest was a charter granted to the Borough of Wilton during the reign of Henry VIII.

the details were different, the demands made upon the individuals were somewhat similar: he had to be able to translate and read to the community any communications from Westminster; he needed to be well-versed in the law and able to argue effectively when disputes arose, not only with Westminster, but also with other boroughs; his penmanship and spelling had to be of high quality, for he generally kept the rolls of the town and made the town's Domesday Book with copies of all deeds, wills and charters; and his ability to manage accounts was often a necessity. Intellectual supremacy was a mark of some Town Clerks.[1] A few, like Ricart,[2] the Town Clerk of Bristol, and Humfrey Burton,[3] the Town Clerk of Coventry, were historians of some stature whose works in local history evidenced accomplished scholarship.

This high intellect and virtual security of tenure enabled some Town Clerks to exercise considerable influence in a community.[4] As might be expected, some people turned the office to their own purposes. One such example was Andrew Bate, a butcher from Lydd, who had continually disturbed the townspeople for years by allowing his herd to overrun the pastures and trespass upon his neighbours' fields and commons. His disputes came to a favourable end for him when his brother, presumably trained in law with this object in mind, was appointed Town Clerk of Lydd and for all practical purposes the controller of the town's affairs.[5] In the many instances, however, it opened up a new and brilliant career for men of professional standing. Thomas Caxton, who began his career at

[1] Mrs J. R. Green, *Town Life in the Fifteenth Century*, 2 vols. (London, 1894), vol. 2, p. 260.

[2] Ibid., vol. 2, p. 20.

[3] F. Smith, *Coventry: Six Hundred Years of Municipal Life* (Coventry, 1945), p. 42. (Note: The author of this book, Mr Smith, was the then Town Clerk of Coventry.)

[4] An example of this security of tenure is the case of Charles Bawdes, who was elected Town Clerk of Nottingham in 1684. In November 1689, he was instructed by the Council to take one Lawrence Athorpe as his deputy, 'or else diligently officiate himself'. Two months later the Chamberlains were instructed to recompense anyone who had to do his work. In June 1690, the Council resolved that as he had divulged Council secrets, he must withdraw from their meetings when anything important was debated. In spite of all this it was not until December 1692 that he was replaced. (Gray, op. cit., pp. 58–9.) Before the reform of 1835 the office of Town Clerk was in many boroughs a freehold office, tenable for life. (J. Redlich and J. W. Hirst, *Local Government in England* (London, 1903), vol. 1, p. 337n.

[5] Green, op. cit., vol. 2, pp. 60–61.

Tenterden and thereafter moved to Lydd and then to Romney, eventually settled down as Common Clerk of Sandwich with a long record of highly successful service to his credit.[1] In York, Nicholas Lancaster performed so well as Town Clerk from 1477 to 1480, that he became one of the King's Council in 1483, and Mayor of York in 1485.[2]

It would be only natural that the holder of a position so influential in the community would take on additional duties and further enhance his position. This was what happened, for Sidney and Beatrice Webb, describing the Town Clerk of 1689, wrote:

> In one borough or another we find the Town Clerk acting as Clerk of the Peace, Prothonotary, Clerk of Indictments, Clerk to the Magistrates, Registrar, and Clerk of all Borough Courts; he would sometimes be Coroner, Under Sheriff, Deputy Recorder, Corporation Solicitor, Keeper of the Records, Steward of the Corporation Manors, and Billetmaster. He might preside at the Court Leet, Court Baron, Borough Court, Court of Pleas or sit as assessor in the Mayor's Court. Almost invariably he acted as solicitor and legal agent to the Corporation, and, in conjunction with the Recorder, as its legal adviser. He was often one of the Corporate Justices of the Peace; but unlike the Recorder and Chamberlain, not usually a member of the Governing Council, to which he acted as Clerk.[3]

The eighteenth century brought the industrial revolution and greater demands upon the close municipal corporations to govern. Generally speaking they were not equal to the task set before them, and as a result the towns and the townspeople suffered. To alleviate such conditions and meet some of the necessities of urban living, Improvement Commissions, deriving their constitution and powers from Local Acts of Parliament, were established in several towns. The Commissions were entrusted usually with no more than the provision of roads and pavements, little or no concern being given to the growing health problems. To the Town Clerk fell the duty of drafting the petition to Parliament and the arguments on its behalf, and it was not uncommon for the Town Clerk to become Clerk to (sometimes also a member of) the newly established Com-

[1] Green, op. cit., vol. 2, pp. 261–3.
[2] Ibid., p. 263.
[3] Webb, op. cit., p. 327.

mission. In fact there were towns in which the Commission was composed of a select body from the Corporation, usually the Mayor and a few aldermen, who were able to control municipal administration without interference even from the council.[1] Had there been any hopes for reform of the local governing structure through these means, such hopes would have been frustrated.

The continued importance of the Town Clerk's office[2] and the expansion of his duties coupled with the inadequacy, and often corruption, of the close corporations, brought irregularities during the late eighteenth and early nineteenth centuries. In Winchester, for instance, two competitors, one a member of the Corporation, actively canvassed for the vacancy in the town clerkship. The governing body, to solve their dilemma, effected a compromise whereby the two would hold the office jointly, the emoluments being divided, the non-member, however, managing all the business.[3] In Boston, three brothers, who were aldermen, supported a candidate for a vacancy in the Town Clerk's office conditional upon their receiving a yearly allowance from the profits of the office. Although several councillors knew about the bargain, they, nevertheless, supported the candidate and he was elected.[4] That the office was one of political importance and often unscrupulously sought after is attested by events in Ipswich in the election of 1827 which was a particularly dramatic affair. The 'Yellow Party' swept their candidates for Bailiffs and Town Clerk into office on the strength of the steamer *Suffolk* which carried a cargo of Free Burgesses and arrived in Ipswich at eight o'clock in the evening to secure victory for their party.[5]

Irregularities brought about by the union of a number of incompatible offices in the Town Clerk were equally evident.[6]

---

[1] Webb, op. cit., pp. 433–4.

[2] 'In Borough Towns, particularly those called "Close", generally speaking, the police are most inert, a deficiency arising from an insufficient Magistracy. A want of education, intelligence, etc. too frequently placed the Corporate Leader in the hands of a crafty Town Clerk.' (Mr George Coles, Tiverton, Devon, to the Secretary of State, March 15, 1827.) Webb, op. cit., p. 697.

[3] Royal Commission on Municipal Corporations (1835), p. 38.

[4] Ibid., pp. 38–9.

[5] Webb, op. cit., p. 563n. Between 1820 and 1833 there were eight exciting contests for the town clerkship in Ipswich (p. 564).

[6] Royal Commission on Municipal Corporations (1835), p. 40.

In Hull and York where the Town Clerk as Clerk to the Magistrates advised on the commitment of offenders, the prosecutions were conducted by his partner. In several places the Town Clerk was elected mayor, and sometimes, though not in all cases, attempts were made to cover the indiscretion by appointing another Town Clerk to hold during the year of his mayoralty.[1] At Reading, the Town Clerk, at the time also the mayor, tried and taxed the costs of a case in which his partner was one of the attorneys.[2] These were but symptoms of the decadence into which the municipal corporation had fallen.

THE ROYAL COMMISSION
AND THE MUNICIPAL CORPORATIONS ACT, 1835

The causes lay deeply imbedded in the self-electing and self-perpetuating municipal corporations, and these bore the brunt of the attack by the reform-minded Whigs. In 1833 the Whigs established a Royal Commission, composed chiefly of young Whig barristers and directed 'to collect information respecting the defects' in the municipal corporations, scarcely in what one would call the traditions of impartial investigations. But even before the Commissioners and their assistants had completed their probings, the chairman of the Commission, John Blackburne, and Joseph Parkes, the secretary and a Whig solicitor from Birmingham, wrote the standing report widely condemning the existing state of municipal affairs.

In dealing with the Town Clerk they were strong but not harsh. They explained that he generally held his office during good behaviour; that he was most frequently appointed by the common council, although sometimes by the Recorder and occasionally by the Crown or by election of the freemen; that he was usually an attorney and acted as a legal adviser[3] to the corporation and recorded its proceedings; that he was usually Clerk of the Peace, Clerk to the Magistrates and Registrar and principal officer of the Court of Record; and that although his salary was generally nominal, he was paid for his legal work on the usual scale of professional fees and further, the position

---

[1] Royal Commission on Municipal Corporations (1835), p. 41.
[2] Ibid.
[3] Ibid., p. 25. The Recorder, however, was the principal legal adviser of the Corporation in most places (p. 24).

provided a good introduction to private practice through his connections with the members of the corporation.[1] They criticized severely the treating of corporate offices, particularly that of Town Clerk, as 'matters of mere patronage' and the strange situations which occurred in the Borough Sessions where the Town Clerk was sometimes judge and prosecutor in the same case.[2] The practice of appointing the Town Clerk as deputy recorder, in which position he might be called upon to act in the capacity of a magistrate or a judge in the Borough Court of Quarter Sessions, they strongly condemned.[3] These irregularities it was asserted were 'a frequent cause of suspicion and jealousy amongst the inhabitants, even where the character of the officer is a security against improper conduct.'[4]

On the basis of the Commission's report the Municipal Corporations Reform Bill was drafted and introduced in Parliament. The central issue was the expropriation of the private property held by the corporations. The position, and more specifically, the tenure of the Town Clerk was subjected, however, to some serious and heated debate. Two separate, but yet intertwined, problems were involved: the one, whether the incumbent Town Clerks should be permitted to continue in office; the other, what precisely should the tenure for the Town Clerks, appointed subsequent to the Act, be.

Speaking in reference to the first, Lord Brougham, the leading supporter of corporation reform in the House of Lords, had this to say:

If, my Lords, there had been a single clause, inserted into some snug and convenient corner of the Bill, to provide that all who are now the incumbents of any municipal office[5] should continue in the same, I doubt if we should have had half so many petitions presented.[6]

Motivated by the self-protective instinct, many Town Clerks

---

[1] Royal Commission on Municipal Corporations (1835), p. 24.

[2] Ibid., p. 40. The more common and also objectionable practice was for the Town Clerk to act as judge and his partner as prosecutor.

[3] Ibid.

[4] Ibid., p. 41.

[5] And he was referring more specifically to the Town Clerks than to any other.

[6] Parl. Deb. (1835), vol. 30, c. 381.

had from the beginning opposed not only the Bill but the Royal Commission before it.[1] The Town Clerks found considerable support for their personal case in the House of Lords. An amendment to ensure the present holders their offices for life was introduced by Lord Lyndhurst and was passed by a vote of 104 to 36. Such a proposal was, however, completely unacceptable to the Whig-controlled House of Commons. As Sir Samuel Whalley put it:

> The Town Clerks had been such participators in all the wrongs that had been inflicted upon the people that their continuance in office would destroy all the utility of the bill.[2]

The final form of the provision was a reasonable compromise; the town council was to have the option to continue the incumbent Town Clerk or grant him compensation for the loss of his job.

It was from the second issue that a provision still valid today emerged. Under the old corporations the vast majority of Town Clerks had held their position for life, or good behaviour, which in fact amounted to the same thing.[3] There were some Whigs who, having witnessed the great power the Town Clerk had been able to amass with life tenure, sought to enable the new corporations to remove their Town Clerks at the expiration of each year, even though they did not intend the frequent use of this power. Nevertheless, in theory the Town Clerk, they hoped, would be appointed on a year-to-year basis and his

---

[1] Mr John Carter, Town Clerk of Coventry at the time, was quite critical of the Royal Commission report and in his own copy recorded some caustic comments, particularly concerning the Commissioners' source of information, a Mr Marroit, who was a discharged clerk of the Town Clerk's. (Smith, op. cit., p. 111.) For his part in opposing the Bill the Town Clerk of Leicester was awarded by the Corporation several valuable pieces of plate. (Webb, op. cit., p. 481). Not all the Town Clerks devoted their efforts to opposing the Bill; Henry Enfield of Nottingham is recorded as having very competently assisted the Commissioners in the inquiries. (Gray, op. cit., p. 80.)

[2] Parl. Deb. (1835), vol. 30, c. 1170.

[3] J. R. S. Vine, *English Municipal Institutions* (London, 1879). Of the 177 pre-1835 boroughs considered, 103 appointed their Town Clerks for life, 44 for good behaviour or during pleasure, 11 annually and 19 did not have a Town Clerk, pp. 110–13. This seems to have been a general practice in regard to public offices; for similar conditions obtained in central government at this time. E. W. Cohen, *The Growth of the British Civil Service: 1780–1939* (London, 1941), chaps. 2, 4, especially pp. 26, 52.

qualifications and performance would be subject to review each year. The Tories at the other extreme argued for tenure during good behaviour, their argument being that only in that way could the local councils be assured of professional men who would proceed with unpopular action without fear of political reprisal. They feared that easy removal would subject the Town Clerk to continuous political pressures, that his fortunes would rise and fall with the shifts in the political wind. The compromise which was struck fell somewhat closer to the Whigs' policy than the Tories': that the Town Clerk shall 'hold his Office during Pleasure' (Municipal Corporations Act, 1835, s. 58).[1] This clause actually had strong support throughout the debate from those who felt that annual approval would deter good men from taking on a town clerkship because of the uncertainty involved, but at the same time thought that 'good behaviour' was too secure because it protected those whose conduct was beyond reproach, but whose competence left much to be desired.

Although the debate centred upon the Town Clerk's tenure, the Act itself had more to say about him. He was to be a 'fit Person', he could not be a 'Member of the Council', nor could he also be Treasurer or Elected Auditor or Assessor; and he was to be paid 'such Salary and Allowance as said Council shall think reasonable' (ss. 37, 58).[2] Orders of payment were to be operative only upon being countersigned by him (s. 59). He was made responsible for the compilation of the Freeman's Roll (s. 5) and the publication and distribution of Burgess Lists prepared by the Overseers (s. 15).

Like all officers he could be required by the council to account in writing for 'all Matters committed to his charge by virtue of this Act and also all Monies which shall have been received by virtue or for the Purposes of this Act . . .' (s. 60). It was also his responsibility to send a summons to attend council meetings to each member at least three clear days before the meeting; the summons was to specify the business proposed for transaction at the meeting (s. 69). And lastly, he was exempted from jury duty so long as he held office (s. 122). Such were the first main statutory requirements made concerning and duties placed upon

[1] The Treasurer and other officers were to be appointed every year.
[2] The salary was to be paid from the Borough Fund (s.92).

what had heretofore been described as the principal officer in local government.[1]

The most apparent immediate effects of the Act manifested themselves in the previously unincorporated towns such as Birmingham and Manchester which sought to bring themselves quickly within the Act. In sharp contrast to the Town Clerks of the old corporations, those of the new corporations were active advocates in the reform movement and were instrumental in securing the charters for their town. William Redfern, Birmingham's first Town Clerk, was active in the Birmingham Political Union, which even was too radical for many of the Whigs. Manchester's first Town Clerk, Joseph Heron, served on the charter committee and journeyed several times to London to block attempts by the opposition to stifle the incorporation move. His success in these ventures was prophetic of his illustrious career during which he became the leader of the council, the inspirer of its actions and the country's most distinguished Town Clerk.[2]

THE EXPANSION OF DUTIES

In spite of this influential position in local affairs which the Town Clerks continued to hold, the era of the full-time official was just dawning. Up to this time almost without exception the Town Clerks had conducted a private solicitor's practice in addition to their official duties. William Redfern, Birmingham's first Town Clerk, resigned after only a little more than a year's service because his legal practice was expanding and was more lucrative.[3] In 1857 plans were laid in Birmingham for a new Town Hall; previous to this the borough records were kept and the administrative work conducted largely in the Town Clerk's private office.[4] Manchester made Heron's position a full-time appointment in 1846.[5] York on the other hand did not take on a

---

[1] For other even more minor duties, see ss. 35, 39, 125. In acknowledgement of the existing circumstances, the Town Clerk was permitted to continue as Registrar of the Borough Civil Courts in those places where the appointment was attached to his office (s. 119).

[2] Lady S. D. Simon, *A Century of City Government* (London, 1938), p. 408.

[3] C. Gill, *History of Birmingham: Manor and Borough to 1865* (London, 1952), p. 260.

[4] Gill, op. cit., p. 421.

[5] Lady Simon, op. cit., p. 407.

full-time Town Clerk until 1886,[1] and even at present there are about forty boroughs which still have only part-time Town Clerks.

With the entrance of local authorities into the fields of public health, sanitation and public recreation, among others, the importance of the Medical Officer of Health and the Borough Surveyor was enhanced and the Town Clerk's functions were complicated. Prior to 1835 the corporations concerned themselves chiefly with the management of their property and administration of justice at the magistracy level; at that time the Town Clerk as a lawyer and a record-keeper could hold all the strands of administration such as they were within his own grasp. Now as the local authorities extended their scope, the newer duties fell upon the technical officers, but at the same time there arose a need to co-ordinate these activities, to visualize the broad implications of each decision.

Whether the Town Clerk stepped in to meet this challenge seemed to depend, and still does, but probably to a lesser extent, upon his personality. Sir Samuel Johnson, Town Clerk of Nottingham during the latter part of the century, obviously took great pleasure in performing this function. He described himself as the professional adviser of the corporation and as the head of the staff of officials. He mentioned in particular that the engineer and medical officer of health frequently consulted with him and that the chief constable often sought out his advice. Further he attributed his controlling position to the fact that all committee directions were channelled through his office by virtue of his duty to record and minute the proceedings and that all the council correspondence with external bodies was conducted by him.[2] Liverpool was particularly fortunate at the same time to have Harcourt E. Clare, who came as Deputy Town Clerk in 1883 and was subsequently appointed Town Clerk. During his sixteen years of service, he played an exceptionally active part in forming Corporation policy and was the

[1] J. B. Morrell and A. G. Watson, *How York Governs Itself* (London, 1928), p. 29.
[2] Royal Commission on the Amalgamation of the City and County of London (1894): Evidence, Q. 9261–9875. '(I am,)' he said, 'a sort of centre. All officials come into my office as it were, and I know, therefore, pretty much what is going on in every department; I have a general ready knowledge of all that is going on throughout the whole municipality so far as the government of the town is concerned.' Q. 9861.

engineer of the successful expansion of the city in 1895. 'His successor, however, was not equally as prominent and it appears that Clare's dominant part was attributable more to his personality than to any general belief that the Town Clerk was [then] required to do more than had been necessary in the past.'[1] In Manchester, Joseph Heron, Town Clerk for thirty-nine years, virtually dominated council policy during this period; and as Town Clerk, he considered himself responsible for all the work of the Corporation, even that technically in the charge of other officials in other departments. He was no doubt an unusual man with great administrative and legal skill, marvellous wit, courteous manner and the very desirable capacity to reach quick decisions.[2] His successor, William Talbot, who had been Deputy Town Clerk for twenty-three years, was not nearly as forceful a personality; and consequently as the duties assumed by the Council became more onerous, it became less unified and more like a collection of individual committees.[3] This tendency was probably quite characteristic of the majority of the councils, and the Talbots more representative of the typical Town Clerk than the Johnsons or Herons or Clares. Indeed in many places at this time the Town Clerk was little more than a legal adviser and parliamentary agent for his council.

By statute, the duties of the Town Clerk increased but slightly. The Municipal Corporations Act, 1882, repealed the 1835 Act and recodified the existing law. To the Town Clerk was assigned the task of keeping the charters, deeds, records and documents of the borough (s. 17), as well as supervising the nomination procedure for local elections (Schedule III) and giving notice of the elections (s. 54). In addition the preparation and submission of an annual return of receipts and expenditures of the Corporation for the Local Government Board was desig-

---

[1] B. D. White, *A History of the Corporation of Liverpool 1835–1914* (Liverpool, 1951), p. 182. During the earlier part of the century, however, the driving force and initiative came not from the Town Clerk, but from the Medical Officer of Health and the Borough Engineer.

[2] Lady Simon, op. cit., pp. 408–9. 'An official, now retired, who remembers Sir Joseph Heron, tells how, when asked to come to a committee as his advice was wanted, he would stroll in smoking a cigar and, balancing himself on the edge of a table, would listen to the chairman's explanation of the difficulty and then say, "You must do so and so." If a member made any objection, he would wave it aside, repeat his instructions and then leave the room' (p. 409n).

[3] Ibid., p. 409.

nated the Town Clerk's personal responsibility (s. 28).[1] To alleviate in some way, nevertheless, the possible financial burdens of these increasing personal responsibilities, the Act provided that the Corporation might undertake to pay any fines incurred by its officers in the performance of their duties (s. 226(3)).

The Local Government Act, 1888, provided for county and borough government, and thereby the municipal corporations, which had been dealt with by statute as one body since 1835, were divided into two groups: the county boroughs and the non-county or municipal boroughs. The distinction between these two kinds of boroughs, which has been widening continually since 1888 and at a quite rapid pace since World War II, has been of some significance in the development of the office of Town Clerk.

A CHIEF ADMINISTRATIVE OFFICER?

In the twentieth century the vast extension of public health activities, the large-scale demand for streets and highways, the increase of municipal trading enterprises, the expansion of state-provided education, the serious undertaking of slum clearance and public-supported housing and the genesis of town and country planning all had a tremendous impact upon local government. The demands on councillors became heavier; the demands by councillors for more officials became stronger. The local government service grew, and so did the concern for its well-being. The responsibility for the co-ordination of local activities, which was assumed by a few outstanding Town Clerks of the nineteenth century but ignored by most, it was gradually recognized must be entrusted to some one official. The situation, which still exists in some localities, where each committee becomes in effect a miniature council, jealous of any encroachment upon its powers or interference with its decisions, could no longer, in the name of efficient local administration, be tolerated.[2] The Royal Commission on Local Government in its final report in 1929 considered the question of office organization and the need for one official to be recognized as head of the

---

[1] The Town Clerk was liable for a fine not exceeding twenty pounds should he fail to comply with this section.

[2] Lord Simon, *A City Council From Within* (London, 1926), pp. 95–100, 188–90.

administration. The Commission concluded that one officer should be in a position to survey the scope of council activities and secure co-ordination with reasonable uniformity and continuity and that the most suitable officer was the Clerk. They emphasized that the Clerk need not interfere with the technical side of the work in other departments, but stressed that the Clerk must be informed of the progress within these departments and of the officers' reports to the committees. The success of the Clerk in these endeavours, they noted, would depend upon his personality and the relations he establishes with the other chief officers.[1]

The Hadow Committee, a Departmental Committee appointed to inquire into the qualifications, recruitment, training and promotion of local government officers, considered the position of the Town Clerk in their report in 1934. The Committee felt that the essential qualification for a Town Clerk was administrative ability and that up to the present time too much importance had been attached to the legal qualification. The Town Clerk, they held, 'should be a person of broad and constructive outlook, interested in the wider issues of local government, skilled in negotiation. And he should ordinarily have had experience of administrative work'.[2] In many places, it was pointed out, the legal qualification was convenient; nevertheless, it should not be insisted upon so that persons of high administrative ability were excluded. The Committee had taken one long, bold step from the position assumed by the Royal Commission five years previous. Not only should the Town Clerk become the centre of the administrative organization, but the heretofore unquestioned tradition of drawing the Town Clerk from the legal profession, generally the solicitors' branch, should be altered. His administrative duties were to take precedence over his technical ones, and his qualifications should, therefore, follow this shift in emphasis.

But these were only recommendations, their implementation has actually never come. The local authorities, on the whole, continue to select a new Town Clerk from those who have risen

[1] Royal Commission on Local Government (1929). Final Report. Cmd. 3436. pp. 130–7.
[2] Report by the Departmental Committee on the Qualifications, Recruitment, Training and Promotion of Local Government Officers (1934), pp. 31–3.

in the legal side of a Town Clerk's department, from Assistant Solicitor to Deputy Town Clerk. Although it is widely claimed that administrative ability and experience are of prime importance in the consideration of the applicants, the selection is inevitably made from the very narrow field of local government lawyers.

There have been, however, certain minor developments since World War II which may be prophetic of more important changes to come. The Conditions of Service for Town Clerks and District Council Clerks, as recommended in 1949 by the Joint Negotiating Committee for these groups, provide that the Clerk 'shall be the chief executive and administrative officer of the Council and shall be responsible for co-ordinating the whole of the work of the Council'.[1] Some provision of this nature seemed inevitable in the development of the Town Clerk and local government administration. Nonetheless, although the Conditions of Service provided the form for a new arrangement, little was done to give content to it. The role and duties of the Town Clerk as chief executive and administrative officer were left to individual interpretation. Moreover, the other chief officers in large measure detracted from the seeming definitiveness of this provision by inserting a section in their own Conditions of Service to the effect that each chief officer, other than the Clerk, shall be the executive and administrative head of his department and responsible therefore to the council through the appropriate committees.[2]

In isolated instances, however, and Coventry is the best example, some content was given to this form. A new organization in Coventry has grown out of the recommendations of the Treasury Organization and Methods Division after an intensive survey of Coventry's administration in 1952 and 1953. The recommendations were embodied in a series of thirty-two reports, the final report being the one most relevant to the present discussion.[3] In this final report it was advocated that

[1] Recommendations of the Joint Negotiating Committee for Town Clerks and District Council Clerks, September 8, 1949, Schedule II, para. 1.

[2] Recommendations of the Joint Negotiating Committee for Chief Officers of Local Authorities, September 12, 1950, Schedule II, para. 1.

[3] For the analysis of the final report and the action taken upon it by the Council, see 'Coventry and Organization and Methods', 32 *Public Administration*, London, 52 (1954).

the Town Clerk become Town Clerk/Chief Administrative Officer. In the simple title there seemed to be nothing new, but in its elucidation the concept was given some practical definition. As Chief Administrative Officer, the Town Clerk was to give continual consideration to administrative arrangements in the hope of securing economy; he was to have full responsibility for securing inter-departmental co-ordination; he was to act as Establishment Officer and arrange common office services; he was to furnish organization and methods for all departments; and he was to maintain a broad view of the policy-implementation mechanism. All these recommendations were directed towards strengthening the Town Clerk's position in regard to the other departments, the executing as opposed to policy formation side of local government. Since it was apparent that even in the supervision of administration, some policy decisions would have to be made, the establishment of a standing committee was recommended. This committee was to be called the 'Establishment and General Administration Committee', the new departure being the emphasis upon the general administration side of its operations, and its duty was to consider the proposals of the Town Clerk in his new capacity. Correspondingly the Town Clerk was to be directly responsible to the committee.

As a means of compensating the Town Clerk for the increase in his duties and responsibility and of emphasizing the administrative nature of his position, the Report took the stand that he should no longer function as the Council's legal adviser, that the legal business of the Council should be handled by a separate department. This proposal drew strong criticism from the Town Clerk who cited the need for legal knowledge in the supposedly non-legal functions of the Town Clerk. In fact the Coventry Council did not accept this proposal although it implemented all the others dealing with the Town Clerk. As to the actual effect of these changes, this is a matter which would be more appropriately investigated in a later chapter.

This development of the chief administrative officer concept was completely outside any statutory delineation of the Town Clerk's duties. Nevertheless during this period certain additional duties were placed upon the Town Clerk by statute. The Local Government Act, 1929, transferred certain powers of supervision over the registration of births, deaths and marriages in county boroughs from the Boards of Guardians to the Town Clerk.[1] The Local Government Act, 1933, superseded the Municipal Corporations Act, 1882, but added little to the responsibilities of the Town Clerk. Other Acts, however, did affect the Town Clerk's responsibilities: the Representation of the People Acts widened the scope of his duties for the registration of electors and assigned to him a key position in the conduct of local and parliamentary elections;[2] the Land Charges Act made him responsible for the registration of local land charges;[3] and the Housing Act[4] and the Public Health Act[5] prescribed certain clerical duties for him. Although these statutory duties do not form a major segment of his work, they have added considerably to the scope of his responsibility.

There are several things which seem to stand out in this very brief look at six to seven centuries of Town Clerks. First of all, the Town Clerk has had a long and close connection with the law. In the early corporations, he was often Steward or Deputy Steward of the Borough Court. A little later he might have been Deputy Recorder, Corporation Solicitor or a Justice of the Peace. Before 1835 it was, and most certainly since then it has been, a fairly general practice to appoint solicitors as Town Clerks. Secondly the Town Clerk, as the name implies, has been a record-keeper, the secretary for the corporation, the recorder of its proceedings. And he has frequently carried his duty beyond its normal bounds and compiled records, preserved documents and written histories. Finally, the Town Clerk has been a type of community leader. He has been the spokesman for his council and his town when disputes have arisen between it and another town, or when it has been necessary to smooth something out with the central government.

[1] Local Government Act, 1929, s. 24.
[2] Representation of the People Acts, 1918–1949.
[3] Land Charges Act, 1925. Generally speaking, local land charges are claims which a local authority acquires against a piece of property for performing some statutory duty, the cost of which can be passed on to the property owner or occupier who benefits from the local authority's acts.
[4] Housing Act, 1936.
[5] Public Health Act, 1936.

These three functions—lawyer, secretary, spokesman—are the legacy of the past, and even today they form the fundamental bases for the office of Town Clerk.

But there is more. There have been shifts, or perhaps better, adjustments, in the last century and half century, and even in the last ten years, which have had a profound effect on the office of Town Clerk. The nineteenth century saw a Town Clerk performing his three fundamental functions. But apart from these, there were growing up other functions in local government, public health, municipal engineering; and to carry out each of these there was a tendency to establish a separate organization, centred around its committee and its department. As functions were added, a new committee and a new department were founded. This may have been adequate to meet the needs of the nineteenth century, but it became apparent to writers early in this century that unless some alteration was effected, many pressing problems in the local government sphere would go unattended.

The call was, therefore, for co-ordination of administration, for someone to be at the centre of things. The Royal Commission on Local Government in 1929 said the Town Clerk should be the co-ordinator. The Hadow Committee in 1934 said the Town Clerk should be co-ordinator, and being such, his qualifications should be primarily those of an administrator, not a lawyer. The Coventry Report in 1953 said the Town Clerk should be styled 'Town Clerk/Chief Administrative Officer' and should be responsible for the establishment, for the organization and methods study, for the inter-departmental co-ordination, and for the maintenance of a broad view of the policy-implementation mechanism.

At the same time Parliament has placed additional duties upon the Town Clerk. He is to keep registers of a variety of things for local and national purposes and convenience. In the main, he is entrusted with the organization and conduct of elections, both local and parliamentary. He is obviously an official who can be entrusted with weighty responsibilities.

At this juncture in history, the office of Town Clerk is an admixture; for in the office, the traditional functions, the special statutory duties, the response to the need for co-ordination in modern local government are merged. How this

30

is done, how these functions and duties are organized and executed by the Town Clerk, the ensuing chapters will attempt to describe.

CHAPTER II

THE TOWN CLERK: THE STATUTORY AND JUDICIAL CONCEPTIONS

EVEN though Parliament has largely moulded the present day structure of local government, the Parliamentary Acts and the court decisions interpreting them say little of significance about the Town Clerk. There is practically nothing in them which contributes to a clear definition of the Town Clerk's relations with the councillors, the other officers, or the public at large.

The statutes in a general way require the appointment of the Town Clerk and authorize payment of compensation to him. The statutes place within his ambit a number of clerical functions and election duties. Similarly a number of court decisions define and expand upon these statutory provisions. And a couple of cases even treat more generally the position of the Town Clerk in the local government system of things. But when all these legal incantations are added together, they say very little about the day-to-day administration of local government, with which the Town Clerk is so intimately concerned.

This is not unusual. It is a common feature of democratic governments, and more particularly of British government, to rely heavily upon the force of custom and tradition and the exigencies of the times rather than upon the careful drafting of constitutions and legislation to define the precise nature and duties of public offices. Nor is this to be deplored. Legislation, and even more, constitutions, react slowly to the particular needs of the times.

This chapter, therefore, is not a preface or legal summary of the more detailed chapters which follow. Rather, it merely organizes the various statutory and judicial references to the Town Clerk. These references will be described under two headings: 'The Statutory Conception' and 'The Judicial Conception'. Under the first will be placed the statutory duties of the Town Clerk and their judicial interpretation. Under the second will be a discussion of the two cases which deal more generally with the position of local government officers, and especially the Town Clerk, in local administration.

THE STATUTORY CONCEPTION

The statutory position, powers and duties of the Town Clerk[1] and the judicial interpretation of them may be divided into four general and broad, but certainly not watertight, categories: those relating specifically to his appointment and remuneration, those relating to his clerical function, those relating to electors and elections, and those dealing with local officials generally, the Town Clerk being one of the wider group.[2]

Appointment and Remuneration

Every borough council must appoint a fit person to be Town Clerk.[3] Precisely what a 'fit' person is has not been more specifically defined, but presumably the person appointed must be capable in mind and body to carry out the duties of the office. The appointment should be under seal; a council resolution recorded in the minutes is not sufficient evidence of his appointment.[4]

The council may pay him 'reasonable remuneration'.[5] This remuneration is payable out of the general rate fund account[6] and is the only compensation to which the Town Clerk is entitled for the discharge of his statutory duties.[7] But although

---

[1] The use of the term 'Town Clerk' is perhaps somewhat misleading, for in almost all instances the reference in the statutes is to the 'clerk of the authority' or more simply the 'clerk'. Nevertheless according to the Local Government Act, 1933, s. 305, 'Clerk of the authority' in application to boroughs means 'Town Clerk'.

[2] These groupings are, of course, quite artificial; they have no relation whatever to the many different statutes which deal with the Town Clerk or the vast range of actual powers and duties which the Town Clerk exercises. They are simply a convenient means for organizing the many statutory references to the Town Clerk.

[3] Local Government Act, 1933, s. 106(1); London Government Act, 1939, s. 76(1).

[4] Arnold v. Mayor of Poole (1842), 12 L.J.C.P. 97; R. v. Mayor et. al. of Stamford (1844), 6 Q.B. 433.

[5] Local Government Act, 1933, s. 106(2); London Government Act, 1939, s. 76(2).

[6] Local Government Act, 1933, ss. 185, 187; London Government Act, 1939, ss. 121, 122.

[7] Jones v. Mayor of Carmarthen (1841), 8 M. & W. 605. And where the council resolves to pay salary for attendance on business of council and committees and usual charges in defending and bringing actions, the salary is remuneration for everything except bringing and defending actions. Thomas v. Mayor of Swansea (1842), 2 Dowl. (N.S.) 470.

a Town Clerk may not accept any fee outside of remuneration, the freedom of the council and the Town Clerk to define by contract the scope of the term 'remuneration' is practically unrestricted. It must be reasonable. However, the courts take a liberal view of what is reasonable, and although the District Auditor may surcharge,[1] his view of 'reasonable' remuneration is subject to judicial review.[2] Thus, whether various fees[3] are to be included as part of a Town Clerk's remuneration could depend wholly upon the contract which is made between the council and the Town Clerk. In actual practice the contract made between these two parties is almost without exception an embodiment of the recommendations of the Joint Negotiating Committee for Town Clerks and District Council Clerks, the details of which will be considered in Chapter Three.

Moreover, the restrictions on remuneration, it has been argued, relate to the Town Clerk as 'town clerk'. When he is registrar of local land charges, or fuel overseer, or supervising the registration of births, deaths and marriages, he is not the 'town clerk'; he is performing special jobs, and fees paid to him are not remuneration for the office of clerk.[4]

The Town Clerk holds his appointment during the pleasure of the council.[5] The council and the Town Clerk, however, may contract for reasonable notice by one or both parties.[6] But a council need give no reason for dismissal and no test of good behaviour can be applied in a challenge of a council's actions.[7]

---

[1] In those boroughs which have replaced the Borough Auditors with the District Auditors.

[2] A recent example of this concerned the remuneration of the clerk to the Rural District Council of Alston-with-Garrigill. *Carr v. District Auditor* (1952), 50 L.G.R. 538. The District Auditor attempted to establish the upper limit of salary contained in the recommendations of the Joint Negotiating Committee for Town Clerks and District Council Clerks as an objective standard of reasonableness. The Court held, per Slade, J., that the courts could not apply these salary limits as objective standards and that in this case the receipt of remuneration over £200 in excess of the upper limit was not objectively unreasonable.

[3] For example, fees as electoral registration officer, registrar of local land charges, fuel overseer and supervisor of the registration of births, marriages and deaths.

[4] The opinion of Goddard, C.J., in *Carr v. District Auditor* see n.2, *supra*.

[5] Local Government Act, 1933, s. 106(2); London Government Act, 1939, s. 76(2).

[6] Local Government Act, 1933, s. 121(1); London Government Act, 1939, s. 88. This provision was written into the Act after the Court held, in *Brown v. Dagenham U.D.C.* [1929] 1 K.B. 737, that any agreement to give notice was *ultra vires*.

[7] *Wood v. East Ham U.D.C.* (1907), 71 J.P. 129.

A vacancy in the office of Town Clerk must be filled within twenty-one days of its occurrence.[1] In practice, if a Town Clerk is suddenly taken ill or dies, twenty-one days is far too short a time to advertise, interview and select a new Town Clerk. Thus the Deputy Town Clerk[2] or an Acting or Temporary Deputy Town Clerk[3] assumes the duties of the Town Clerk until a successor is appointed. In the normal cases, when a Town Clerk resigns to take up a new post or retires, ample notice is usually given to allow the local authority to meet the statutory requirement.

The Town Clerk may not be Treasurer, nor may he and the Treasurer be connected in business.[4] This section does not forbid the Town Clerk from holding the position of Chief Financial Officer, which many of them in the smaller boroughs do. The Town Clerk, as are all members and officers, is also forbidden from holding the office of elective auditor.[5]

Clerical Functions

The Town Clerk's clerical function may be divided conveniently into four categories: the reception and dispatch of notices, the keeping of records and registers, the submission of statements and returns, and the signing of documents.

Notices. The Town Clerk must send a summons at least three days before the council meetings. This summons should specify the proposed business and should be sent to the residence of each member. The failure to send the summons to any member does not invalidate the meeting.[6]

---

[1] Local Government Act, 1933, s. 106(3); London Government Act, 1939, s. 76(3). According to Jenks, *Outline of English Local Government* (London, 1930), p. 184, this provision (carry-over from Local Government Act, 1882) was inserted because the Town Clerk must countersign orders of payment and a discontinuance of more than twenty-one days would be too much of a delay for the efficient operation of local government.

[2] Appointed under Local Government Act, 1933, s. 115; or London Government Act, 1939, s. 82.

[3] Appointed under Local Government Act, 1933, s. 116; or London Government Act, 1939, s. 83.

[4] Local Government Act, 1933, s. 106(5); London Government Act, 1939, s. 76(4).

[5] Local Government Act, 1933, s. 237(2). Nor may a Town Clerk be a juror in the county or borough in which he serves. Juries Act, 1870 Schedule.

[6] Local Government Act, 1933, Third Schedule, Part II (2); London Government Act, 1939, Third Schedule, Part II (3).

Notices of resignation from a corporate office must be delivered to the Town Clerk. Resignations take effect only upon receipt of the notice by the Town Clerk.[1]

Councillors must give notice of any pecuniary interest in any matter before the authority. Usually verbal notice is given when the matter is first raised in council or committee, but a general notice given in writing to the Town Clerk stating that the member is affiliated with a specified company or group is regarded as sufficient disclosure. The Town Clerk must record each disclosure in a book which must be open to inspection by any member.[2]

Records and Registers. The Town Clerk, subject to any general directions which the council may give, has custody of, and is responsible for, all charters, deeds, records and other documents belonging to the borough or to the council.[3] A very literal reading of this section brings to mind a Town Clerk who at his very best is an archivist; at his worst, the one who knows the combination to the safe. An interpretation of more liberality would envisage the Town Clerk as general secretary of the corporation, responsible for the minutes of all its meetings, and for the conduct of its correspondence. But this is a very broad interpretation, and even it falls far short of accurately describing the Town Clerk's place in the scheme of things. Nevertheless, this section comes closer than any other to clothing much of what the Town Clerk does with statutory authority.

Consistent with this provision, the Town Clerk is directed to receive and retain, and endorse, acknowledge and issue receipts for any map, plan or other documents deposited with him pursuant to any law, statutory order or the standing orders of either House of Parliament.[4] These documents may be inspected by any person, and obstruction to inspection by the

---

[1] Local Government Act, 1933, s. 62; London Government Act, 1939, s. 37.
[2] Local Government Act, 1933, s. 76; London Government Act, 1939, s. 52.
[3] Local Government Act, 1933, s. 279 (2); London Government Act, 1939, s. 169 (2).
[4] Local Government Act, 1933, s. 280(1); London Government Act, 1939, s. 170(1). There are a number of statutes which provide for maps and plans to be deposited with local authorities, e.g. Land Clause Consolidation Act, 1845; Railway Clauses Consolidation Act, 1845; the Land Charges Acts; the Town and Country Planning Acts.

Town Clerk makes him liable for a small fine.[1]

The Freemen's Roll is the responsibility of the Town Clerk.[2] This roll which was once of great importance in the pre-1835 era of municipal corporations now lists chiefly the very small number of people upon whom the borough has bestowed this honour. As a result it makes little claim on the Town Clerk's attention, even though some boroughs continue to maintain Freemen's Rolls as they were historically kept.

It is in connection with the preparation of various registers that the wide compass of the Town Clerk's statutory duties are most evident.[3]

He is responsible for keeping a register of mortgages created by the authority, and he must enter within fourteen days the details of each mortgage in the register. He must be notified of any changes and must hold the register open for inspection under the usual conditions.[4]

The Land Charges Act, 1925,[5] as it was subsequently defined by the Local Land Charges Rules, 1934, designated the Town Clerk as the proper person to act as local registrar for those charges created in his authority's favour or enforceable by it.[6] His major responsibilities as registrar are the maintenance of an accurate register and the provision of official certificates of search.

In a somewhat different way the Local Government Act, 1929, placed certain responsibilities concerning the registration of births, deaths and marriages on the Town Clerks of the county boroughs. With the abolition of the Boards of Guardians this registration function was transferred to the counties and county boroughs, not as a poor law function to be exercised by the Public Assistance Committee, but under the direct super-

[1] Local Government Act, 1933, s. 280(2), (3); London Government Act, 1939, s. 170(2), (3). This section corresponds to s. 283 (and s. 173 of the London Government Act) which require that council minutes, orders of payment, local authority accounts, local authority abstract of accounts and the borough freemen's roll be open to inspection.

[2] Local Government Act, 1933, s. 260; London Government Act, 1939, s. 159.

[3] Electoral registration, one of the Town Clerk's more important registration duties, will be dealt with in the more general consideration of the Town Clerk's statutory connection with elections, both local and parliamentary.

[4] Local Government Act, 1933, s. 207; London Government Act, 1939, s. 130.

[5] Land Charges Act, 1925, s. 15(6).

[6] Statutory Rules and Orders, 1934, No. 285/L.4.

vision of the Clerk. Thus the Act required that each county borough and county council prepare a scheme for the administration of the registration and that every scheme give the Clerk general powers of supervising the registration, particularly setting of hours of attendance for officers, distributing business between officers and transferring officers from one district to another.[1]

Statements and Returns. A return of income and expenditure of each authority must be made annually to the Minister of Housing and Local Government.[2] The Town Clerk has a personal responsibility to make this return; the Borough Treasurer, or the person whose duty it is to keep the accounts of the authority, must certify the return.[3] Should the Town Clerk fail to make the return, he is liable for a small fine.[4] In addition the Town Clerk must, within one month of a Minister's request, send him a return indicating what provisions the local authority has made for the repayment of its borrowings.[5] Once again, should the Town Clerk fail to comply he personally is liable for a fine.[6]

In January of each year the Town Clerk, in those boroughs with a separate commission of the peace, must submit a statement to the Clerk of the Crown in Chancery which must contain the names of the newly appointed justices and the names of those who have died during the preceding year.[7]

Documents. Not only must the Town Clerk receive a number of documents and provide for their care, he must also sign quite a number if they are to have any legal effect. Perhaps the most important of these are the orders of the council for payments, which must be signed by three members of the council and

---

[1] Local Government Act, 1929, s. 24.

[2] Local Government Act, 1933, s. 244(1) as amended.

[3] Ibid., s. 244(3).

[4] Ibid., s. 246.

[5] Local Government Act, 1933, s. 199(1); London Government Act, 1939, s. 141(1).

[6] Local Government Act, 1933, s. 199(5); London Government Act, 1939, s. 141(6).

[7] 21 *Halsbury's Laws* (2nd ed.) 518. This is a rule made pursuant to the Crown Office Act, 1877, s. 5.

countersigned by the Town Clerk.[1] All payments out of the
general rate fund of the borough, except those pursuant to the
specific requirements of law, or to an order by a judicial
officer, and those which are remuneration to certain specified
officials, require an order of the council.[2] The requirement
theoretically places a great deal of power in the Town Clerk's
hand, for without his signature only a very few expenditures
could be made by the council. But in practice, no Town Clerk
would consider using this duty to issue vetoes.

Under the Public Health Act, 1936, the Town Clerk is
authorized to sign for the council any notice or other document
required by the Act for his council. Other chief officers—the
Surveyor, the Medical Officer of Health, the Public Health
Inspector and the Chief Financial Officer—are granted the
same authority, but only for documents concerned with matters
within their province. The council may, however, authorize any
officer to sign documents of a particular kind, or a particular
document.[3]

The Housing Act, 1936, is more restrictive: orders must be
under seal and must be authenticated by the signature of the
Town Clerk or his deputy;[4] and notices, demands and other
documents must be signed by the Town Clerk or his deputy,
but they need not be under seal.[5]

[1] Local Government Act, 1933, s. 187(2); London Government Act, 1939,
s. 122(2). The Town Clerk's duty to countersign orders of payment extends his
responsibility only to the validity of the members' signatures.

[2] Local Government Act, 1933, s. 187(2); London Government Act, 1939,
s. 122(2).

[3] Public Health Act, 1936, s. 284(1). Note that the widest authorization is given
to the Town Clerk. The expression 'sign' includes facsimile and rubber stamp
signatures and would probably extend to a printed name. (*Clerk of the Council*, p. 7.)
Public Health Act, 1936, s. 284(2). Where an act does not include authorization
for the use of facsimile signatures, the validity may depend upon whether the
Town Clerk was present when the facsimile signature was affixed. (*Canterbury City
Council v. Boarman* as reported in *Clerk of the Council*, p. 7, from the 'Official Circular
of the Urban District Councils' Association', November 1948, p. 279.)

[4] Housing Act, 1936, s. 164(1).

[5] Housing Act, 1936, s. 164(2). The courts have interpreted this very literally.
In *West Ham Corporation v. Benabo* [1934] 2 K.B. 253 a demand notice was held
invalid because it had not been signed by the Town Clerk or the Deputy Town
Clerk. The court, per Atkinson, J., said, 'If the notice comes from the recognized
agent, the Town Clerk, a recipient must be bound to assume that the demand is
made with authority and that the conditions of payment have been considered by
the local authority and that he is under an obligation to obey the demand. But if
it comes from anyone else there is no reason why he should be bound to make such

For the proof of documents in court the Town Clerk's signature is sometimes required. A by-law is proved by producing a printed copy together with a certificate signed by the Town Clerk. This certificate is then sufficient evidence of the facts stated in it, and the validity of the Town Clerk's signature need not be proved.[1] Similar sections provide that documents certified or signed by the Town Clerk under the Public Health Act, 1936, and the Housing Act, 1936, should be received in evidence without further proof.[2]

Elections. The majority of the Town Clerk's duties relating to elections could be very accurately classified as clerical; yet the comprehensiveness of his election responsibilities are such that it was felt more appropriate to consider them separately. These duties may be categorized conveniently under three headings: registration, local elections and parliamentary elections.

Registration. The registration for parliamentary and local elections is, so far as practicable, combined.[3] The responsibility rests upon a registration officer. Whether this office is filled by the Town Clerk depends upon the extent of the parliamentary constituency in the area: only where there is a constituency coterminous with or wholly contained in a Borough is the Town Clerk automatically the registration officer.[4] But where the Clerk of the County Council is registration officer, he is empowered to require any Town Clerk or District Council Clerk within the area to perform the registration duties, that is, the preparation and publication of electors lists, for the Town Clerk's or District Council Clerk's own area.[5]

an assumption. The demand may have been made on the writer's own initiative without any instructions from the corporation. . . .' (Ibid. at 261–62). But see, London Government Act, 1939, s. 184.

[1] Local Government Act, 1933, s. 252; London Government Act, 1939, s. 149. Cf. with Local Government Act, 1933, Third Schedule, Part V (3), under which the proof of a council or committee minutes is established on the basis of the signature of the presiding officer.

[2] Public Health Act, 1936, ss. 248, 286; Housing Act, 1936, s. 165. And under the Housing Act, 1936, s. 166 any notices to be served on a local authority under the Act may be served by delivery to the Town Clerk or to someone employed in his office.

[3] Representation of the People Act, 1949, s. 7.

[4] Ibid., s. 6.

[5] Representation of the People Regulations, 1949, Reg. 21.

The principal duty of a registration officer is the preparation and publication of a register of electors, both parliamentary and local government, each year for his constituency.[1] His other duties are exceedingly numerous.[2]

Local Elections. At least twenty days before the election the Town Clerk must prepare and publish an election notice. Publication consists of exhibiting it in some conspicuous place, on or near the outer door of the town hall, or in the case of a by-election in a ward, wherever he thinks is adequate.[3]

For borough elections nomination papers must be supplied by the Town Clerk. Further, the Town Clerk has a duty to prepare, when requested, any paper for signature, which means that he must fill in the form stating the name of the electoral division and county, the date of election, the name of the candidate, and the candidate's place of residence and description.[4] Each candidate must notify the Town Clerk of the name and address of his election agent and the Town Clerk must then make this information public. When a candidate fails to make the required declaration, the Town Clerk simply publishes the notice listing the candidate as his own agent.[5]

In all boroughs except the metropolitan boroughs, the mayor or the aldermen—where the borough is divided into wards— act as the returning officers.[6] In the metropolitan boroughs, the Town Clerk is the returning officer.[7] In the handling of the

[1] Representation of the People Act, 1949, s. 7.

[2] The following duties are to be found in the Representation of the People Act, 1949. The apportionment of the gross value land and premises in the case of non-resident qualifications for local government elections (s. 5); the holding of a house-to-house survey in order to ascertain the persons entitled to be registered and the determination of all claims for registration and objections to any persons registered (s. 9); the receipt of applications and the recording of absent voters (ss. 13, 24); the appointment of proxies and the issuance of proxy papers at parliamentary elections (s. 14); and the compliance with any specific or general directions given by the Secretary of State (s. 41). Moreover the Town Clerk as clerk shall make up a corrupt and illegal practices list for local electors (s. 40). Failure to perform these duties or any others connected with registration or elections constitutes a breach of official duty and is punishable upon conviction by a fine not exceeding one hundred pounds (s. 51).

[3] Local Election Rules r. 1, 4.

[4] Local Election Rules r. 6(3). A. N. Schofield, *Local Government Elections* (London, 1950), 2nd ed., p. 82n.

[5] Representation of the People Act, 1949, s. 55.

[6] Ibid., s. 27.

[7] Ibid., s. 28.

election the returning officer has the control of almost all matters.[1] At the conclusion of the election the returning officer forwards the ballot papers, counterfoils and certificates concerning poll employees, ballot paper accounts, statements of rejected ballots, tendered vote list and other documents, together with a return of those elected, to the Town Clerk. The Town Clerk must retain them for six months and then destroy them.[2] During those six months the Town Clerk must keep the papers open for inspection and must, on request, supply copies of them, or extracts from them.[3]

Within two months after the election a declaration of acceptance must be delivered to the Town Clerk.[4] The Town Clerk generally will prepare the form in readiness so that as soon as the councillor is selected he makes the declaration and thus avoids the possibility of disqualification.[5]

All expenses properly incurred by the Mayor, returning officer or the Town Clerk are paid by the council, as are expenses incurred by the Town Clerk as registration officer.[6]

In connection with elections within the council—that is, those of mayor and aldermen—the Town Clerk has again only minor statutory duties. At the conclusion of the voting for aldermen, the mayor or presiding officer must deliver the voting papers to the Town Clerk, who retains them for six months.[7] And where there is a casual vacancy in the office of mayor, the Town Clerk may convene a meeting for the election of a successor.[8]

Parliamentary Elections. For parliamentary elections the returning officer for a borough constituency is either the mayor or the sheriff.[9] The duties are numerous, but in general the returning

[1] W. O. Hart, *Introduction to the Law of Local Government and Administration* (London, 1957, 6th ed.), p. 103.

[2] Local Election Rules, r. 49, 51.

[3] Local Election Rules, r. 51, 52. Ballot papers, counterfoils and certificate of employment are not open to inspection.

[4] Local Government Act, 1933, s. 61; London Government Act, 1939, s. 36.

[5] Schofield, op. cit., p. 272.

[6] Representation of the People Act, 1949, ss. 27, 43.

[7] Local Government Act, 1933, s. 22; London Government Act, 1939, s. 22.

[8] Local Government Act, 1933, s. 66; London Government Act, 1939, s. 41.

[9] Representation of the People Act, 1949, s. 17. It is the sheriff in those constituencies which are wholly contained in, or co-terminous with, a county of a city or town.

officer is to do everything necessary for conducting the election in the manner provided by the parliamentary election rules.[1] The vast majority of these duties, however, are performed by the registration officer, that is, the Town Clerk, as acting returning officer. In fact by statute, except for those duties specifically mentioned in Parliamentary Election Rule 3[2] and those which the returning officer reserves to himself by written notice to the acting returning officer and undertakes to perform himself, the acting returning officer is charged with all the duties of returning officer.[3] Thus the Town Clerk, at least by statutory acknowledgement, has a much greater part in the conduct of parliamentary elections than he does in the conduct of local elections.

Local Officials. The Town Clerk is of course a local officer and as such is subject to all the provisions of the Local Government Acts which apply to them generally. The number and variety of these is great; only the most important, however, need to be mentioned here.

Officers cannot become members of the same local authority. The law provides that a person is disqualified from being elected or being a member of a local authority if he holds any paid office, other than mayor, chairman or sheriff, for that authority or for any authority whose members sit on a committee which directs his work.[4] But although a year must elapse between the withdrawal of a member and his appointment as an officer,[5] officers may, and some do, resign their posts and immediately become members.

A matter which more directly concerns the Town Clerk is the institution and defence of legal proceedings. A local authority may prosecute or defend any legal proceedings so long as such course is deemed expedient for the promotion or protection of the public interest, and the local authority may authorize generally or particularly any member or officer to

---

[1] Ibid., s. 16(2).
[2] These generally deal with the delivery of the writ of election.
[3] Representation of the People Act, 1949, s. 18.
[4] Local Government Act, 1933, s. 59; London Government Act, 1939, s. 33.
[5] Local Government Act, 1933, s. 122; London Government Act, 1939, s. 89.

act in these proceedings on its behalf.[1] Except in courts of summary jurisdiction, however, a solicitor or a barrister, in the same way as for other corporations, must appear for the local authority; thus the width of selection is somewhat more limited than it first appears.

THE JUDICIAL CONCEPTION

Only two cases have dealt in a broad way with the relationship between a chief officer and his council. In both cases—*Attorney General v. DeWinton* and *Re Hurle-Hobbs ex parte Riley and Another* —the courts recognized certain basic duties of the chief officers which extend beyond the master-servant concept. Only the second of these concerned a Town Clerk.

First let us consider the case of *Attorney General v. DeWinton*.[2] The facts of the case are relatively simple. The Borough of Tenby had exhausted its power to borrow and had beyond this carried a large fluctuating overdraft with its bank. The accounts of the Borough were kept in the name of the Borough Treasurer. During 1903 and 1904 the bank charged quarterly interest on the overdraft, and the Borough Treasurer in his accounts with the Borough debited the Borough and credited himself with the charges of interest. The Attorney General sued, impeaching the Borough Treasurer's accounts for the interest charges on the overdraft and seeking an injunction to restrain him from making further such payments from the Borough Fund.

It was held, first of all, that the Borough Fund is a trust fund, that the Borough Treasurer knew that the monies he credited to himself were trust monies and that, therefore, he could not escape by pleading the wrongful orders of his employers, the Council. Further, and more important, it was held that the Borough Treasurer was not a mere servant of the Council; that he owed a duty and stood in a fiduciary relation to the burgesses as a body; and that, as a result, he could not plead the orders of the Council for an unlawful act. This ruling was, of course, notwithstanding the fact that the Borough Treasurer

---

[1] Local Government Act, 1933, ss. 276, 277; London Government Act, 1939, ss. 176, 177. Note that two resolutions are involved here: (1) to institute or defend an action; (2) to authorize some member or officer to act on the corporation's behalf.

[2] [1906] 2 Ch. 106.

held his position completely at the pleasure of the Borough Council.

This decision, as was to be expected, has enhanced the position of the Borough Treasurer.[1] He must disobey any order of the Council which calls for an illegal payment. The responsibility for illegal payment rests upon him personally.

Does the *DeWinton* case, or the principle decided in it, apply to the Town Clerk? It is obvious that the Town Clerk cannot be said to stand in a fiduciary relation to the burgesses, for the Town Clerk is not statutorily responsible for the receipts into and payments from the general fund of the borough.[2] Nevertheless, if the Borough Treasurer is said to not be a 'mere servant of the Council' and to 'owe a duty to the burgesses', might it not be argued that the Town Clerk also has some duty to those outside the council chamber? Might it even be said that he is Clerk to the Town and not just Clerk to the Council?

The matter has not gone judicially unnoticed. It was considered in the unreported case of *Re Hurle-Hobbs ex parte Riley and Another* in 1944.[3] The case arose on a surcharge by the District Auditor on the majority leader of the Finsbury Borough Council, Alderman Riley, and the Finsbury Town Clerk with regard to certain expenditures upon an air raid shelter in 1939. The basis for the surcharge was section 228 (1) (d) of the Local Government Act, 1933, which directs that any loss incurred by a local authority must be surcharged upon the person whose negligence or misconduct caused it.[4] The precise

---

[1] Whether this decision extended to local authorities other than municipal corporations need not be settled here. There seems to be good support for both sides of the argument. On the one hand, the governing precedent cited in this case, *R. v. Saunders* (1854), 24 L.J. (M.C.) 45, dealt with county treasurers. On the other hand, there is good reason for saying that in local authorities other than municipal corporations the officers are more directly the servants of their councils and have little claim of any duty to members of a corporation or electors.

[2] The Town Clerk's duty to countersign orders of payment extends his responsibility only to the validity of the members' signatures.

[3] The complete transcript of the decision in this case is included in the appendix of *The Law Relating to District Audit* by C. R. H. Hurle-Hobbs (London, 1955, 2nd edition).

[4] This section reads as follows:
  '(1) It shall be the duty of the district auditor at every audit held by him . . .
    (d) to surcharge the amount of any loss or deficiency upon any person by whose negligence or misconduct the loss or deficiency has been incurred.'

facts of the case are somewhat complicated, but they may be abbreviated for the purposes of this discussion.

In 1939, with war impending, the Finsbury Council decided to build some deep shelters, and a very large scheme was drawn up and submitted to the Home Office and the Ministry of Health in order to secure a government loan. Both Departments turned down the request because the plans for the shelters had some serious technical defects. Thereupon the Town Clerk, at the bidding of Alderman Riley, proceeded to negotiate with private investors in hopes of obtaining a loan from them. The question of whether private financing was *intra vires* arose and counsel's opinion was taken. Counsel advised that private financing was legal, but suggested strongly, in view of the position taken by the Home Office, that an engineering expert be consulted. Consequently, a professor of engineering at London University was asked to review the plans and submit a report on them. Before the report was received, however, the Town Clerk signed an agreement with Shops Investments Ltd to finance the project. Two committees under Riley's direction approved this agreement, but the council, in accordance with its standing orders, deferred consideration of it. Shortly thereafter the report of the expert, Professor Collins, was received by the Town Clerk who read it and sent it on to Alderman Riley. Whether Riley read the report or not was in doubt. But it was established that the Town Clerk had read it and was of the opinion—as he later admitted —that it was a 'devastating and scathing report which would have meant the abandonment of the whole scheme'. In any event, it was established that Riley knew the general nature and import of the Collins' report. Nevertheless neither he nor the Town Clerk disclosed its contents to the Council which met a few days later and approved the agreement with Shops Investment Ltd. The work began almost immediately, but was discontinued about a month later at the outbreak of the war, when the contractor elected to take advantage of a 'war clause' which had been included in the agreement and of which the Town Clerk had also neglected, inadvertently or purposely, to inform the Council. As a result the Council owed £10,474 from the rate fund for which they and the ratepayers received no tangible benefit. The District Auditor surcharged Alderman Riley and the Town Clerk for this loss, and the two of them brought this appeal to the courts against the District Auditor's decision.

On behalf of the Town Clerk, it was argued that, while he knew that fuller information, particularly the Collins' report, should be given to the Council, he was under Alderman Riley's domination. Alderman Riley, it was claimed, had at least once threatened the Town Clerk with dismissal, if he disclosed more information to the Council. It was emphasized that the Town Clerk had no security of tenure and that he had no right to address the Council. Further it was maintained that neither the finance agreement nor the deep shelter was *ultra vires* and that the reason no benefit had flowed from the project was that the war had broken out too soon. Consequently, it was said, the Town Clerk could not be held for negligence or misconduct.

But the Court was unmoved by these contentions and unanimously agreed with the District Auditor. The Lord Chief Justice summed the case up, at least as far as the Town Clerk was concerned, in this manner:

> . . . the Town Clerk seems to me wholly to misconceive his duty when he says that although he thought that the matters I have discussed ought to have been disclosed to the Council he was entitled to stand by without taking such steps as were open to him merely because he would otherwise have been liable to dismissal from his office without notice. It was a little surprising to me that such an argument should be advanced on his behalf. It seems to me to be tantamount to an admission of misconduct. It suggests that the Town Clerk put his private interests above his duty in his office. . . .

This line of reasoning, of course, follows directly from a basic tenet of officer-councillor relations, that each officer is a servant of the entire Council, not a part of it. An officer's primary and over-riding duty is to the Council as a whole, not to one committee, or one party, or one very influential alderman.

The Lord Chief Justice also had some interesting remarks about the extent of a Town Clerk's duty to the ratepayers as well as the Council, *obiter dictum* to be sure, but food for thought nonetheless. He said:

> . . . The office of Town Clerk is an important part of the machinery of local government. He may be said to stand between the

Borough Council and the ratepayers. He is there to assist by his advice and action the conduct of public affairs in the Borough, and if there is a disposition on the part of the Council, still more on the part of any member of the Council, to ride roughshod over his opinions, the question must at once arise as to whether it is not his duty forthwith to resign his office or, at any rate, to do what he thinks right and await the consequences. This is not so dangerous or heroic a course as it may seem. The integrity of the administration of public affairs is such that publicity may be safely relied upon to secure protection for anyone in the position in which the Town Clerk was said to have been placed.

This is certainly the DeWinton rationale, stated perhaps in even broader terms. For in that case the Borough Treasurer's responsibility was limited to legality or illegality of payments; under this case, the Town Clerk's responsibility, as envisaged by the Lord Chief Justice, extends to his opinions of what is best for the ratepayers, of what constitutes the good conduct of borough affairs. But, it must be emphasized, this view as here expressed by Lord Caldecote was *obiter dictum*. To date, no court has specifically applied the *DeWinton* case, even in the limited sense, to the actions of a Town Clerk.

To conclude, the law—both statutes and court decisions—adds but a few sketchy lines to any portrait of a Town Clerk. The actual duties, responsibilities and character of the office depend more on custom and necessity than on written law. Do these customs and traditions, these new duties taken on by or devolved upon a Town Clerk, find written expression in places other than legislation? To a certain extent they do. There are, in fact, extensions of the constitutions and legislation, which are made within the bounds and limits established by them. In the case of the Town Clerk, his position is governed by Whitley negotiations, by individual contract, by a local authority's Standing Orders and its instructions to committees and sometimes to officers and by local authority resolutions. These may be general in their application or only apply to a specific case or to a specific officer.

But by and large, the customs are uncommitted to paper and often unexpressed. The office has some flexibility; it is adaptable to the differing needs in different localities and at times alterable to meet new conditions and demands. This is as it should be in government and particularly in local government.

CHAPTER III

THE TOWN CLERK:
HIS TRAINING AND CAREER

In England and Wales there are 431 boroughs[1] and in each there is a Town Clerk. There are eighty-three county boroughs, 319 non-county boroughs, and twenty-nine metropolitan boroughs, including the City of London. Each kind has its own place and powers within the local government scheme of things. County boroughs are as a rule the very large boroughs. But most important, they are all-purpose authorities responsible for the administration of all local government services within their boundaries. Non-county boroughs, on the other hand, are part of a two-tier system. They have a good number of powers to exercise, but some of the more important services, particularly education and town planning, are provided by the county councils.[2] Similarly metropolitan boroughs share the total local services of the Administrative County of London with the London County Council.

Moreover, there are a variety of distinctions, other than legal ones, between boroughs: a large number are middle-sized market towns; some are the centres and many others the outlying portions of the large conurbations; some are seaside resorts or spas; others are cathedral cities; and a few are really small villages in the remote parts of Cornwall, Cardiganshire and Caernarvonshire. The major distinction is in terms of population. The table (next page) illustrates the very wide variations.

Nearly one-third of the boroughs have populations under 20,000 and about 12 per cent have populations under 5,000. At the other end of the scale, a quarter have populations over 75,000, and about 18 per cent have over 100,000 people living

---

[1] As this is being written, the review of local authority areas has been put in · hand, which may bring about significant changes.

[2] In some instances, however, they do acquire additional powers through delegation from the county. See generally, P. G. Richards, *Delegation in Local Government* (London, 1956).

Population* Range	Non-county Boroughs	County Boroughs	Metro- politan Boroughs	Total
Under 5,000	50			50
5–10,000	36			36
10–15,000	28			28
15–20,000	25			25
20–30,000	35	1	1	37
30–45,000	59		1	60
45–60,000	40	7	5	52
60–75,000	20	11	3	34
75–100,000	10	15	4	29
100–150,000	11	23	6	40
150–250,000	5	13	6	24
250–400,000		7	1	8
400–600,000		3		3
Over 600,000		3	2	5
Totals	319	83	29	431

* The ranges are those employed for the purposes of salary scales by the Joint Negotiating Committees. The populations were taken from the *Municipal Yearbook*, *1958*.

within their boundaries. Almost a majority of the boroughs lie between the 20,000 to 75,000 range, and, if the London boroughs are excluded, the median population is about 36,000.

There are thus 431 Town Clerks in England and Wales whose scope of duty and responsibility varies enormously according to the size of the borough, the extent of the council's powers, and the nature of the town itself.

Most Town Clerks spend their full time at the job of Town Clerk. In the very smallest boroughs, however, there often is not enough business to keep a Town Clerk busy on a full-time basis. These boroughs, therefore, employ a part-time Town Clerk who combines his municipal work with some kind of business outside. Normally he is a solicitor, living within the borough and carrying on a private practice there or in a larger nearby town. According to figures given in 1957, at that time there were forty-four part-time Town Clerks.[1] Some conflicts of interest may arise in this kind of situation and may lead to some unseemly results, but by and large it is a good solution for

[1] Argument of the Society of Town Clerks in *Re Town Clerk of Newcastle-upon-Tyne Corporation*, Industrial Disputes Tribunal, Award no. 963 (1957).

those boroughs with limited resources and a desire for talent in their Town Hall.[1]

A similar situation exists in the slightly larger, but still very small, boroughs, in which the offices of Town Clerk and Chief Financial Officer are held by one man. Although the Town Clerk is forbidden by the Local Government Act, 1933, s. 106 (5), from being Borough Treasurer, there is nothing which prohibits a council from appointing the Town Clerk as the Chief Financial Officer to manage the finances of the corporation, and from allowing someone else to hold a largely nominal post of Borough Treasurer. This someone else is often the local bank or Bank Manager. This is the situation in fifty boroughs, none of which is over 18,000 in population and forty-seven of which have less than 10,000 inhabitants.[2] By combining the two posts these boroughs are able to secure one man of better than average qualifications and talent instead of two men with less ability and inferior qualifications. But part-time Town Clerks and Chief Financial Officer-Town Clerks are the exceptions: the general rule is a full-time man who spends the whole of his time on the job of Town Clerk.

EDUCATION AND TRAINING[3]

The great majority of—but certainly not all—Town Clerks are solicitors; some are accountants; a few are barristers; and a substantial number have no such profession, many of whom, however, possess a secretarial or similar qualification. The size of each of these groups in percentage form is shown overleaf.

Since the solicitors form such a large segment of the Town Clerk population, it is well to consider in some detail the education and training of a solicitor, particularly the local govern-

---

[1] For a contrary view, see W. A. Robson, *The Development of Local Government* (London, 1948, 2nd ed.), pp. 333–34.

[2] Figures according to *Municipal Yearbook, 1958.*

[3] Except where stated otherwise, the figures, percentages, etc. given in the remainder of this chapter were derived from a questionnaire circulated with the help of the Society of Town Clerks to all the Town Clerks as of January 1958. Certainly there have been changes since that time, though one doubts whether any of the changes would have radically altered the conclusions reached. Of the 431 distributed, a total of 381 or 88·4 per cent were returned. The figures here advanced are done so with the reservation that there may be some biases caused by the absence of the remaining 11·6 per cent and the return of partially completed questionnaires.

	per cent
Solicitors	82·4
Barristers	1·6
Accountants	3·9
Others	12·1
	100·0

ment solicitor. In short, how does one become a solicitor? First of all, each aspiring solicitor must serve as an articled clerk to a practising solicitor. The period of articles varies, but essentially it is five years with certain concessions being made to barristers, university graduates, bona fide solicitors' clerks of ten years' standing and students who have achieved a predetermined standard in the G.C.E. examinations.[1] But all must serve articles of some duration. Thus the choice is open whether to serve them in local government with a Town Clerk, Clerk of the Council or some other qualified solicitor, or to serve them with a solicitor in private practice. Some Town Clerks feel that the more experience one can get in local government work, the better it is, and therefore these people strongly advocate serving articles to a local government officer. Others feel that it is well for the local government solicitor to have had some experience outside, and therefore they advocate serving articles to a solicitor in private practice. Both sides have their following, for of the solicitor Town Clerks it is found that 57 per cent served articles to a full-time local government officer (almost without exception, a Town Clerk), 34 per cent served articles to a private solicitor, 5 per cent to a part-time local government officer, and 4 per cent had a divided articled clerkship between local government and private practice. It does not seem to make much difference which path an aspirant chooses to follow.

But there is another choice which may face the Town Clerk aspirant which does seem to make some difference. This is the question of a university education. Approximately 35 per cent of the Town Clerks have university degrees, and all but about 1 per cent of these are solicitors.[2] Thus 41 per cent of the Town Clerks who are solicitors have university degrees. Moreover,

[1] Law Society Regulations, reg. 5, and Schedule I.
[2] In the 1 per cent were two university graduates in law who became neither a solicitor nor barrister and one barrister with a law degree.

there are several further observations which can be made. First, in the larger boroughs, where the position of Town Clerk is more important and better paid, the councils tend to prefer the man with a university degree. This point may be illustrated by the following table:

PROPORTION OF TOWN CLERKS

Population Group	With a University Degree (per cent)	Who are Solicitors (per cent)
Under 5,000	13	36
5–10,000	13	37
10–15,000	25	71
15–20,000	36	92
20–30,000	34	94
30–45,000	29	94
45–60,000	34	93
60–75,000	48	100
75–100,000	45	100
100–150,000	47	100
Over 150,000	58	100
Metropolitan Boroughs	48	78

Secondly, the overwhelming majority have taken a law degree of one kind or another, and some have taken two law degrees. This fact is indicated by the following percentages:

Degrees	Proportion of Total Degrees (per cent)	
LL.B.	48	
LL.M.	14	
M.A. (law)	6	
M.A. and LL.B.[1]	18.5	
Law Degrees		86·5
M.A. (other)	8	
B.A. (other)	4	
B.Sc.	1·5	
Other Degrees		13·5
Total		100·0

[1] Includes two Town Clerks with B.A. and LL.B and two with M.A. and B.C.L. Some, but a minority, with M.A. and LL.B. read classics or history for the M.A.

Thirdly, there does not seem to be any outstanding preference as to which university. London is at the top of the list, probably because it is possible to take an external LL.B. degree there. Cambridge and Oxford follow in that order and the other universities divide the remainder with reasonable evenness.

University	Per cent of Total Degrees
London	25
Cambridge	21
Oxford	14
Manchester	10·5
Sheffield	9
Birmingham	5
Liverpool	5
Leeds	4·5
Durham	3
Wales	3
	100·0

It is interesting to compare these figures with a sample taken from the recent applicants for membership to the Local Government Legal Society. This Society was founded in 1947, and its membership is open to any solicitor in the service of a local authority. According to its application circular its principal objects are 'to promote the professional and legal knowledge of solicitors in local government and to confer on all matters concerning the status, duties and remuneration, responsibilities and interest of members'. It is thus an organization of a large number of the Assistant Solicitors in local government generally, not only boroughs, and it is from this group that most of the Town Clerks of the future will come. From a sample of over a quarter of the Society's membership, one finds that over 63 per cent have university degrees, a figure to be compared with 41 per cent for the present Town Clerks who are solicitors.

It seems safe to conclude, first, that in general the most successful Town Clerks—that is, most successful in terms of securing the higher paid positions—have been those who have taken a degree, and, second, that this tendency will be even more pronounced in the future. There are several reasons for this. Since the war the process of securing a university education has been less dependent upon one's family resources and more dependent upon one's ability. With the advent of state scholarships, county grants and a more universal basis for grammar school education, it has become much easier for the talented, but poor, student to make his way to and through the university. In addition the Law Society has, for the modern generation of solicitors, made the choice between taking articles straight from school or going to the university infinitely easier. The holder of a degree from a recognized university need serve only three years' articles, in place of the normal five.[1] Furthermore, the holder of a degree in law from one of these universities is exempted from the law portion of the Solicitors' Intermediate Examination and need only take the Final and the Trusts and Bookkeeping examinations to be admitted.[2] And finally, those who do not go to the university must spend during the period of their articles at least one year in attendance at a Law School, either the one conducted by the Law Society or one approved by the Society. Consequently, the person who goes to university and who intends to become a solicitor takes only one year more to reach the goal than the one who takes his articles immediately upon leaving school. Taking all into consideration one year does not seem to be a great deal of time to exchange for a degree and the many other benefits of a university education.

The university degree and articles, of course, are not all that is required of one before one is admitted as a solicitor. There are examinations: Preliminary, Intermediate and Final. The Preliminary is of little consequence since most aspiring solicitors are exempted from it in one way or another. The Intermediate is of more consequence, although it is chiefly to ascertain whether an articled clerk is making the necessary progress towards becoming a solicitor.[3] As was pointed out, those with degrees in law are exempted from all but one paper—Trust Accounts and Bookkeeping—of this examination. Nonetheless, for many it is a hurdle to be surmounted on the way to becoming

[1] Law Society Regulations, Schedule 2. The recognized universities are Aberdeen, Birmingham, Bristol, Cambridge, Durham, Edinburgh, Exeter, Glasgow, Hull, Leeds, Liverpool, London, Nottingham, Oxford, Reading, St Andrew's, Sheffield, Southampton, Wales, Victoria University of Manchester and the Queen's University of Belfast.
[2] Law Society Regulations, reg. 54.
[3] Regulation 33.

a solicitor. The final examination is, however, the major obstacle. And it is worthwhile, therefore, to investigate what kind of obstacle it actually is, since presumably the major portion of a solicitor's training is spent upon preparation for this examination.

The final examination consists of five compulsory papers and two optional papers.[1] The compulsory papers are concerned with the major areas of law with which solicitors generally deal:

1. Real and Personal Property with special emphasis on conveyancing.
2. (a) Contracts.
   (b) Torts.
3. Wills and Intestate Succession; and Equity, including Trusts.
4. Taxation—Income, Death Duties and Stamp Duties.
5. Company Law and Partnership.

The optional papers offer a varied selection, but there are two which the local government solicitor normally selects:

1. Local Government Law and Practice.
2. Planning Law (although this is concerned with matters affecting the general public, as distinct from those affecting a public authority).

This appears to be an excellent background for the local government lawyer, and even for the local administrator, if one concedes that some kind of legal training is proper for the administrator. But the subjects of the examinations are only one side of this problem. On the other side is the question of what kind of examination it is and of what kind of preparation is necessary to be successful in it. In this connection I was impressed by the remarks of a recently admitted local government solicitor who had experience of both the Solicitors' Final and one of the Oxford Honour Schools. As he explained it, each paper in the Solicitors' Final contains twelve questions, ten of which must be done—three compulsory and seven optional—all in three hours. There is, therefore, little choice, no time for long thinking and a demand for short and direct answers. The stress, he felt, was upon the ability to memorize a vast amount of 'bitty information' and to put it on paper as the occasion demands. Consequently, little scope is given for one's intelli-

[1] Regulation 58.

gence. This means, in his opinion, that the intelligent man has a far smaller advantage in the Solicitors' Final than in an Oxford Honour Schools; that the indifferent-minded persevering man might get honours in the Final, but would never get a First in Schools; that the indolent genius might get a First in Schools, but would probably fail the Final completely. The distinction is perhaps somewhat overstated, but it is nevertheless a valid distinction. It is difficult to avoid the conclusion that learning law as a collection of factual information, statutes which exist and points of law which have been decided, is not productive of a creative imagination; the kind of imagination which, it is often said, is required of a successful administrator. Nonetheless, this is the kind of professional training which the vast majority of Town Clerks have experienced.

But what of the remainder of Town Clerks? What are their professions and standing? First of all, there are a very few barristers—slightly less than 2 per cent. Generally they tend to be Town Clerks in the smaller boroughs; the largest borough with a barrister Town Clerk has a population of about 59,000.[1] If the local authorities want or need lawyers (not just solicitors) as Town Clerks, why has the barrister been by-passed? This question has a special significance in that a barrister's training need last but three years, substantially less than a solicitor's, and further in that he serves no articles. (It is not uncommon for a student of an Inn to hold a full-time job and study for the Bar Examination in his spare time.) The easy answer to this question is, of course, that the Town Clerk has traditionally been a solicitor and the usual inertia has made the departures from this convention rare. But then come the questions: why the convention? and why so few departures if sound reasons for departure exist?

Originally, one would suspect, when local government meant the management of the corporation's property, the Town Clerk's legal functions centred upon transactions in property—sales, leases, purchases, wayleaves or, more generally, conveyancing. Private transactions of this kind were, and still are,

---

[1] This figure, of course, relates only to Town Clerks. A greater percentage of barristers serve the urban and rural district Councils, and there are three barristers among the clerks of County Councils. One of these is Clerk of the London County Council, the largest local authority in the country.

generally handled by solicitors, and, since the Town Clerks in earlier times were only part-time, the corporation quite naturally looked to a local solicitor. More recently as the Town Clerk's duties and functions, except in the smallest authorities, have ranged over a far wider ambit, such an explanation, however, loses some of its logic, but not its effect.

Much of the legal work which a local authority expects its young lawyers to do, and in the very small authorities expects its Town Clerk to do, centres around conveyancing. Whether barristers in local government may perform this work is a matter about which there has been, and apparently still is, considerable dispute and confusion. On the one hand, the Bar Council has required local government barristers to secure the Council's permission (or as it is commonly called 'dispensation') before engaging in conveyancing for the local authority. On the other, the Society of Local Government Barristers disputes the Bar Council's authority. To the contrary, the Society claims, the Bar Council does not represent the Bar as a whole, and that consequently whether acting for his authority, employer, or simply as a barrister, the Bar Council lacks any power to restrain a local government barrister who wishes to do conveyancing. Whatever the eventual resolution of the dispute may be, in the past the Bar Council's requirement has probably discouraged both young barristers from seeking local government employment and local authorities from seeking barristers for junior legal positions.

The more recent snag, therefore, has not been so much at the Town Clerk level, but somewhat lower on the promotion ladder among the junior lawyers. But since most Town Clerks climb the ladder from junior lawyer to Deputy Town Clerk to Town Clerk, the young barrister's situation probably explains in large measure the present paucity of barrister Town Clerks.

There are a few more accountant Town Clerks than barrister Town Clerks, but only a few more—the total number is about 4 per cent of all Town Clerks. One metropolitan borough with a population of about 50,000 has an accountant Town Clerk, but the largest borough outside of London with an accountant as Town Clerk has a population of about 11,000.

In almost every case the accountant performs the dual capacity of Town Clerk and Chief Financial Officer so that, although as Town Clerk he must fulfill certain statutory obligations and tend to the usual committee business, such as it is, his major concern is to ensure the sound financial position and structure of his corporation. For the very small borough this approach is without doubt sound, for it increases its chances of getting a trained person to manage its finances. In the main this training involves becoming an Associate Member of the Institute of Municipal Treasurers and Accountants, although a few have Certified Accountant or similar qualifications.

The remaining segment, almost 12 per cent of the total, is comprised of Town Clerks who have been trained in a wide variety of ways, and who have acquired a similar variety of qualifications. As a few examples, there are some who are Fellows of the Corporation of Secretaries (F.C.C.S.); others who are Fellows of the Chartered Institute of Secretaries (F.C.I.S.); a few who are Fellows of the Rating and Valuation Association (F.R.V.A.); a number who are Associates of these various bodies; and a larger segment who hold no qualification but long experience in their work. Again this group is concentrated in the small authorities. The largest borough outside of London with a Town Clerk of this background has a population of about 47,000; but even this is an exception, for nearly three-quarters of this group are employed in boroughs under 10,000 population. In London, there are at least five in the metropolitan boroughs, the populations of which reach 90,000. On the whole, however, this kind of Town Clerk is found in the small borough which is limited in its resources, powers and activity.

To summarize briefly, therefore, all Town Clerks of boroughs (other than metropolitan boroughs) above 60,000 population are solicitors; and in fact, in all but those boroughs under 10,000, solicitors hold the majority of town clerkships. Over 40 per cent of these solicitors have university degrees, the greater concentration of degree-holders being in the larger authorities. The overwhelming majority of degrees have been taken in law, a study of law which in this sense—that is, the academic sense—is reasonably broad and theoretical. This training then has been followed by the restricted approach demanded by the Solicitors' Final examination. The remaining 60 per cent of solicitor Town Clerks have been trained solely with the restricted approach. Aside from solicitors, there are barristers, accountants and others with a variety of qualifications who serve as Town Clerks, mostly in the very smallest authorities. But their number is small, their influence among Town Clerks as a group even smaller. In general, the best start on the road to a town clerkship is a good university degree followed by a successful Solicitors' Final. What happens after this start depends upon the system of promotion.

THE SYSTEM OF PROMOTION

Except in a very small minority of cases, the road to a town clerkship has been through the various positions in a Town Clerk's department. Moreover, within that department there are four usual roads to the position of Town Clerk, one or another of which nearly all the present Town Clerks have travelled. First of all, there are the ones who, straight from school or university, serve their articles to a private solicitor and subsequently take positions as Assistant Solicitors, then Deputy Town Clerks, and finally Town Clerks. Secondly, there are the ones who straightaway serve their articles in local government, normally to a Town Clerk, and then, having been admitted, become Assistant Solicitors. This is the most numerous segment. Thirdly, there are those who enter the local government service as a junior clerk, subsequently become articled to a Town Clerk, and then, being admitted, take a position as Assistant Solicitor. There is, in many cases, little to distinguish one in this category from one in the second group. Some Town Clerks have begun as a junior clerk, worked for a year or two in that position and then have taken up their articles. Others have worked on the administrative side of the department for as much as twelve years before they began serving their articles. Consequently, some may have intended right from the time of their entrance to become local government lawyers and eventually Town Clerks, whereas others may have turned to law when they seemed to have exhausted their opportunities for advancement early in life. In the fourth group are those who enter as junior clerks and work their way up the administrative side, through appointments of Committee Clerk, Senior Committee Clerk and Chief Clerk, and are eventually appointed Town Clerk without having become qualified solicitors. Also in this group are those who are accountants and who may have begun in the Treasurer's rather than the Town Clerk's department. The major exceptions to these practices are the part-time Town Clerks who have been appointed to their positions without any previous local government experience; but even among part-time Town Clerks, their number is not great.

Quite expectedly, the lawyer entrant is more common in the large authority, essentially because it is only when an authority reaches about 50,000 in population that the need for a third lawyer, hence an Assistant Solicitor, on the staff arises. Moreover, university graduates, except those who take an external degree somewhat later in their career, invariably take their articles immediately after graduating and therefore enter local government as solicitors, again in the larger boroughs. In the smaller places where the non-solicitor Town Clerk is most prevalent, the junior clerk entrant is, as a result, not unusual. But much more often than not the path to a town clerkship leads through the legal side of a Town Clerk's department.

This is illustrated by the following table which shows the proportion of Town Clerks who obtained their first full-time appointment in local government as either a junior clerk or as an Assistant Solicitor.

Population Group	Assistant Solicitor (per cent)	Junior Clerk (per cent)
Under 5,000	4	96
5–10,000	21	79
10–15,000	50	50
15–20,000	64	36
20–30,000	48	52
30–45,000	68	32
45–60,000	75	25
60–75,000	83	17
75–100,000	74	26
100–150,000	81	19
Over 150,000	88	12
Metropolitan Boroughs	71	29
	64	36

(These percentages are based upon a total sample of 296.)

The keystone of the system of promotion is, however, inter-authority mobility, the movement from a position in one authority to a better one in another authority. This mobility is not something which is peculiar to the Town Clerks; rather it is a feature of the entire local government service, and movement is particularly commonplace among the professional officers. Ease of movement from place to place has been improved by the Local Government Superannuation Act, 1937, which established compulsory superannuation throughout the service and provided for the transfer of accrued benefits from one authority to another when an officer moves. On the other hand, certain post war factors have reduced this ease.

There are some Town Clerks who have served in only one authority, but their number is small. The overwhelming majority have moved at least once and usually more than once. On average, the present Town Clerk has served with between three and four local authorities, which means that the average Town Clerk moves two to three times.[1] For example, the Town Clerk of a small borough in the south with twenty-four years in local government held the positions of Assistant Solicitor and then Deputy Town Clerk in the middle-sized Lancashire borough where he was also articled to the Town Clerk. He then moved to a larger non-county borough on the south coast to become Deputy Town Clerk there and five years later acquired his present position, Town Clerk of a borough of about 23,000 population, the smallest in which he has worked. Another example is the Town Clerk of a county borough near Manchester. He began his career twenty-six years ago as an Assistant Solicitor in a Midlands county borough. Four years later he moved to a similar position in a larger corporation in the Midlands, and three years after that became Assistant Town Clerk in a county borough near London. He was promoted to Deputy Town Clerk in the same borough seven years later. He held this post for two years and then moved northward to take his present position. These are two very typical examples of the kind of movement made by the aspiring Town Clerk on his way up the ladder.

There are several very general observations which can be made concerning this inter-authority movement. The most

[1] This average is based upon a total sample of 176.

striking is that the amount of movement from non-county boroughs to county boroughs, particularly at the Deputy Town Clerk and Town Clerk levels, is not very large. County boroughs usually fill vacancies with those who have had county borough experience. Consequently unless one, early in one's career, secures experience with a county borough, one's chances of eventually becoming Town Clerk of one of the large authorities are substantially reduced. Furthermore, of the present Town Clerks, only a very few have had experience with urban or rural district councils, and those who have are chiefly the Town Clerks in the smaller authorities. And even fewer have ever worked for a county council. The vast majority of Town Clerks have worked only for borough councils, and as often as not for only one kind of borough.

There are several factors in the present system of salary scales which now operate against a great deal of movement. According to the latest scales recommended by the Joint Negotiating Committee for Town Clerks and District Council Clerks in February 1959,[1] the salary spread is from £860 minimum in the authority under 5,000 population to a £4,600 maximum in an authority of 400,000 to 600,000 population, and at the council's discretion in authorities over 600,000 population. This is a substantial differential. But it is well to remember that almost a majority of authorities lie between 20,000 and 75,000 and in these ranges the differentials are considerably smaller, the average salaries running from £1,775 to £2,642. Couple this with a tendency towards limited movement from non-county to county boroughs and the high rates of income tax, and it is seen that essentially the salary differentials are not as great once one becomes a Town Clerk or even a Deputy Town Clerk. It is often easier for a Deputy to wait until the Town Clerk retires in anticipation of moving into his position than to undertake the trouble and expense of moving and finding a new home for at most a few hundred pounds. The problem for Town Clerks is the same and perhaps more acute. As an example, take the Town Clerk of a borough of 25,000 with a salary of £2,000 and his annual increments exhausted. A position in a borough of 65,000 is advertised. Should he apply?

[1] The salaries referred to in the scales dated, February 9, 1959, are at present under review.

His starting salary will be about £2,500 which in three years will become £2,830. Thus the move would be worth £830 gross, but after taxes, not much more than say £350. He must bear the expense of moving, selling his present home and buying another one, and the difficulties of adjusting to a new environment, both living and administrative. For the young Town Clerk under forty years of age, such a move may be worthwhile; for the older one, probably not. Consequently, when one becomes a Town Clerk, the chances are reasonably good that he will remain with that authority until retirement. Most of the mobility is at the Assistant Solicitor level and to a lesser extent at the Deputy Town Clerk level.

Excluding solicitors' articles and war service, twelve years is the average time it takes for the young entrant to attain his first town clerkship. In general, it takes the junior clerk entrant somewhat longer than the person who enters as an Assistant Solicitor. This figure, however, is based upon the present generation of Town Clerks, many of whom lost six to eight years during the war. As a result, although measured by actual years of service in local government their movement up the ladder may have been quicker than normal; their movement to the top in terms of age has been somewhat slower. In normal times, therefore, one would expect the average Town Clerk to serve about fifteen years in local government before being appointed a Town Clerk, the average age on appointment thus being thirty-eight.

It is quite unusual for a Town Clerk to have worked outside local government at all. Except for those who served their articles to a private solicitor and remained in private practice for a few years before entering local government, the number who have spent any time working outside the local government service is infinitesimal. As it was emphasized above, unless one enters the legal side of local government early in one's working life, the opportunities for becoming a Town Clerk are extremely limited.

METHOD OF APPOINTMENT

When a vacancy for a Town Clerk occurs or is about to occur—and there are about thirty vacancies each year—the council advertises for applicants. It generally advertises in the more popular local government journals, *Justice of the Peace and Local Government Review*, *Municipal Journal*, *Local Government Chronicle* and occasionally in *The Times* and the *Law Weekly*. The applications are considered by a committee and a short list of candidates to be interviewed is drawn up. The initial screening committee may be variously composed: it may be a standing committee, usually either the Finance or Establishment Committee, or a special sub-committee, or a committee of ex-mayors, or in the small places, the entire council in committee. In almost every case its composition includes the senior and most respected members of the council. The initial screening committee generally interviews the first short list of about twelve, from which six are selected for a second interview. This second interview is usually conducted by a somewhat larger committee which generally recommends to the council one candidate and perhaps one or two alternatives. The choice, therefore, usually lies with the second interviewing committee. However, some authorities do require a final short list of three to five to come before open council and address the group for five to ten minutes. In these instances the final decision rests with the whole council. In any case, the successful candidate is usually expected to attend the council meeting at which his appointment is approved and to address the council briefly at that time. The council resolution is normally the final stage in the process of appointment. The appointment of the Town Clerk of Richmond, Yorkshire, however, in accordance with the Borough's charter of 1668 granted by Charles II, must be approved by the Sovereign. After the Council makes its choice, application for approval is made to Her Majesty through the Home Secretary by the Mayor, and in due course the approval is granted.

It is not unusual, during the process of drawing up the short lists and considering the various applicants, for a council to send representatives into the towns of these applicants in order to determine the general public feeling about them. Enquiries are sometimes directed to the local party organizations as well. One Town Clerk was confronted by both party leaders for advice when they received letters from their counterparts in the borough in which the Town Clerk was applying, asking for information on the applicant. There can be no doubt that councils take the job of finding a new Town Clerk very seriously.

SALARIES AND CONDITIONS OF SERVICE

In 1948, to meet what was described as a 'chaotic and difficult' position in regard to the salaries and the conditions of service of the chief officers in local government, two Whitley Councils were established: one, the Joint Negotiating Committee for Town Clerks and District Council Clerks; the other, the Joint Negotiating Committee for Chief Officers of Local Authorities.[1] The establishment of a separate committee for the Clerks was in a sense a recognition of the Clerk's senior status among the chief officers and was the final result of what was no doubt a heated dispute behind the scenes among the various officer organizations and local authority associations, a dispute resolved in the end, it would seem, by the strong pressures applied by the Society of Town Clerks upon the sources of influence in the Association of Municipal Corporations.

The Joint Negotiating Committee for the Town Clerks and District Council Clerks is composed of the following representatives:

Employers
Association of Municipal Corporations   3
Urban District Councils Association   3
Rural District Councils Association   3
Metropolitan Boroughs' Standing Joint Committee   1

Employees
Society of Town Clerks   3
Society of Clerks of Urban District Councils   3
Local Government Clerks Association   3

In addition the County Councils Association sends two non-voting representatives for liaison purposes.

Once established, it took about a year for the Joint Negotiating Committee to produce the initial set of recommendations. These were issued on September 8, 1949, and consisted of a preamble and two schedules—one for salary scales and the

[1] For a description of the evolution of Whitleyism in the local government service, see generally, J. H. Warren, *The Local Government Service* (London, 1951).

other for conditions of service. The salary scales were and still are based on the principle of ranges with a different range applied to each population group. The ranges have in fact been kept quite wide so that the appointing authority has considerable latitude as to the initial salary it gives its Town Clerk. In the smaller authorities, the range has gradually increased from £150 to its present £180. In the largest authorities covered by the scales the range initially was £250; it is now £330. The use of ranges for minimum salaries is justified on several counts. First of all, the scales apply to Clerks of all kinds of authorities except county councils. The responsibilities of the Clerks, however, differ considerably from one class to another even when the populations are similar. Consequently some flexibility is needed, or the reliance upon population as a means of gradation is unfair. Moreover, there are numerous special or local conditions which make the job of one Town Clerk differ greatly from that of another, especially such things as the higher cost of living in the London area, the additional council-operated enterprises in seaside towns, the Clerk who doubles as Chief Financial Officer or who holds several appointments additional to those held by a Clerk, and the professionally trained officer in the very small authority. All of these conditions merit some special consideration and instead of permitting a number of exceptions to be made from a rigid scale, the Committee thought it best to install a certain amount of flexibility in the original system. The Joint Negotiating Committee for Chief Officers of Local Authorities adopted the same principle in its recommendations, first used September 12, 1950.

Since the first recommendations, the salary scales have been revised upwards three times; once in November 1954; again in May 1956; and the last time in February 1959. At present the recommended maximum salary for authorities up to 600,000 population is £4,600, the minimum for an authority under 5,000 is £860. The general gradations of salaries according to population are shown in the table overleaf.

The salary, however, is not the only remuneration to which a Town Clerk is entitled. According to the negotiated Conditions of Service, he is entitled to certain fees: those which he receives for his duties as acting or deputy returning officer and as registration officer or deputy registration officer; those pre-

Population	Average Salary*
	£
12,500	1,310
25,000	1,775
50,000	2,310
85,000	2,977
125,000	3,312
200,000	3,642
500,000	4,307

* These figures are based upon the mean between the lowest starting salary recommended and the highest salary (after increments) recommended.

miums which he receives from articled clerks if he is a solicitor; and his salary for carrying out the duties of Clerk of the Peace, if he holds that office. These fees may amount to quite considerable sums. The Town Clerk of a very large city, for instance, receives a salary of £4,100 plus from £1,000–£1,200 in fees. The premiums paid by articled clerks may be as high as £300 per clerk and each solicitor is permitted to have two articled clerks, though few have. As for the salaries of Clerks of the Peace, in Andover the Town Clerk has received an extra £50 for this job; in Northampton he has received £150; in Newcastle £315. In all but a very few instances, therefore, the Town Clerk's basic salary is supplemented by fees, premiums or secondary salaries, which may prove to be quite substantial sums.

The other Conditions of Service negotiated by the Joint Negotiating Committee for Town Clerks and District Council Clerks very generally outline the Town Clerk's duties and responsibilities and set out the requirements for annual leave and sick pay. By way of brief summary, the Town Clerk's duties are to perform the council's legal work; to convene all council and committee meetings; to advise the mayor; to assist members in the drafting of resolutions; to advise on standing orders and local government legislation; to conduct the council's official, but not technical, correspondence with outside bodies; to supervise ceremonial arrangements; to conduct all important inquiries; and to oversee all public notices and advertisements. Beyond this it is agreed that no political group shall seek his advice and that no major negotiations shall be carried on by any other officer without his knowledge. In addition he is entitled to a minimum of four weeks' annual leave and very liberal allowances in event of sickness. And most important, he is described as 'the chief executive and administrative officer of the Council' and is responsible for 'co-ordinating the whole of the work of the Council'.

But these salary scales and conditions of service are only recommendations; they do not have the force of law. Nonetheless there are ways of enforcing them. If an authority advertises a vacancy for a Town Clerk and does not offer the recommended salary or conditions of service, the authority is black-listed, the Society of Town Clerks appeals to its members not to apply for the open position. Moreover the Law Society discourages its members, the solicitors, from applying.[1] Consequently the two most fruitful sources of Town Clerks are cut off, and the area of choice open to the black-listed authority is severely restricted. For those authorities who refuse to implement the negotiated recommendations for their present Town Clerks the sanctions are somewhat different. The Town Clerk places a complaint before the Society of Town Clerks. The Society, now a registered Trade Union, then reports to the Minister of Labour that a labour dispute has arisen. Following this the Minister sends a mediator, who investigates the situation and attempts to bring about a settlement. If he is unsuccessful, the Minister thereupon declares that a dispute has arisen, and the matter goes before the Industrial Disputes Tribunal. The Industrial Disputes Tribunal hears the arguments of the Society of Town Clerks and the involved corporation and then hands down the decision. At least three Town Clerks have had disputes brought before the Tribunal and in each instance the Tribunal has enforced the recommendations of the Joint Negotiating Committee.[2] Thus enforcement of the 'recommendations' is possible.[3] And the vast majority of authorities

[1] (Anonymous) 'Law Society Supports Society of Town Clerks, etc.' 60 *Municipal Journal*, 61 (1952).

[2] Industrial Disputes Tribunal, Award nos. 665, 778, 963.

[3] But these means have not always been available. In *R. v. National Arbitration Tribunal ex parte South Shields Corporation* (1951), 2 A.E.R. 828 it was held that a Town Clerk could not have a 'dispute' between himself and his authority referred to the Tribunal because by interpretation of the Ministerial Order establishing the Tribunal a 'dispute' must involve more than one workman and his employer. Subsequently the Society of Town Clerks registered as a Trade Union and thereafter the 'disputes' referred to the Tribunal were between the Society and the

have accepted the recommendations without necessitating resort to the enforcement methods.[1]

From all these facts and figures, negotiations and recommendations, emerges the outline of the major problem concerning the Town Clerk in the present-day local administrative structure. His training is invariably that of a solicitor. But his job is described as legal adviser *and* chief administrative officer. He is trained as a lawyer. Should he also be trained as an administrator? Or should legal adviser and chief administrator be separated, be two distinct offices with other professionals as well as lawyers being tapped for the chief administrator's job?

Over the past thirty years various recommendations have been advanced on this problem. The Royal Commission on Local Government (1929) recognized the need for high administrative ability in a Town Clerk but saw the balance of convenience weighted in favour of legal qualifications. The Hadow Committee (1934) stressed administrative ability as a much greater requisite for a Town Clerk than legal training or proficiency. Professor Robson strongly advocated the administrative qualifications almost to the exclusion of any need for legal background and suggested that the chief administrator be drawn from those 'men of imagination and proved administrative ability' within local government or without, no matter what their training has been.[2] In the Coventry Report, the Treasury (O. and M.) Division recommended the separation of legal adviser and chief administrator and the complete recognition of the Town Clerk as chief administrative officer.

Despite these and many other suggestions of reform or recasting, the office of Town Clerk has remained essentially unchanged over this period. The Town Clerk continues to function in the dual role of a part-lawyer and part-administrator, trained and largely experienced on the legal side of

employing Corporation. A Divisional Court in December 1957 upheld the Society of Town Clerks' contention that it represented a section of trade or industry and that it was able to have 'disputes' referred to the Tribunal. 29 *Municipal Review* 113 (1948).

[1] As of March 1957 of the 387 Boroughs employing full-time Town Clerks (the recommendations do not apply to part-time Town Clerks), 345 were applying the recommendations in their entirety, and 374 were applying all recommendations except the increased salaries scheduled to take effect April 1, 1956. (Argument of Society of Town Clerks, Industrial Disputes Tribunal, Award 963 (1957).)

[2] Robson, op. cit., pp. 317–20.

local government operations. Some Town Clerks are more administrators than lawyers. Others are more lawyers than administrators. But all of them play the role of both in some way and at some time. The following five chapters are devoted to an attempt to describe how and to what extent this dual role is played.

CHAPTER IV

THE TOWN CLERK AND THE ELECTED REPRESENTATIVES: THE COUNCIL AND AND ITS COMMITTEES

THE TOWN CLERK AS AN OFFICER: AN INTRODUCTION

IF one were to select a single phrase to describe the Town Clerk, it would necessarily be—'a local government officer'. A Town Clerk may be a number of things in addition to this; he may be the principal officer or the chief executive officer or, without confusing him with the Prime Minister, the *primus inter pares*, but none of these disturb the basic and essential fact that he is first and foremost an officer and that he works within the scope and limitations prescribed for officers in the administration of local government.

What, then, is the place of an officer in local government? Very succinctly, it is the job of the councillors, collectively as a council or a committee, to decide matters of policy; it is the duty of the officers to execute[1] this policy. This theory in its general form is very simply drawn.

In fact, perhaps it is too simply drawn. What precisely is meant by this distinction embodied in the words—policy and execution? A closer look at this theory is desirable, for maybe it has no meaning. These words—policy and execution—stand for ideas which can be very easily distinguished if one clings to the extremes, the poles as it were, of decisions to be made on the continuum of human activities involved in running a local authority. At one pole we might put the decision to levy a 25s. rate for the year 1961—definitely a matter of policy; at the other pole perhaps the decision to lick a stamp and post a letter—definitely a matter of execution. But in the middle, where the Town Clerk and other higher officials operate, the

---

[1] Preference is given to the word 'execute' in this context, rather than 'administer', since the word 'administration' has consistently been used to signify the entire operating machinery of a local authority.

dichotomy loses its definitiveness. Nothing automatically separates matters of policy from matters of execution for a Town Clerk. Neither he nor the councillors have an electronic sorting machine. Thus, if one hoped, by using the theory, to place labels on an activity and then assign responsibility for the activity to either the council or an officer, one is mistaken. He would only be chasing himself in semantic circles.

In the simple practical terms it is impossible that 'policy' and 'execution' have absolute meanings. There are circumstances which vary greatly between one authority and another and which make an activity a matter of policy in one authority and a matter of execution in another. There is the status of a local authority, whether it is a county or a county borough or a county district; this determines to a large extent what services it will provide, and this in turn affects what becomes policy and what becomes execution in the administration of the local authority's affairs. Secondly there is the size of a community. Although a local council may increase in size as the population it serves increases, there are obvious practical limits to this so that a town of 10,000 population like Bideford has sixteen members on its Council and a city like Birmingham, with a population of well over a million, has 152 members. Birmingham has a population one hundred times the size of Bideford, but a Council less than ten times its size. Certainly the amount of work involved in administering the needs of a million inhabitants is more than ten times as heavy as that involved in a town of 10,000. From this it follows that since the amount of time which one councillor can allow to his local government work is roughly the same the country over, what is a matter of policy in Bideford may be a matter of execution in Birmingham. Next, the differences in the various local services themselves affect the distinction between policy and execution. To administer efficiently some services and to make effective decisions in their administration, it is often necessary to have a fair amount of technical knowledge, whereas for other services a good mixture of local knowledge and common sense generally suffices. An example of the former would be the waterworks; of the latter, housing. Similarly in those trading enterprises where the committee is able to supervise effectively the operation by watching the running accounts of income and expenditures, the scope of the elected representatives in deciding policy can be quite limited. Thus the terms of this theory are relative terms. They have no fixed meaning.

To say this is not to join the cynic who says policy matters are the things councillors decide, execution matters are the things officers decide, and that this business of there being any qualitative difference between policy and execution is ridiculous. We need not go that far.

There is a general idea which lies behind this theory. It is this: that matters of policy involve a much wider area of discretion than do matters of execution, that the areas of choice, the scope of action, of the elected representatives greatly exceed those in which the official moves and works. Certainly even here much ambiguity remains, for what is meant by wider areas of discretion or choice or action? But this idea is a general guide.

It gives both officers and councillors pegs on which to hang their claims that either they or the other group *should* perform a certain function or activity. Thus the distinction has more than a descriptive or 'is' use; it has prescriptive or 'ought' use. Although one may say deciding policy is what councillors do, and executing policy is what officers do, and this is a policy matter because councillors handle it, and this is an execution matter because officers handle it, this solves nothing when it comes to deciding who does some new activity. To follow the cynical path, one would have to say that is a decision made on the basis of power or leverage or capability or knowledge or however in human relationships one person or group prevails over another. But this is not a completely true description of what happens. The idea behind the words as a guide between policy and execution has some use, if not some precision.

At the same time wider area of discretion cannot always be equated with greater importance or greater influence on the course a matter may take. A council may lay down the general lines along which it wishes its officer to proceed. The officer's discretion is thus limited. But whether the matter succeeds or fails may depend on how the officer 'executes', for instance, the approach he uses to a Ministry, the tone of a letter, the structure and content of an argument. Execution of policy is not a mechanical thing. People are not machines. People can react to

74

logic, persistence, flattery, favour or a host of other things. When executing a policy involves getting people to do something (as it usually does), the policy decision may not be the prime factor in answering the question: did the council succeed or fail?

The policy-execution distinction is used to justify other propositions concerning the relation between councillors and officers. As policy is the scope of the councillors, so execution is the scope of the official. It follows, therefore, that councillors as individuals have no right to participate in the execution of any policy, nor do they have a right to inspect the work of any officer. This, of course, does not deny the right of the council to inquire into the efficiency of a department or even to inspect the work of a particular official; but the council or one of its committees must authorize such an enquiry or inspection. It also follows that the responsibility to the public for policies adopted is borne by the elected representatives. Generally speaking, no officer can be taken to task for any decision taken by the council or one of its committees. Although complaints from the public may be sent to the Town Clerk or lodged personally with a local official, these complaints are directed not at the official, but at the council. There is an exception to this rule. The Treasurer stands in a special relation to the council, and may be held personally responsible if he permits the council to spend money for an illegal purpose.[1] But aside from this, the responsibility rests squarely upon the elected representatives.

So far in this discussion attention has been focused upon councillors and officers as decision-makers. Obviously more is involved in the taking of a council or committee decision than merely counting 'yeas' and 'nays'. One must usually recognize the facts of a situation, then one must consider the various alternative actions which spring from these facts, actions which must be considered in light of past performances and successes and forecasted results. A councillor, or even the councillors collectively, could not be expected to have all the relevant facts in his or their hands, to think out the various alternatives, or to supply information on past performances or predicted results. This illustrates another aspect of the relations between coun-

[1] See discussion concerning *Attorney-General v. DeWinton supra*, p. 44 ff.

cillor and officer, an aspect arising chiefly because the increase in the technical complexities of human life requires that a great deal of knowledge and competence be applied to the government of democratic peoples. The problem has been to apply this knowledge and competence without abrogating the principle of popular control, through representation, of government. The solution, at least as far as local government in England is concerned, lies in entrusting the major decisions to the elected representatives, but retaining the officers not only to execute the policy but also to advise on the formulation of it. This principle is based upon the belief, as the late Lord Lindsay put it, 'in the inherent soundness of the reactions of the common man, the good judge of men and of horses'.[1]

Co-existent with this belief has been a tendency to distrust experts. There is a feeling—a feeling one must readily admit is too often supported by actual examples—that the expert exaggerates the importance of his own field of expertise and tends to lose a proper perspective on things in general. Of course one must be careful, as Dr K. C. Wheare has warned, about placing labels on the various functionaries within local government administration. The advisers, as they are being referred to here, are generally the chief officers of the local authority. A chief officer is less likely to be an expert, in the sense of those whom many people distrust, than he is a general practitioner; that is, in possession of a good general knowledge of one profession. His lack of specific and detailed knowledge of one area within his profession and his breadth of rather general knowledge should make him, first of all, a more acute and discerning adviser and, secondly, less prone to excesses ascribed to experts.[2] Even so, even though this offers less cause for distrust, it does not alter the general principle that councillors decide, officers advise.

Again a caveat: the distinction between deciding and advising is not a clear-cut one. Councillors vote, officers do not. If one holds that a decision is taken when a vote is made, only then would the distinction acquire clarity. But it would be a misleading clarity. When in the course of reaching a decision

[1] Quoted by E. C. R. Hadfield and J. E. MacColl, *British Local Government* (London, 1949), pp. 128–9.
[2] K. C. Wheare, *Government by Committee* (Oxford, 1955), pp. 12–20.

does a group stop discussing and begin deciding? Actually most people have their minds made up before a vote is ever taken. Where the discussion is free and open, the officer's advice, pitched or coloured to strike favourable responses among the audience, clothed in the aura of disinterested reflection, may in actual fact be worth more than the one vote he does not have. One needs to be wary of over-simplifying how decisions are taken in the way drawing lines between deciding and advising induces one to.

In this very brief introduction something of the basic theory of democracy as it applies to local government has been explored. It is well, therefore, to keep this theory and its limitations in mind as the examination of the actual relations existing between the Town Clerk and the elected representatives proceeds.

THE TOWN CLERK AS CLERK OF THE COUNCIL AND ITS COMMITTEES

Before launching into a detailed discussion of the Town Clerk's relations with the council and its committees, one should note several major variables which play a large part in determining the exact nature of the relationship in any given town. The most obvious, probably the most important, is the size of the town. Municipal corporations vary in size from Montgomery with under 1,000 population to Birmingham with well over a million inhabitants. These are quite naturally the extremes. Almost a majority of the corporations lie between the 20,000 to 75,000 range.[1] At the same time it should be noted that even though variations in size are extremely great, all these corporations have councils, all have Town Clerks; but all do not have the same powers and functions. The major distinction is between county and non-county boroughs. The county boroughs, in terms of powers and scope of operation, may be closely compared with the county councils; both are largely all-purpose authorities. Similarly there is little which distinguishes a small borough from an urban district except the Mayor, the mace and the Town Clerk.

The variations in size and functions or powers are vast. But what general impact does this have on the office of Town Clerk?

[1] See, *supra*, p. 50.

The large corporations are big businesses. Their operations involve often ten or more thousand employees and net expenditures of several millions of pounds.[1] As with large businesses, the hierarchy of organization must be properly defined, procedures must be established and followed. The amount of detailed day-to-day management is immense and complex. All this means that the Town Clerk becomes more involved in running a machine and less involved in carrying out specific duties within the machine. Contrast him with his counterpart in the small town of 15,000 to 20,000. There the employees may number not more than 200; and everyone on the office staff will more than likely work in one building; hierarchy of organization gives way to a network of more or less informal relationships; procedures may be altered to meet the unusual case; the details of day-to-day management may often be carried in the head of the chief official.

Not only does population vary among municipal corporations, but so does the size of council. Generally speaking this variation is fairly well correlated to the differences in population. Yet there are certain limits: only three authorities have less than sixteen members, and none has more than 160. From this it is apparent that a Town Clerk will get to know the members of a small council, their ambitions and their eccentricities, more quickly and better than will a Town Clerk of a large council. The relationship in a small council will no doubt be closer and more informal; the Town Clerk will assume proportions more human and less divine or otherwise in the councillors' minds. This is not to say that business will move on better, for it is a curious thing that very often in the small council the gulf in ability that exists between officials and councillors is much larger than the one existing between officials and councillors in the large councils. It is in such situations that experts tend to be more greatly distrusted, possibly because of a feeling of inferiority on the part of the councillor, or perhaps a fear that the council's prerogative to control may be lost to the official.[2]

[1] As examples, Bristol, population 442,500, had a net expenditure in the 1956–57 fiscal year of over five million pounds; Northampton, population 102,800, had a net expenditure of almost one and a half million pounds for the same period.

[2] F. H. Smith, 'The Expert in the Local Government Service', 22 *Public Administration*, London 30 (1944), p. 38.

To a certain extent the tendency towards unfamiliarity in large councils may be mitigated when the membership turnover is not great, when councillors tend to hold office term after term. The paradox, however, is that this tendency is probably more marked in the small authorities, particularly in those that are unorganized politically. Where the political balance in a local authority is very close, conceivably there might be a great number of changes each year. A case in point is a middle-sized borough in the north, where a political balance has shifted from one party to the other several times in recent years: of fifty-two councillors only ten have had *more* than ten years' experience and more than thirty have had *less* than four years on the council. The Town Clerk has scarcely had time to become acquainted with a councillor before a political rival supplants him.

The political composition itself is a variable which may greatly affect the functioning of a Town Clerk. Generally it may be said that councils are divided politically; normally it is along lines similar to national politics, Conservative and Labour. Both national party headquarters contain local government sections which assist in the organization of local election campaigns and distribute circulars on national policy and its local implications. On the whole it is safe to say that the Conservatives inspire less cohesiveness from the national level and create less at the local level. As a result the division in many councils is one of Labour and anti-Labour, the latter group being less likely to have a definite programme. But simple division is not really the crux of the matter so far as the Town Clerk is concerned. First of all, the party spirit may vary in intensity. Thus in some councils one group or the other may seize upon almost any issue at all and make it a political one.[1] In these circumstances a Town Clerk must be very careful concerning the kind of advice he tenders and the amount of influence he exerts on policy formation. And this is even more true where the division between the party is but a few seats. It is altogether possible, where the minority party is weak and its chances of gaining a majority remote, that the Town Clerk

[1] For example, a middle-sized borough in the Midlands recently divided politically over the question of whether to have litter baskets in the town centre area.

might show a little bias at times without subjecting himself to charges of favouritism. But where the majority is slim the Town Clerk must be particularly guarded, for an impropriety of one year may be the source of his discomfort the next if the offended minority comes to power. Party composition, intensity of spirit, size of majority—certainly all these factors in some way help to fashion the office of Town Clerk in a particular locale, but one must take care not to over-emphasize this effect. For the most part housing is the only major problem upon which the parties consistently divide at the present time, and here it is an easy task for a Town Clerk or any official to frame his advice so as to avoid the areas of party conflict.

An aspect closely related to party composition, but not necessarily dependent upon it, is what might be described as a council's general attitude or outlook. A council may be aristocratic and, as one writer has explained, tend to treat its professional officers as if they were gamekeepers. Or a council may be working class, and in a sense be in a position of boss to people who in outside employment would be their superiors.[1] Councils may be independent-minded and have a tendency to rebel against any outside advice from officers or joint negotiating committees or more especially the central government. On the other hand, a council may be quite happy to follow anyone's lead. To be sure the council is reflecting a community attitude if one could say that communities have attitudes. And yet there does seem to be something peculiar to itself in these council attitudes in that they may cut across party divisions and the class lines in the community. It is just as if the council were a club and there were a set of unwritten rules which every member of the club religiously observed. It is not difficult for a Town Clerk to get along with a council attitude. In most instances it is simply a matter of recognizing it and adjusting one's habits of thought accordingly. It is predictable.

There are, therefore, four general conditions which affect a Town Clerk's relations with his council: the size of the town or city, the size of the council, the party complexion of the council and the general outlook or attitude of the council so far as it is discernible. These conditions are in the background of any Town Clerk–council relationship, whether in council meeting

[1] E. C. R. Hadfield and J. E. MacColl, op. cit., pp. 126–7.

itself, in the committee room or across a desk in the Town Clerk's office. In the main, however, it is in the committee where these forces and certainly a number of others have their freest play.

THE TOWN CLERK AND THE COMMITTEES

To quote Dr K. C. Wheare, 'local administration in Britain is administration by committees'.[1] In local government, committees abound—standing committees, non-standing committees, statutory committees, special committees of all sizes, purposes and descriptions. One large city has listed in its year-book eighteen standing committees, two non-standing committees, two advisory committees, two ex-officio committees, four joint committees and twenty-eight regular sub-committees plus governing bodies for schools and advisory councils on education. In an average month forty-eight of these committees were scheduled to meet according to the municipal calendar prepared at the beginning of the year. In one middle-sized non-county borough, there are eighteen standing committees, three joint committees and twenty-two regular sub-committees, A small southern town, however, has only nine standing committees and two special committees. Roughly speaking, the size of the borough and its status determines the number of committees it has.

The common practice is for each standing committee to meet once a month and to make a report with recommendations to a monthly council meeting. There are, as would be expected, numerous exceptions to the common practice. Some boroughs operate on a five week cycle. A few others have a monthly committee cycle but bi-monthly council meetings; in other places a special council meeting is held to consider the yearly budget. May—the month of elections—and August—the month of holidays—are often exceptions to this monthly cycle procedure. A survey of county boroughs has shown that committees average one to two hours in length; the more important committees such as Housing, Town Planning and Finance tend to last somewhat longer.[2] There is always one

[1] K. C. Wheare, op. cit., p. 165.
[2] D.N.C., 'Council and Committee Meetings in County Boroughs', 32 *Public Administration*, London 429 (1954).

officer, and usually several more, sitting in on a committee; thus over the course of a year the number of man-hours spent by officials in committee adds up to an extremely large amount.

The Town Clerk, nominally, and to a very great extent in practice, is clerk to all committees of the council just as he is clerk to the council. This simply means that he supervises the organizational aspects of committee work, the preparation of agendas, the summoning of meetings, the recording of decisions and recommendations. This work is normally carried out within the Town Clerk's department.

There is, nevertheless, one major exception to this principle. In those boroughs in which the councils are the education authorities, that is, the county boroughs, a large majority of the Education Committees have as their secretary the Chief Education Officer. According to figures compiled in January 1955, sixty-four Education Committees in county boroughs have the Chief Education Officer as their secretary. This number may be slightly, but not significantly, smaller at the present time.

One middle-sized borough council gave this practice a thorough look recently and the result of its study and the action it took aptly summarize the problems this exception poses. The sub-committee instructed to re-examine the policy reported that when education became a municipal function in 1902 a few local authorities placed the committee work under the Town Clerk's supervision and other authorities have in recent years switched to this procedure. Nevertheless, a large majority of county boroughs started with and continue to have the Chief Education Officer as clerk to the Education Committee. The sub-committee could see no logical reason for handling the Education Committee work differently from that of other committees and recognized that doing so created a tendency towards independence on the part of the Education Committee and department. Thus committed in principle to the consolidation of committee work under the Town Clerk, the sub-committee went on to consider the practical aspects of the transference. It found that one and a half to two committee clerks would have to be added to the Town Clerk's staff to cope with the additional work, which would involve the one full committee, seven sub-committees and five sections and joint sections of sub-committees. This addition would have to be made without an equivalent reduction in the Education department staff since the committee work there was handled by five senior assistants who also had other duties. The Town Clerk advised that although no practical difficulty would be presented by the transfer, the present system worked reasonably well and his co-ordinating function was not unduly hampered.

Balancing the additional cost against the principle of consolidation of committee work, the sub-committee recommended that the transfer not be made, but that the position be kept under review. Moreover it was emphasized that the Town Clerk should continue as legal adviser to all committees and should co-ordinate the work of all committees including that of the Education Committee, even though in practice he might find this difficult in respect of a committee for whose work he is not responsible. The council approved the sub-committee's recommendation. In substance what the sub-committee's recommendation amounted to was that the principle of consolidation, and whatever improved efficiency and co-ordination which might be expected to flow from it, were not worth one thousand pounds or more a year. No doubt other authorities whose Education Committee work is handled by the Education department have been faced with the same problem and have reached the same conclusion. It is significant that councils do consider this problem, and presumably when a transfer can be made without such serious financial implications, it will take place.

According to the recommended Conditions of Service negotiated for Town Clerks and District Council Clerks, the Town Clerk is entitled to attend all committee meetings of the council.[1] In practice it would be a most unusual case when either he or one of his representatives—the Deputy Town Clerk or an Assistant Solicitor or a Senior Committee Clerk— were not on hand to advise a committee in its work; and in most cases two representatives of the Town Clerk's Department, a solicitor to give advice and a committee clerk to record the proceedings, are present.

The number of committees a Town Clerk personally attends

[1] Recommendations of the Joint Negotiating Committee for Town Clerks and District Council Clerks, Schedule II, para. 6.

is dependent upon a number of conditions: his personal inclination, the councillors' wishes, the particular matters up for consideration, the size of the town. In general, the size of the town seems to have the most effect. In towns of less than 10,000 population it is a rarity for a Town Clerk not to attend all the committees of his council. This would in most cases amount to four to six per month, though in some places perhaps more. In the slightly larger authority with 10,000 to 30,000 population, although some Town Clerks attend all the committees, the tendency is to have the Deputy Town Clerk, where there is one, or an Assistant Town Clerk or solicitor take care of a few of the minor ones. On the average a Town Clerk in this size authority attends seven to eight committee meetings a month. When one reaches the 30,000 to 50,000 class there is a noticeable tendency on the part of a Town Clerk to reduce the proportion of committees he attends. Thus he might divide them equally with his Deputy or Assistant, or take two-thirds or three-quarters of them himself leaving the remainder to his representative. Yet the total number he attends remains on the average about seven to eight. In the middle-sized authority of 50,000 to 100,000 almost all Town Clerks divide the committees among the solicitors in their department. At the lower end of this class this might be only the Town Clerk and his Deputy and perhaps one Assistant Solicitor, but nearer the 100,000 mark it would probably entail a four or five-way division. In this class authority there is also a tendency to break committees into sub-committees and to create special committees to deal with a temporary problem. In short, the committee structure becomes more complicated and more man-power is needed to manage it. There are also wide variations between Town Clerks as to the number of committees they regularly attend; some attend fifteen or twenty; others may reduce their regular attendance to one or two. The average number, however, is about seven, just slightly less than in the smaller boroughs. In the large authority the tendency is to reduce the number attended even more. Thus in boroughs of 100,000 to 200,000, the average Town Clerk attends five to six committees in the normal month; in those over 200,000 the average is just five. As a result, not only does the proportion of committees which the Town Clerk personally attends decline as the size of the

authority increases, but the actual number he attends also
decreases. These figures, however, relate only to regular attendance; that is, those committees which the Town Clerk plans to
attend as part of his normal working schedule. In fact a Town
Clerk may appear at a large number of committees if there is
something on the agenda which he feels particularly demands
his attention or on which he would like his views heard, or if
a councillor requests him to be present.

Where a Town Clerk does limit his attendance, which committees does he attend? Almost invariably he will attend the
Finance Committee or Finance and General Purposes Committee, where the two are combined. Beyond that he will
usually attend the Legal and Parliamentary Committee, or
whatever committee is entrusted with overseeing the general
legal work of the corporation; the Establishment Committee;
the General Purposes or Co-ordinating or Policy Advisory
Committee; and less frequently the Planning Committee.
Where the Town Clerk is Civil Defence Controller-Designate,
he probably attends the Civil Defence Committee. In other
instances, his attendance depends on the type of town—for
example, in a resort town he might attend the Public Relations
Committee; or on the Town Clerk's own personal interests—in
which case he might attend the Entertainments Committee or
Water Committee or Archives Committee. The variety is
infinite, but in the main the nature of his office compels him to
be most interested in the committees dealing with finance,
establishment, law and general policy advice.

The Town Clerk and his representatives are not the only
officers who attend committees. In general there is at least one
and quite frequently two or three officers from other departments in attendance. Again much depends upon the size of
the authority and the nature of the committee. In the small
authority almost every committee will be attended by the
Borough Surveyor and the Borough Treasurer as well as the
Town Clerk and a Committee Clerk. Not infrequently each of
these chief officers will be accompanied by his deputy or assistant. As authorities become larger, committees tend to become
more specialized and only the officer most directly concerned
with the work of the committee will attend; consequently at the
Housing Committee there will be the Housing Manager; at the

Transport Committee, the Transport Engineer; at the Baths Committee, the Baths Manager. The Treasurer in most authorities, however, like the Town Clerk, sends a representative to each committee. Nevertheless, even in the larger places, officers are officers of the council, not of a particular committee, and they should, therefore, regard themselves as available for consultation by any committee. The trend towards independent departments and committees, about which more will be said below, is closely related to this feeling often held by an officer and a committee that an officer is only responsible to that one committee.

PREPARATION FOR COMMITTEE MEETINGS

Preparation for a committee meeting begins with the formulation of an agenda. As the Town Clerk is the clerk to all committees, the agenda is for the most part formulated within the Town Clerk's department, except of course the Education Committees in county boroughs. Before describing the actual mechanics of this preparation, it is well to consider some of the more theoretical, but nonetheless important, questions: what is the significance of the agenda in the Town Clerk-committee relationship? What kind of items are placed on an agenda? What is the origin of items placed on an agenda?

The formulation of an agenda is the procedure by which matters of policy are separated from matters of execution. The former become items on the agenda, the latter, problems which are solved within the confines of the departments without reference to a committee.[1] And although it is common to think of local government in terms of councils and committees administering services, in all but the very smallest of authorities the number of officers far outweighs the number of councillors, and an even more striking difference occurs between the amount of time officers spend on their work and the amount of time spent by the councillors. It is apparent that matters of policy are less frequent in the normal course of administration than are matters of execution. A Town Clerk in a middle-sized borough in the Midlands estimates that for every twenty

---

[1] There is, of course, the in-between stage where the officer consults the Chairman and secures his approval or disapproval. This is discussed *infra*, p. 120.

matters which cross his desk only one ever touches a committee agenda. Similarly a Chief Public Health Inspector of a small town in the north asserts that of the complaints received by his department from the public, 99 per cent are handled by his department, only one in a hundred ever comes before a committee for advice or a decision of some kind.

The initiative as to whether a matter is placed on an agenda rests very largely with the officers, and since it is within the Town Clerk's department that most agendas are prepared, the Town Clerk is capable of influencing their contents. Some Town Clerks may exercise a great deal of control over what is included, often redrafting and revising the agenda after the initial draft is prepared by someone in his department. In other places the Town Clerk may include on an agenda any item another officer desires: thus a Treasurer of a medium-sized borough in the north explained that he simply sends a letter to the Town Clerk stating, 'I would like the following items to be included on the agenda of the —————Committee,' and followed by an enumerated list of items. The Town Clerk then puts these items on the agenda verbatim, without change or comment. The Town Clerk's control in this respect is one of scrutinizing those items which another officer would like placed on an agenda. This is not the same as deciding, from the vast number of problems which have arisen during the past month, which should be decided by the committee and which should be dealt with by the members of the staff on their own. Taking the instance of the Public Health Inspector referred to above, the decisions on the ninety-nine complaints rest with the Public Health Inspector; it is only in connection with the one in a hundred that the Town Clerk is likely to exert any control; that is, by re-phrasing the question to be decided, or postponing its reference to the committee, or advising the Public Health Inspector to handle the matter without reference to the committee. Of course the departments do not work in complete isolation from each other; therefore in a number of the ninety-nine cases, the Public Health Inspector might quite expectedly consult the Town Clerk for legal advice, or perhaps simply general advice, in which case the Town Clerk's influence would be felt. The Town Clerk moreover makes decisions concerning matters which cross his desk, and since he is the authority's chief correspondent, his decisions may often be of some importance. In general the Town Clerk's influence upon the content of most committee agendas is neither continuous nor all-encompassing but it is, nonetheless, greater than the influence exercised by any other officer of the corporation.

Now assuming an item or problem or issue comes before the Town Clerk, or for that matter, before any officer of the authority, what considerations would affect his decision to place or not to place it on a committee's agenda? First of all, the council or committee may have already established its policy on the issue. As an example, the Town Clerk of a small and ancient borough cited the instance of a letter he had recently received from the Member of Parliament which discussed the conditions of a woman living in an unfit house in the borough. The problem had only recently been before the committee in another context, so the Town Clerk answered the Member of Parliament straightaway without referring to the committee. Examples such as this could be multiplied a thousand-fold, for where the council has established its policy, it is the duty of its officers to act in concert with that policy until it is changed. This is in essence a simple manifestation of the division between policy and execution.

Nevertheless, there are other considerations which leave the dividing line less clearly defined. Matters of urgency sometimes necessitate official action when the normal recourse would be to get a committee decision first. A storm may have caused a road embankment to subside or trees to fall and block the road. Quite obviously no one is going to wait for a committee to approve the money to repair the road. The Borough Engineer will see that it is done and then report the matter to the committee. Likewise it would be more common for something of this nature to arise in the operations of a department other than the Town Clerk's department. On the other hand in any major emergency which involved the possibility of alternative action the head of the department involved would most likely consult the Town Clerk.

To a certain extent the officer's decision is affected by the work of the committee. Certain committees by their very nature must consider more important problems, and the less important issues thereby come within the purview of the officers. The Town Clerk of a very large city commenting on this said that some committees do not have enough to do so that one must be careful not to bypass them too much, whilst other committees have all they can do to decide major issues of policy. A comparison of the agenda papers of two small boroughs seems to lead to the same conclusion. In the one, a town of about 16,000 population, the Housing Committee considered the purchase of several temporary bungalows, the sale of certain houses and the housing of tubercular patients. The Parks and Properties Committee, with a much shorter agenda, considered the lease of some Corporation property to the Sports and Social Club and the temporary use of part of a park as a car park during a garden fête. In the other, somewhat smaller, town the Estates Committee considered such things as an architect's modifications in the Guildhall staircase doorway, the joy-riding of bicycles, the lease of a room to the Pensioners' Associations, and the date and time of the next meeting. The Finance Committee on the other hand considered the Corporation's position on bank overdraft facilities, a Ministry circular on the restriction of capital investment, the financial implications of a council housing rent review and the proposals of the standing committees involving expenditure. It is difficult to avoid concluding that in these instances at least the officers concerned possessed wider discretion in regard to the Housing and Finance Committees than they did in regard to the Parks and Properties and Estates Committees.

Not only does the general scope of the committee work exert its influence, but the membership on the committees does also. New councillors tend not to recognize what decisions might be prudently left in the hands of an official. A Town Clerk of a medium-sized borough in the north illustrated this tendency in connection with a recent issue over street lighting. He contended that once a committee had decided that a certain street should be lighted, the officers concerned should select the lamps and posts and decide upon their placement. In this instance, however, the committee members, most of them recently elected, took it upon themselves to visit other towns in order to compare the various types of lamp posts in use and then to make the choice themselves. This perhaps is an example of an over-zealous official as well. But one cannot doubt the contention that new councillors may tend to concern themselves with matters which are better left within the province of an officer. When this happens the officer has a double duty: one, to guide the new members to an understanding of their proper function; two, to prevent the discouragement of this initial enthusiasm which new councillors often bring to the council.

Less frequently a consideration of a much more personal nature must be made. A certain issue may affect some councillor personally and its omission from committee consideration may lead to some agitation by him. Although this is a rare happening, it is nevertheless to the officer's advantage to watch for such items, for thereby he ensures a smoother and happier relationship between members and officials. Similarly past practice has some effect upon what an officer brings before a committee. A committee which has become accustomed to deciding a matter is certain to raise some questions if it is suddenly dropped from the agenda.

Thus far the discussion has centred upon what considerations an officer and particularly the Town Clerk makes in selecting agenda items: the emphasis has been, however, on the amount of officer discretion involved. It would be a gross distortion to present the limits of this discretion as being exceedingly wide, for in fact there are strong limiting factors. In a small local authority many councillors as a rule have an intimate knowledge of what is happening in their community gained from their associations at work, their contact with their neighbours—that is, their constituents—and more often than not their wife's daily conversations in the shopping queue. Any attempt by an officer to keep some information from a committee in these circumstances would be hazardous and probably unsuccessful. In the larger authority the situation may be different, but not radically so. It is compensated by the fact that no longer can committees concern themselves with the detail which the committees of smaller authorities often do, so that the forces of circumstance, not the misplaced intentions of the officers, lead committees to frame policy on more general lines and to allow officers to fill in a greater amount of detail. More particularly, the officer usually keeps in close touch with the Chairman of the committee. He may go over the agenda with the Chairman before the meeting. He does consult the Chairman when he is in doubt about a matter or wants a confirmation of an action so he can go ahead. In a large authority in the Midlands it is the custom in sending out committee agenda to include also a list of decisions made by the officer concerned on his own, decisions made by the officer and confirmed by the Chairman and Vice-Chairman of the Committee, and decisions made by the Chairman and Vice-Chairman themselves. Where the officer is in close contact with the chairmen and they in turn have the confidence of their committees, there would seem to be little reason why an officer would attempt to by-pass the elected representatives on any doubtful matter.

But by far the greatest limitation is the self-restraint of officers themselves. A Town Clerk in almost every instance has reached his position after a number of years of service in local government. From the start the division between officer and councillor has a firm hold on his thinking. Thus any Town Clerk is quick to impress upon an observer that the councillors do the deciding and that the Town Clerk is there to carry out these decisions. There is no doubt that the Town Clerks have a clear appreciation of their place in the English system of democratic local government. More than one Town Clerk when presented with the question as to how he distinguishes between matters of policy and matters of execution has stressed that the ability to distinguish comes from an instinctive or intuitive sense built up by many years of experience. It is this sense nurtured on the traditional belief about a Town Clerk's proper place in the scheme of things which is the ultimate restraint upon the improper use of his discretion.

What is the origin of the agenda item? How does it come into the Town Clerk's hand? A quick perusal of almost any agenda would lead one to the conclusion that most of the items originated at a previous meeting of the committee or perhaps at the meeting of another committee, or, less frequently, from a motion in Council. But of course even these items had their origin in some earlier stage in the administrative machinery.

The Town Clerk each day receives a considerable amount of correspondence. A letter from the local station officer of the Fire Service about housing accommodation for a part-time fireman, one from the District Valuer concerning the acquisition of some land, one from the Chamber of Trade concerning a clause in a new local bill, a circular from the Ministry concerning the interpretation of an Act of Parliament—these are but a few examples. In addition, there are calls and deputations from clubs, associations, tradesmen, and ratepayers, each of which may introduce some new problem which needs to be solved. Each of these is potentially a matter for some committee.

Some agenda items have their origin within the administrative machinery itself. The majority of new ideas, the innovations in practice or policy, emanate from the officer in local government. The increased complexity and technicality of local government require that a greater understanding of various operations be acquired before one can, with any assurance, put forward a new idea. The officers have this necessary understanding; the councillors by and large do not. Further a councillor normally, unless he is a Chairman, sees the work of a particular phase of local government once a month. The time and effort he can give even to digesting the particular issues placed before him is quite limited; that he might have additional time to think out new approaches or policies is not very common. The officer, on the other hand, is immersed day by day in this work; when the good officer sees something which appears to have some fault or be in need of revision, he applies himself to finding the best way to eliminate the faults or effect the revision. In this way most, but certainly not all, new ideas are begun.

The ways these ideas reach the agenda of a committee and then become new policies are quite varied. Very often it is by way of a report to the committee. The Town Clerk might prepare a report on the printing contracts entered into by the corporation during the past year and at the same time suggest that the corporation establish its own printing shop. Or he might receive a number of complaints from council house tenants to the effect that their rents are high when compared with their friends' rents on another estate, which might prompt him to prepare a report suggesting a rent review and a new basis for computing rents. Or he might hear from the manager of a local factory that the corporation's sewers are continually backing up and causing damage to some valuable machinery and that if something is not done a law suit may ensue, in which case the Engineer would be brought into the picture and asked to report on the situation and to suggest some remedies. Or perhaps at the Town Clerks' Conference he meets his good friend, the Town Clerk of Northingworth, who tells him about the new system of mechanized record-keeping they have instituted in Northingworth, which might prompt him to assemble the facts and figures on a mechanized system for his own council.

To summarize, the germ of an idea may come from a number of places: the review of an existing system, the complaint of a ratepayer, the practice of another local authority. The next step is usually a report, sometimes prepared by the Town Clerk or, more usually when it is a technical matter, by the officer concerned—a report which reviews the present situation and suggests several possible courses of action which the committee might take.

Occasionally the new idea is not significant enough to merit a report, or perhaps a report might be expected to meet with some strong opposition. The Town Clerk might then choose to work through a Chairman or a respected councillor. The method would be to convince the Chairman of the wisdom of the new proposal, or less frequently to develop the idea with the Chairman so that he takes it up as his own. Sometimes a committee is very hesitant about some radical departure suggested by an officer, but less hesitant about the same thing if it comes from a councillor.

But the Town Clerk must also be careful as to whom he consults. On almost every council there will be one or more popular councillors who, because everybody likes them, can get almost anything they support passed; likewise, there will be the unpopular chap whose most merited suggestions are rejected without the slightest consideration. But again the actual situation would vary from one Town Clerk to another, from one council to another. Some Town Clerks have a very convincing way of placing their ideas before a committee, others lack this gift or have never cultivated it. Some councils trust their officials implicitly, others resent any attempt by an officer to lead them. Nonetheless enlisting the support for a new idea rarely hurts a Town Clerk.

The issues which committees consider, therefore, have their

origin from outside sources—the Ministry, the County Council, a ratepayer; and from within—the new idea or proposal of an officer or, somewhat less frequently, an individual councillor.

Much of the Town Clerk's actual work in preparing for a committee is purely mechanical: the sifting and gathering of items for each committee, the establishment of priority for certain items, the printing or duplication of the agenda paper, its distribution with the summons to the meeting. No doubt one could deal with these mechanical processes in a very detailed fashion, weighing the pros and cons of the different systems used in the various authorities. What will be done here, however, will be to discuss only very generally the common system and its implications, leaving the detail to one's imagination or further investigation.

The first step is the separation of the various items which arise so that they may be considered by the proper committee. Thus when a letter comes to the Town Clerk's desk, he notes its contents and directs it to the file of a certain committee. If he wants other officers to see it, he might have copies made and sent around to them; or if it is a small authority the original itself might be circulated. The same would be true of a matter arising by 'phone. The Town Clerk would make a note of the call and the note would be directed to the file of the appropriate committee.

The committee files may be of several kinds, two of which are mentioned here as examples.[1] There may be a series of boxes or trays marked with the name of each committee and sub-committee. As a letter is received it is placed in the appropriate box or tray, as are notes of calls and deputations and the like. A different system is to keep a folder for each committee. When a piece of correspondence arrives, its contents are noted on a sheet in the folder together with its file reference. The actual letter then goes into the files. The latter system has the advantage of keeping the file on any particular matter completely up-to-date and of preventing the annoyance of having to check both the file and the committee box to ascertain the latest development in a matter. The former system, however, is simpler, involves less paper work and probably reduces mis-

[1] Society of Clerks of Urban District Councils, *The Clerk of the Council and His Department* (1953), pp. 119–20.

takes since the possibility of overlooking a matter by forgetting to record it in the committee folder will not arise. In addition to the committee files there is usually a committee diary which contains a list of recurring items such as the expiry of leases and the elections of representatives for special committees, each entered beside the date when they should be considered. Normally the diary is projected twelve months ahead.[1]

With the items thus collected the next step is to draft the agenda. Agendas in their formats vary considerably from place to place. But one can recognize two extremes in format between which the practices of all authorities fall. The one is comprised of a list of all items which the committee is to consider. The other is a list of reports by the various officers connected with the committee; invariably the Town Clerk, bringing the correspondence from the outside; the Treasurer, bringing matters of financial concern; and the Technical Officer,[2] bringing whatever else the committee should consider. Under the first system everything that goes on to an agenda must go through the Town Clerk or his department. This, in turn, has two ramifications. First, the Town Clerk may exercise a power of review; that is, he may defer items or refer them back to the officer who has raised them. In practice this type of review would not be frequently used.[3] Secondly, and more important, however, the Town Clerk with this system is kept in touch with the occurrences and progress in other departments. The other system may be slightly more efficient in that officers do not have to go through the Town Clerk. No time is wasted in collecting items from several officers and organizing them on a single agenda sheet. The agenda itself would be quite simple: it would list the recurring items and then simply enumerate the various reports to be given. Yet the system has the disadvantage of allowing the officers to go too much their own way. It might happen that conflicting proposals would be advanced by two officers in their separate reports. To some extent this difficulty may be mitigated by submitting the

[1] Ibid., pp. 121–2.

[2] By 'Technical Officer' is meant the professional officer who is most directly concerned with the executive work arising from a committee's decisions, e.g. for the Finance Committee, the Treasurer; for the Works Committee, the Engineer; for the Legal and Parliamentary Committee, the Town Clerk.

[3] See, *supra*, p. 87.

reports to the Town Clerk before the meeting, but often the stage when the Town Clerk should be brought into the picture is somewhat prior to that. In practice, most authorities use some system somewhere in between these two extremes, probably, one would guess, nearer to the first than the second. Often major items are listed in the body of the agenda, and the officers' reports on day-to-day progress or issues settled in the department, usually for the purpose of giving information and inviting criticism, are considered separate from the main agenda. Where an item is of great importance the officer most directly concerned, or when a joint effort is required, the Town Clerk, will send with the agenda a full report on a problem. This would normally occur when a major shift in policy is being contemplated, but may, depending on the officer and the authority, be used often in other circumstances.

Another aspect of agenda formats may be treated quite briefly. The items on an agenda may be simply listed as headings or they may include a synopsis of the background of the issue being raised. The heading type is obviously much easier and less time-consuming to prepare. The synopsis type, on the other hand, provides the councillors with some background material before they come to committee. Which should be employed would therefore depend upon the desires of the councillors.

The agenda drawn, the next step is usually to circulate it to the members of the committee along with the summons to the meeting. The systems vary (for example, one town allows four days before each meeting; in another all agendas for the next week are distributed on the Friday previous), but the chief aim is to give the members a few days to think about the matters that are to be brought up. In at least one authority the agendas are not circulated before the meeting. The Town Clerk gave two reasons for this practice: first, that members often would not come to the meeting if there was nothing on the agenda which interested them, and second, that when some matter came up between the date of circulation and the date of the meeting, which could not be deferred until the next meeting a month hence, a complaint was certain to be made by someone saying, 'If I had known this was coming up I would have been at the meeting.' Thus in balancing these disadvantages against the advantage of prior knowledge, this authority has decided against circulating the agendas.

The final step in the preparation for the committee meeting is the assemblage of the relevant documents—correspondence, reports and the like—to be taken to the committee meeting. It is of utmost importance that these papers should be close at hand for the Town Clerk or his representative to refer to in committee. Without them relevant questions may go unanswered and needless delays become inevitable.

THE COMMITTEE MEETING

Even though the agenda represents the division between policy and execution, the Town Clerk's association with matters of policy is not ended when the agenda is prepared. It is around the committee table that the councillor and officer, lay and professional minds, are brought into intimate contact, and the policies of a local authority fashioned in detailed completeness.

The setting is the committee room. Its actual physical characteristics vary enormously, but its basic essentials are a table, some chairs around it, and an atmosphere of informality —not the informality of a tea party, for there must be order and procedure, but at the same time the atmosphere must be free from over-guarded speech and the restrictive rules of parliamentary debate.

The Chairman is seated at the head of the table. On his one side is the Town Clerk or his representative, on the other the Technical Officer of the committee. The other officers— deputies and clerks mainly—may be seated around the table or may be seated behind the Chairman and Town Clerk. Their seating is generally dictated by the size of the room and the table rather than any theory of councillor-officer relations. The councillors are seated at the remaining seats around the table: preference may be given to aldermen or to the more senior members by seating them nearer the Chairman. It may also happen that the members of the same party will sit together. So far as the Town Clerk is concerned, either he or his representative invariably has the ear of the Chairman; he is in the perfect position to whisper advice to him and to slip notes and papers before him as the meeting is in progress.

This then leads to the question of the role of the officer in a committee. Opinions as to what this role *should* be differ greatly. A Chairman of some experience, Dr R. M. Jackson, takes the view:

> Officials have no right to speak and they may not vote. A Chairman should, however, see that officials get a full opportunity to speak.[1]

Contrarily the Society of Clerks of the Urban District Councils is of the opinion that:

> At committee meetings, the scope and quality of the Clerk's intervention can be greater. Here, in the privacy of the committee room, where the cut and thrust of debate is almost absent and party passions are normally subdued, the Clerk can safely assume that active role made possible by his experience and comprehension of municipal affairs.[2]

The conflict over the officer's role, moreover, does not end with the decision that officers may speak only when spoken to or that officers may speak when their knowledge and wisdom lead them to believe that something should be said. Beyond this, questions are raised concerning what it is proper for the officer to say. One school of thought takes the view that the officer's duty is to present the facts of the situation reduced to terms the layman can understand, to suggest several possible solutions assessing the relative merits of each and their probable results. The other school recognizes that officers quite expectedly will have strong feelings about matters which have become their life's work and that it is unreal to expect that an officer would have no preference among the several solutions he offers. They reason, therefore, that he should state his preference to the committee, but, of course, not force it upon the committee. The difference in viewpoints may seem somewhat subtle, but the distinction is real. Underlying it on the one side is a strong faith in democracy, the feeling that once given the facts the layman is a better judge than the expert; on the other side is a stress on the increased technicality of

[1] R. M. Jackson, *The Machinery of Local Government* (London, 1958), p. 76.
[2] Society of the Clerks of Urban District Councils, op. cit., p. 34.

governmental work, the feeling that no longer is the layman able to digest all the facts needed to reach a rational decision, that, therefore, more reliance must be placed upon the judgment of the trained technician.

This is all fine, one might say, but these problems are very theoretical. Just how does this interplay of expert and lay minds work in practice in the committee room? How much does the Town Clerk or his representative participate? How great is his influence? To give a simple and direct answer to these questions would be misleading, for in fact, there are a number of variables at work in a number of ways in every committee.

To begin with there is the Chairman. The Chairman, if he is to be at all effective, must know what is going on in connection with the work of his committee. He may secure this knowledge through a conference with the Town Clerk or his representative or the Technical Officer before the meeting, at which time the agenda paper is thoroughly covered and the course the Chairman plans to take in introducing each item well defined.[1] Or again he may prefer to keep in contact with the officers on a more continuous basis, say once a week or more frequently, in order to see things as they develop throughout the month. The necessary element in all Chairmen is interest in the committee's work. If he is interested he will take the trouble to find out how various matters are progressing and what new developments may be expected. If he is genuinely interested, he will come into the meeting prepared. If he is not prepared, the part played by the officer becomes more prominent. Instead of the Chairman introducing each item or calling on the officers for advice, the initiative will fall into the Town Clerk's or the Technical Officer's hands. The Town Clerk may introduce each item, offer some advice on his own, perhaps ask the Treasurer or Surveyor or Baths Superintendent to comment, and before one knows it the issue is settled, and the Town Clerk is introducing the next item.

As important as preparation is the ability to be a good Chairman, to guide and direct the debate to the main issues without limiting free and useful discussion or dictating the lines of a decision. When the Chairman allows the debate time after time to wander from the point at issue or permits four coun-

[1] Jackson, op. cit., p. 74.

cillors in a row to say in very certain terms that they agree wholeheartedly with Councillor Brightwell, who opened the debate, the way may be open for an officer to assume control. Officers spend a great deal of time in committee; few things are more enjoyable to them than a good, reasoned debate which indicates that both sides have a firm grip on the major issue; but when the debate lapses and the issue becomes lost or obscured, officers often become impatient to get home to their supper and act to put the debate in order. The Chairman, therefore, is an important part of the machinery; if he fails in his responsibilities, it is more than likely that the Town Clerk or the Technical Officer will act in his default.

The Town Clerk himself—his attitude, his bearing, his approach—all are of importance in any assessment of his influence on a committee. Some Town Clerks take the view that their job is to advise on legal matters; if the committee does not take the advice, it must suffer the consequences; but the Town Clerk's job is finished once the advice is given. At the other extreme there are Town Clerks who claim confidently that never on a major issue has a committee ignored their advice, legal or otherwise. There can be little doubt that these differing attitudes produce quite dissimilar Town Clerks in the committee room.

The Town Clerk's bearing in committee is of some significance as well. This fact was greatly stressed by the Town Clerk of a large borough in the Midlands. He felt that the Town Clerk must maintain an air of slight aloofness in committee; he himself would laugh and joke with them but he would never allow them to feel that he was one of them, for if this should happen, much of his effectiveness would be lost. At the same time he would not stand too aloof, because if he did he would lose contact with his councillors. Similarly some Town Clerks will preface all their remarks to a committee with phrases like 'with all respect' or 'of course this is a policy matter, but my feelings are', both of which serve as reminders to the councillors that the Town Clerk is not one of them.

But the Town Clerk's approach is of most importance. He must suit his proposals and advice to the temperament and personalities of his committee. He must, above all, be understandable; his advice must be cast in terms that are readily grasped by the members. If he resorts to a professional jargon he may mystify some but others will rebel. He must be flexible; he must recognize when one of his proposals does not gain support and be ready to modify it to save the principle underlying his advice. A good example of this occurred in the Highways Committee of a small borough in the south. The Town Clerk had noticed a certain service road in the town which had been started but never finished. The County had allowed several options to complete the work at the residents' expense under the Private Street Works Act to expire. Thus unless some new proposal was put forward the unsightly and practically useless road would remain that way. The Town Clerk therefore suggested that the Borough Council approach the County Council with a plan to complete the road, under which the County would pay half of the whole cost, the residents would pay half of the cost of the road and the borough would pay half of the cost of the pavements, drains, sewers and other necessary amenities. Certain councillors objected on the grounds that this was the County's mistake and that it should be their duty to remedy it. The Town Clerk then modified his proposal to the effect that the borough pay nothing but simply take the lead in organizing the matter. By sensing the attitude of the committee and modifying his advice to meet their objections, the Town Clerk's purpose was not lost. But flexibility does not imply that the Town Clerk should necessarily adapt his views to what he feels will be most welcome.[1] If the Town Clerk has no considered views on a matter he generally finds it better to leave the entire matter to the councillors. Conversely there are times when the Town Clerk should show no flexibility at all; that is, when the committee appears desirous of taking an illegal step or one that is legally foolhardy. The only position a Town Clerk should take in this instance is the one which his knowledge of the law dictates.

Closely related to the idea of flexibility is the one of timing. The pointed remark inserted at the proper instance in the debate is often more effective than a continual barrage of opinions and advice. The successful Town Clerk has usually mastered the art of well-timed remarks.

---

[1] See, 'Essex, More Local Government Reforms', 116 *Justice of the Peace* 324 (1952) for a rather extreme view as to what to do about this type of advice.

If the Chairman's preparation is important, the Town Clerk's, or for that matter any officer's, preparation is more important. One of the major functions of the layman in local government is to question the expert. One cannot sit through many committees before he is aware that almost as much time is spent questioning the Town Clerk and the other officers as is spent debating. Questions like 'How much will this cost?' or 'What are other boroughs our size doing on this kind of thing?' or 'Why was this piece of equipment preferred to this other one I saw advertised in a journal the other day?' are quite common. The Town Clerk who has the answers at his quick disposal and who can put the questioner at ease, will find his position with the committee much stronger and his relations smoother. The one who, however, puts off the answers or asks for some time to consider the matter delays the work of the committee and slows the processes of local government. Of course no Town Clerk can anticipate all the questions he will get from his councillors, but a little thought beforehand, a little foresighted preparation, is an invaluable asset, for often it is simply a matter of having brought the right maps, plans or tables of figures to committee.

Likewise, the Town Clerk represents the continuing element in local government. His knowledge of how an issue arose and what progress has been made on it is one of his strengths. Much of councillor uncertainty arises from an incomplete knowledge of the history of a particular item. The Town Clerk who can erase these doubts with a concise but accurate account of the relevant past events influences his committee accordingly.

One should not receive the impression that because the Town Clerks are in the position to exert great influence upon a committee that they purposefully attempt to direct the affairs of local government. Town Clerks, as it was said before, have a great respect for the imaginary dividing line between the functions of the councillors and those of the officers. The Town Clerk of an average-sized borough explained that on one occasion he reprimanded committee members for taking his advice too readily and for not expressing their own opinions on matters. Another Town Clerk of a much larger borough said that he from time to time emphasizes to a committee its duty to decide policy and that he himself has experienced some dis-satisfaction when advice which he may have been doubtful about was accepted without query or debate. Town Clerks bear uneasily the responsibility attached to their position of influence, and often when they do exert their influence they are not fully conscious of it.

It is quite apparent from the preceding that the extent of the Town Clerk's influence depends in some manner at least upon the individual councillors apart from the Chairman. It is not uncommon for a councillor to speak out in committee after the Town Clerk has interjected and say, 'Mr Town Clerk, we've heard all we want to hear from you on this, now we'll do the deciding.' Some councils and some councillors show more independence of spirit than others. This may be attributed to a clear acceptance of councillor responsibilities. But it may also be a feeling of insecurity on the part of the councillor, a feeling that the officers are trying to take advantage of the councillors' relative lack of knowledge.[1] Nonetheless this type of councillor, until the Town Clerk can win his confidence and trust, may have a debilitating effect on officer-councillor relations.

A special problem which a Town Clerk may be faced with from time to time is that of a lawyer, that is a rival expert, on a committee. Dr K. C. Wheare has carefully weighed the advantages and disadvantages of councillor-experts and has concluded that where a committee has a good supply of good laymen, there is little advantage in having councillor-experts.[2] Although a judge is quite astute in resolving the conflicting arguments of lawyers, councillors are not judges and such conflicts can be more mystifying than illuminating for the layman. Notwithstanding this undesirability, Town Clerks do at times have to cope with the problem of lawyers on the council and in committees. Often there is no problem; the councillor recognizes that the Town Clerk is the legal adviser and any effort by a councillor to secure legal advice from a fellow councillor meets with an immediate rebuff and deference to the Town Clerk. Where the understanding is not as firmly based, however, the Town Clerk's influence may be decreased.

Moreover, it is equally apparent from the preceding that the Town Clerk's influence in committee depends greatly upon his strength *vis-a-vis* the Technical Officer of the committee.

[1] Jackson, op. cit., p. 76.
[2] Wheare, op. cit., p. 191.

Where a committee is occupied mainly with establishing policy upon matters which arise chiefly from technical considerations, the Technical Officer is in a better position to influence than the Town Clerk. Where the matters are likely to involve several other committees or where they may affect general council policy, the Town Clerk may be in the better position. But even this broad statement is subject to many qualifications: the attitude of the councillors towards the officials in question; the relative lengths of service of the Town Clerk and the Technical Officer with the particular authority; the extent of the 'committee mind' attitude among the councillors; and, in general, personalities.[1] In addition, as was noted above, the Town Clerk, except in the smaller authority, attends personally only a small minority of the total committee meetings.[2] In all the others in which he is represented, his Deputy or an Assistant Solicitor or a Senior Committee Clerk handles his functions. Consequently in these situations, it is to be expected that the Technical Officer has a much greater influence upon the course of the committee meeting than the Town Clerk's representative. This is why, when an item of general importance is to be taken up by a committee which is not normally attended by the Town Clerk in person, most Town Clerks make a point of being in attendance at that particular meeting. This is also why, in the smaller authorities where a Town Clerk's personal attendance is more widespread, the Town Clerk's influence upon individual committee decisions throughout the authority is generally greater than the influence of his counterparts in the larger places.

The advice of a Town Clerk to a committee—what is its range? First, and generally foremost, he is the council's, and hence each committee's, legal adviser. When a question of law arises the councillors quite naturally look to him for advice. Questions of law arise in every committee from time to time, but some committees have a greater share than others; and there are some councils which have a Legal and Parliamentary Committee to supervise the legal work of the council, particularly those instances where the council may be a party to an important action, the promotion of local bills, and the scrutiny

[1] These qualifications are further discussed in Chapter 7, *infra*.
[2] See, *supra*, pp. 83–85.

of general legislation affecting the work of the council. With this work the Town Clerk is most directly connected as adviser.

The Town Clerk also advises on the Standing Orders of the council. When a committee appear likely to violate one of their own rules for the proper conduct of business, it is the Town Clerk's job to advise them of the implications of their action. Recently the Highways Committee of a borough in the West Country invited tenders for the purchase of two lorries. One tender arrived after the meeting held to consider the tenders but within the time specified in the letter inviting tenders, so that although the committee had awarded the contract it had not given fair consideration to all those firms submitting tenders. The Town Clerk in a special meeting observed that the Standing Orders in respect of tenders had been violated and therefore advised that invitations to tender be made a second time in conformity with the Standing Orders but that the terms be varied so as to provide a new basis for tendering. The Committee did not adopt this course. As a result the Town Clerk stated that he had no alternative but to ensure that a report of the irregularities be made to the council, which he did. The council after a debate of some length voted to follow the Town Clerk's advice and overturned their committee's recommendation. As a respected alderman said during the debate: 'The Town Clerk's advice on the Standing Orders should be supreme. He is the custodian of the Standing Orders.'

In addition, the Town Clerk gives what could only be termed 'general advice'. Possibly this advice tends to be concerned with certain areas of local administration more than others, but few Town Clerks would feel themselves confined to these. For instance, the Town Clerk's contact with the central government usually makes him reasonably adept at predicting a department's feelings on whatever items seem likely to concern it. His advice on matters of establishment and administrative organization and efficiency are also common. But one may also observe a Town Clerk, particularly in a small authority, advising on the best method of providing a loan for a local sports club or on the proper basis for a rent rebate scheme or the best way to provide a pavilion for the local sports ground. Sometimes these may involve comments on the advice given by the Technical Officer, comments which may consider the general policy implications of the technical advice or may attempt to clarify the technical language so that it may be readily understood by the layman members. Town Clerks recognize that conflicting advice by officials is to be avoided if at all possible; and if not, that conflict should be stated clearly to the committee so that they may resolve it. They refer mainly to major disputes concerning policy. In committees, however, on relatively minor matters officials do provide conflicting advice during the course of the discussion, depending upon the disposition of the members and the fact and attitudes brought to light in the discussion. The point to be taken is that although the advice may conflict, it must not appear to do so openly, in such a way that an issue becomes a debate between two officers rather than two rival factions on the committee.

The mechanical operation of the committee is under the guidance of the Town Clerk. The Standing Orders of the council usually charge the Town Clerk with the responsibility of keeping a record of attendance at committee and sub-committee meetings and of preparing an annual statement of each member's attendance. As clerk to the committees it is also the Town Clerk's responsibility to note the proceedings carefully, giving particular attention to the character of each decision. Committee decisions are often taken merely by the nod of a few heads or a word of assent from two sides of the table. The Town Clerk's job is to translate these signs into a direction which captures the sense of the meeting, and which is easily understood by those who must act upon the direction. This probably sounds more difficult than it actually is. From the way the agenda is drawn it is reasonably certain what the character of various resolutions emerging from the meeting will be. And where an issue has been hotly contested, particularly where party lines have been sharply drawn, the Town Clerk may easily ask the members to help him frame the resolution. From the notes then the committee minutes are drafted; and upon their approval by the officers concerned with the committee they are entered into the committee minute book.

THE PREPARATION FOR COUNCIL MEETING

The Town Clerk is responsible for the preparations for the council meeting. The procedure is simpler than that involved in the preparation for a committee. The major portion of the agenda is comprised of either reports from the committees or the minutes of the committees. There may also be included mayoral communications, correspondence, orders for the sealing of documents, and notices of motions. In addition councils usually provide a procedure whereby questions may be directed to the Chairman of a committee.

The major controversy, which concerns the Town Clerk, in these matters is whether committee reports or committee minutes should be placed before the council. The controversy, in the main, springs from the fact that committees have delegated powers to act on their own without council approval. Thus committee recommendations as opposed to committee resolutions are the only items which must come before the council. In practice, however, it is well to keep the council informed from time to time concerning how the various committees are exercising their delegated powers. In substance the arguments for minutes are that minutes must be prepared so that labour is saved by drafting and reproducing them once only, and that the council is informed of all proceedings of its committees. Against minutes it is said that they are bulky and that their form makes it far from easy to understand what the committee has been doing. As for reports it is argued in support that only major matters need be reported; thus formal, routine and adjourned matters should be eliminated and that a well-drafted report can give the history of the subject, summarize the arguments, and convey the committee's views so as to give sufficient information on which the council can base its decision. The main argument against reports is that they entail additional expense both to draft and to reproduce.[1] It is interesting to note that the Metropolitan Boroughs' (O. & M.) Committee found that both systems were in operation in London (of twenty councils, two submit minutes, eighteen submit reports), each is strongly supported by its respective users and each works satisfactorily, and that the success depends

---

[1] Jackson, op. cit., pp. 80–1; and Metropolitan Boroughs' (O. & M.) Committee, *Form of Officers' Reports to Committees, Committee Reports to Councils and Minutes of Committees and Councils* (London, 1952), pp. 8–9. See also J. H. Warren, *Municipal Administration* (London, 1948), pp. 127–133 for a more extensive discussion of the problem, a refutation of the attempt to over-legalize the problem by *Justice of the Peace* and general support for submitting minutes to the council.

not on any detached reasoning but simply on the acceptance of a thoroughly familiar practice or well-established tradition. Moreover one can draw too distinct a line between the two systems. The advantages of both could be secured by drafting those committee minutes which should come before the council in a report-like fashion and eliminating the routine minutes from the council agenda. In this way only one set, the minutes, is drafted; sufficient detail is included in the council agenda; and the problem of bulk is avoided.

Standing Orders usually direct that notices of motions shall be given to the Town Clerk, that he shall enter them in a book properly numbered and dated, and that he shall insert the notice in the summons for the council meeting.[1] In practice the Town Clerk usually advises the member in the drafting of his motion, advice which in theory should extend only to the form and the manner of the wording, not to the content, but actually a Town Clerk finds it difficult to separate the two.

Correspondence can be a tricky problem for a Town Clerk. Generally, correspondence is best handled in committee meetings. However, there is usually some correspondence of a wider nature, as, for instance, a petition from a group of rate-payers. In deciding whether to bring such a petition before council or to hold it until the next committee meeting, the Town Clerk is usually governed by the status of the item concerned. If a committee is still considering the matter, it would be untimely to bring the petition before the council. Where the petitioners demand that the matter be brought before the council, the Town Clerk might mention the petition and indicate that it will be placed before the appropriate committee at its next meeting.

Standing Orders usually provide a procedure by which a member may question the Chairman of a committee upon the proceedings of the committee then before the council. Notice in writing given to the Town Clerk at least two clear days before the meeting may be required, although it is possible for the Chairman to waive this requirement.[2] The burden of preparing the answer often falls upon the officers.

[1] See Model Standing Orders, *Proceedings and Business*, no. 4. Ministry of Housing and Local Government (H.M.S.O., 1950, reprinted 1954).
[2] Model Standing Orders, op. cit., no. 6.

By statute the Town Clerk is required to summon each member to the council meeting, specifying the business proposed for transaction, at least three clear days before the meeting.[1] The summons need not accompany the agenda, but generally, unless there has been some unusual happening, it does. The committee cycle is so arranged that there is time after the last committee meeting to prepare its minutes or report and have the entire agenda printed or duplicated, and still meet the three clear days requirement.

The final step in preparing for the meeting is the Town Clerk's briefing with the Mayor. The Mayor and the Town Clerk go over the agenda together noting the various actions to be taken, making certain that where two committees have considered the same matter, usually a spending committee and the Finance Committee, the two recommendations will be considered at the same time. It should be noted that the major emphasis in this meeting, as contrasted with an officer-chairman meeting, is upon matters of procedure rather than matters of content for, unlike a chairman of a committee, the Mayor is not expected to take sides or in any way descend to the field of battle.[2]

THE COUNCIL MEETING

The setting of the council meeting is the council chamber, which may be a most elaborately-styled room like the House of Commons or a very simple room, often the same room in which committee meetings are held, with only a long table surrounded by chairs.

The Mayor is seated at the centre of the dais or at the head of the table. The Town Clerk is seated close to the Mayor. Generally this means at his side and frequently at a slightly lower level. In about one of every ten authorities the Town Clerk sits in front and below the Mayor much as a clerk of a court. This arrangement presents certain difficulties, for the Town Clerk's advice is frequently needed during the course of the meeting and the whisper in the ear is certainly more effective and less obtrusive than having the Town Clerk

[1] Local Government Act, 1933, Third Schedule, part II (2).
[2] Jackson, op. cit., pp. 84–5.

jumping up in front of the Mayor or continually passing notes over his head, or even worse, having the Mayor leaning over his desk in a very un-Mayorlike fashion to catch a few words from the Town Clerk.[1] The more general practice is certainly preferable.

The Mayor accompanied by the mace and the Town Clerk enter the chamber together. They both may be robed, the Mayor in a scarlet robe trimmed with brown fur, the Mayoral chain and badge about his neck; the Town Clerk in a black silk robe trimmed with a velvet band and robe lace trimming and wearing a barrister's wig.[2] The councillors also may be wearing gowns. In some authorities this dress is worn for each council meeting; in others it is limited to the four statutory meetings; and in still others it is worn only for the annual meeting on Mayor-making day.

The Town Clerk actually takes very little part in the conduct of the meeting. Some evidence points to the fact that in the past the Town Clerk played a more active part, or at least felt he was completely within his rights if he did so. Before the Royal Commission on the Amalgamation of the City and County of London in 1894, Sir Samuel Johnson, the Town Clerk of Nottingham, was asked whether he had a right to speak at council meetings. He replied:

> I have a right of audience; that is our ancient right. A right to speak; a right to be heard. If there is anything of importance I have a right to be heard. In full Council it is not exercised once a year hardly, but if I find someone grievously misleading the Council as to a fact, it is my duty not to let the Council come to a conclusion upon a false statement of facts. . . .[3]

[1] Lord Simon had these comments on this arrangement in Manchester:

'The Lord Mayor sits on a raised chair, with the Town Clerk, who must constantly advise him on points of order, well out of hearing at his feet. It is difficult and undignified for the Lord Mayor to keep shouting to attract the Town Clerk's attention. I installed a little red electric lamp on his desk, with the idea that when I wanted to consult him I would switch it on, and he would then get up and speak to me with apparent spontaneity. Unfortunately he was always looking somewhere else when I pressed the button!' *A City Council From Within*, p. 185.

Since Lord Simon's term of office, Manchester has built a new council chamber in which the Town Clerk's seat is at the Lord Mayor's left side.

[2] J. F. Garner, *Civic Ceremonial* (London, 1957, 2nd ed.), p. 93.

[3] Royal Commission on the Amalgamation of the City and County of London (1894): Evidence, Q.9850–3.

Lady Simon recalls several incidents from the town clerkship of Joseph Heron which illustrates the exercise of this right. On one occasion Heron intervened in the debate and said, 'Councillor X, you know nothing about this matter. Please sit down.'[1] Another time a councillor annoyed by the Town Clerk questioned him: 'What right have you to speak? What ward do you represent?'[2] Heron quickly met the challenge with: 'A larger ward than yours, sir. I represent the entire city.'[3]

It would be quite unusual to find a Town Clerk today following Mr Heron's example; at the same time Town Clerks do not remain completely silent in council meeting. The Town Clerk of a small borough said that he would intervene when it appeared that the council was about to do something illegal or when the Mayor called upon him. He gave as examples of the latter, two instances: one where the Mayor, attempting to explain a complicated question of property law, became entangled himself and called upon the Town Clerk to extricate him; the other, where a member living in a council house seconded a motion on housing tenancies, the question of the member's interest was raised and the Mayor called upon the Town Clerk to state the legal position. Thus the Mayor usually calls on the Town Clerk to elucidate certain points of procedure or law which arise during the debate. In this connection the value of clear and detailed Standing Orders are realized by the Town Clerk, for as the former Clerk of the London County Council said:

> When feelings run high ... in Council chamber debate and appeal is made to the Clerk for a ruling as to whether a member or committee can do this or that, it is very convenient for the Clerk to have at his elbow a book of Standing Orders which deal with every point of that kind ... (since) they do not represent the Clerk's personal view and he cannot therefore be criticized for what is in them.[4]

The Town Clerks of two larger boroughs pointed out that they would intervene if something was said that was patently false

[1] Lady Simon, op. cit., p. 408.
[2] Ibid.
[3] Ibid.
[4] Sir Howard Roberts, 'Too Many Rules—or Too Few', 58 *Municipal Journal* 249 (1950).

and there was reason to believe that the statement was misleading the council and if the council seemed to be making a mistake by not considering one aspect of a problem that was particularly relevant. Even so such interventions are not frequent, and it is probably true, as one Town Clerk who has had experience in both small and large boroughs observed, that in the smaller authorities the atmosphere in council is less formal than in the larger authorities, and as a consequence the Town Clerk tends to speak more frequently in the smaller places.

The Town Clerk's influence on the course of the meeting does not depend entirely upon the number of times he speaks. Where he is at the Mayor's side his influence is probably more effective since his advice can be proffered without difficulty and since he avoids the risk of alienating the several councillors who regard any remark from the Town Clerk as an intrusion upon their private sanctity.

The Town Clerk's duties concerning the mechanics of the council meeting are essentially the same as those concerning the committee meetings. He is required to make a record of attendance. He is responsible for having the proceedings properly noted. Where a time limit is placed upon members' speeches he is responsible for establishing and operating the timing system. He usually counts votes when voting is by hand; and he calls the roll and records the vote, when voting is by roll-call. From the notes of the meeting he or his staff drafts the minutes. Minutes may be of two styles—a long form which includes whole agenda plus decisions taken or a short form which merely lists the decisions with a reference to the previous agenda. The short form is more economical and not much less desirable.[1] The full minutes of the committees and council of the past month, with decisions or memoranda embodying the decisions and directions of the committees and council, are then circulated by the Town Clerk to the executing departments, and execution of the established policy begins. One cycle is at an end—another is about to begin.

---

[1] Metropolitan Boroughs' (O. & M.) Committee, op. cit., p. 10.

CHAPTER V

THE TOWN CLERK AND THE ELECTED REPRESENTATIVES: RELATIONSHIPS WITH THE PARTICIPANTS

THE previous chapter described the position and duties of the Town Clerk throughout one turn of a committee cycle. But council and committee work as such form only one side or phase of a Town Clerk's contacts with the elected representatives. The Town Clerk has frequent dealings outside the committee room and the council chamber with the councillors in their various roles of Mayor, Chairmen, party leaders or simply ordinary aldermen or councillors. It is the description of these relationships and the analysis of the Town Clerk in this role to which attention is now turned.

THE TOWN CLERK AND THE MAYOR

The Mayor during his term of office combines a rigorous social schedule with his duties as presiding officer of the council and other duties of an incidental nature to produce a most curious mixture of prestige without power. It is characteristic that a Mayor will hold office for only one year, and this practice tends to emphasize the Mayor's social function. But at the same time one cannot say that the introduction of a longer term of office would necessarily strengthen his powers, for practice also holds that the Mayor during his term shall withdraw from the political life of the council. He thus becomes a kind of King and Speaker of the House combined in one on a smaller and time-limited scale. And where does the Town Clerk fit in the Mayor's realm? The Town Clerk is the Mayor's personal adviser.[1]

[1] This is true in most places, but there are always exceptions. In one ancient borough the Mayor has his own special adviser and secretary called the 'Mayor's Sergeant'. The Sergeant also fills the positions of Sergeant-at-Mace and Superintendent of the General Market. The office is one of early origin stemming from the time when the Mayor was responsible for assuring honest weights and measures in the market. He would hire a Sergeant to do the actual work for him and the

H 113

Taking most important things first, what is involved in the Town Clerk's function as social adviser? The Mayor gets invitations to parties, to dinners, to meetings; he gets an allowance or a salary; and at times he gets bewildered. The Town Clerk's task is to lead him out of his bewilderment. He helps the Mayor select the invitations he will accept, prepare the speeches he will give, and decide about the money he will spend.

The Mayor's allowance can be a touchy problem. Recently a Mayor caused quite a bit of concern about the way he was spending his allowance and using the Mayoral car. The Town Clerk approached the Deputy Mayor, who had held the Mayoralty the year before, and the Finance Chairman, and asked them to have a talk with the Mayor. They did and the Mayor agreed to cut down on his activities. Thus, although the Mayor and the Town Clerk were on the closest of terms, he felt that any advice of this nature should come from two respected members of the council and not an officer. In spite of this it should be noted that the Town Clerk initiated the action.

If the Mayor is inexperienced in matters of protocol, the Town Clerk may be called upon to advise on many insignificant things, which often become important to the Mayor who is trying earnestly to uphold the dignity of the borough during his term of office. One Town Clerk tells the story of a Mayor who, meeting the Queen for the first time, leaned heavily upon the Town Clerk's views about personal attire. Likewise Mayors can often provide embarrassing moments for Town Clerks. Another Town Clerk describes a Mayor who was a strict teetotaler; so strict, in fact, that he refused to serve any alcoholic drinks at his receptions. Things seemed to go well until the Mayor held a reception for a group of R.A.F. officers. As the Town Clerk wandered among the officers with their orange squash, he gathered a number of disgruntled looks and a comment or two about the paucity of gin. But at the same time one can be certain that there are a number of Mayors who are more at ease when being received by the Queen than are their Town Clerks. And even more who are more at home at a large

Sergeant grew to be his personal adviser as well. Consequently the relationship between the Town Clerk and the Mayor is less close there than is generally customary, but even so, the Town Clerk's contact with the Mayor is reasonably frequent.

reception or before a large audience than their Town Clerks are; for many Mayors are quite accomplished political figures who enjoy these occasions which are so much a part of public life.

The organization of the various ceremonial functions of the Mayor and the council comes within the scope of the Town Clerk's operations as well. It is his job to see that all details—halls, caterers, invitations, and the like—are attended to in the proper manner. Where it is the usual reception or dinner affair, the preparation is very much a routine matter handled by one of the Town Clerk's staff. But when Her Majesty or one of the Royal Family is planning to visit, much of the Town Clerk's daily life for several months may be consumed by the arrangements and organization of the programme. The Town Clerk needs to be an authority on the order of processions and seating and on programmes. Last-minute bickering about who should follow whom can easily turn a serious and orderly procession into a parade of clowns. All these things can be exceedingly tricky as the Town Clerk of a Midlands borough illustrated in recounting a visit by the Queen Mother. During her visit she was scheduled to open a new technical college and a new wing of a hospital. While she was on corporation property —that is in the technical college or riding through the streets of the borough—the civic precedents were applied; while she was on the hospital property, another set of precedents was used. The Town Clerk was charged with working this out to everyone's satisfaction.

The Town Clerk, holder of an ancient and honourable office, is himself an active participant in the various civic ceremonies. As a general rule whenever the mace accompanies the Mayor, the Town Clerk is along too. In procession the Town Clerk, attired in wig and gown, is often at the Mayor's side.[1]

As presiding officer the Mayor also has a close contact with the Town Clerk. The preparation for the council meeting and the procedural and other advice during the meeting, described above, are the foremost of these contacts. But they are not the entire extent of them. The Mayor's neutrality is an asset for a Town Clerk, for it is a neutrality which differs from that of the Town Clerk. Whereas the Town Clerk is expected to provide

[1] J. F. Garner, op. cit., pp. 55, 122.

advice completely free from political bias, the Mayor is capable of providing leadership which is free from political bias. It is often desirable to combine this advice and leadership. For instance a certain problem may arise which either does—or in the best interests of the citizenry should—transcend party politics. Yet to secure full co-operation, the assent of the two party leaders is essential. Some Town Clerks feel that they are treading on difficult ground if they call the two leaders together in their office. To avoid this difficulty they therefore arrange for the Mayor to call the leaders to his parlour and, with the Town Clerk in attendance, the four of them discuss the problem and attempt to arrive at some satisfactory solution.

Although the Mayor's power may be limited, when the reputation or prestige of the borough is in some way involved, his word is often important. The Town Clerk of Redcar discovered this not too long ago. He was invited on short notice to represent the council at the opening ceremony of the Festival of Britain in 1951, which he did. But when he submitted his expense statement of slightly over £20, the council balked and advised that the Town Clerk pay his own expenses. The major complaint seemed to be that although he could not have consulted the council or a committee because of the short notice, he should have secured the Mayor's permission. In the end the Town Clerk apologized and paid the £20 out of his own bank account.[1]

In the pursuance of his statutory duties the Mayor relies almost entirely upon the Town Clerk. The Mayor is charged with the duty of examining the nomination papers for local elections, deciding which candidates have been validly nominated, and giving notice of his decision to each candidate.[2] In practice the Town Clerk checks the nomination petitions thoroughly and passes them to the Mayor for a few random checks and signing. Much of the same division of labour is employed in those boroughs where the Mayor is returning officer.[3] The complexity of election rules and law make it

[1] (Anonymous) 'Clerk must pay £20 to settle town's account', 59 *Municipal Journal* 2125 (1951).

[2] Hart, op. cit., p. 104. The relevant statute is the Representation of the People Act, 1949, Second Schedule, Local Election Rules, 9.

[3] For boroughs not divided into wards, the Mayor is the returning officer; where the borough is divided into wards, an alderman is returning officer for each ward.

imperative that the Town Clerk advise the Mayor at every step, and in many cases the bulk of the duties of returning officer are delegated to the Town Clerk. In urban and rural districts and metropolitan boroughs, the Clerk is the returning officer by statutory enactment. One Town Clerk has pointed out this anomaly which exists concerning borough returning officers and has advocated most strongly that the boroughs should follow the practice of the urban and rural districts, for, according to him, under the present system the Town Clerk has to do all the work and put up with the nuisance of the unenlightened returning officers as well.

THE TOWN CLERK AND THE COMMITTEE CHAIRMAN

Since English local government is government by committee and every committee needs a Chairman, it is a fair assumption that the Chairmen of committees are important persons in the local administrative framework. As such they may have contact with the Town Clerk for a number of reasons, but basically these contacts fall into three classes: the preparation for meetings, both committee and council; the ratification of urgent actions; the examination of new ideas. In some respects these contacts have been discussed in detail above. The purpose here, therefore, is only to bring the relationship into focus and to point out some of the problems involved.

First, however, it should be noted that, although a Town Clerk has frequent contact with the Chairmen, he is by no means the only officer who is in contact with them. The Treasurer invariably has a very close relationship with the Chairman of the Finance Committee, and in places where the Finance Chairman is the strongest member of the council, a not unusual situation, this relationship may be the source of considerable influence for the Treasurer. Furthermore, in the preparation of the annual budget, the Treasurer comes in contact with the Chairman of each committee. Here again he is in a position to make his influence felt. Likewise, the Surveyor sees the Highways Committee Chairman frequently; the Medical Officer of Health, the Health Committee Chairman; the Housing Manager, the Housing Chairman; the Planning Officer, the Planning Chairman; the Chief Constable, the

Watch Chairman; the Water Engineer, the Water Chairman; and so on. And the larger the authority, the closer these relationships, as compared with the Town Clerk-Chairmen relationships, become.

But at the same time the Town Clerk is responsible for co-ordination, and he ought to be acquainted with the general course of events in all departments.[1] As a Town Clerk of a large borough explained, he has a general knowledge of what every department is doing and either he, or someone in his department responsible to him, has specific knowledge of the work in the other departments. Consequently on general problems the Chairmen often come to the Town Clerk for advice, for the Town Clerk is in the best position to see the problem as it affects the whole corporation. But this is a reasonably strong position for a Town Clerk. Although some Town Clerks are so placed, there are probably some who rarely see a Chairman on a general problem unless it is fraught with legal complications. In any event, however, the majority of Town Clerks have, by means of the agendas and other committee documents, the opportunity to keep themselves informed of the work in the other departments. And, generally speaking, many avail themselves of the opportunity.

Concerning the preparation for meetings, the advantages of the Chairman being the most knowledgeable member of the council on the affairs of his committee are obvious. The Chairman should be able to lead his committee during the committee meetings and be able to guide the recommendations of his committee through the council. The position of the Chairman *vis-a-vis* the council is a curious one. Attempts to draw an analogy between a Cabinet Minister and a Committee Chairman are somewhat misleading. It is true, it is the Chairman's job to move the acceptance of his committee's report in the council meeting, and usually it is his function to offer some comments in support of the various controversial issues contained in it. But a Chairman may not, and at times does not, agree with or support the recommendations of his committee; indeed one would have some doubts concerning the efficacy of committee government if the Chairman was always in agree-

[1] G. H. Etherton, 'Employment and Organization of Committees in Local Government Administration', 2 *Public Administration* 389 (1924), p. 396.

ment with his committee. As a result a Chairman is perfectly free to state his disagreement where he has one.

The purpose of a Chairman's contact with the Town Clerk is twofold: to secure information and to receive advice. The scope of each depends upon both the Chairman and the Town Clerk. Where a Chairman has a strong mind or will of his own, he will probably seek more information and less advice. Where the Town Clerk has a firm grasp upon the reins of control, he will tend to offer more advice and less information. In either case a good admixture of the two is unavoidable. The contact may be a regular meeting at which time the committee agenda or the committee's report to the council is reviewed. One Town Clerk estimates that this is the practice in about half the local authorities; and that in the half that do, it is practised by about half the Chairmen. In other words, about one quarter have regular meetings. In some authorities the contact may be of a more irregular nature—an occasional 'phone conversation supplemented by a meeting in the Town Clerk's office if a major problem is under consideration, the purpose being to keep the Chairman informed rather than advised. The regular meeting at which the agenda is reviewed item by item is the best way for the Town Clerk to ensure that his advice will at least be received. For this reason most Town Clerks would agree that the regular meeting type of contact is preferable. But not many Chairmen can spare the time from their employment for a regular meeting with either the Town Clerk or the Technical Officer. In the smaller towns, particularly where the officers are able to have close relationships with the Chairmen, the need for the regular meeting diminishes accordingly. In these circumstances the meeting may amount to a fifteen-minute discussion in the committee room before the meeting or a similar one after the meeting to plan the report to be made to the council. In the larger authorities, moreover, the Town Clerk's own time is more circumscribed so that the regular meetings with Chairmen are normally conducted by the Technical Officer alone or sometimes by a member of the Town Clerk's staff in conjunction with the Technical Officer. If the Town Clerk in these places takes any part in these pre-committee consultations, it is only in connection with those committees he attends personally.

The ratification of urgent actions by Chairmen is becoming increasingly important because of the general increase in the tempo of local government. The Town Clerk of a middle-sized Midlands borough gave an example of the obvious virtues of this method. A request was sent to the council for permission to give a demonstration in the market square. The chief officer in charge, acting on his own initiative, directed a portion of the square to be roped off for the demonstration. At the next committee meeting the Chairman voiced a very pointed criticism of the action, for it seemed he was in the habit of parking his car in the market square parking area, and the officer was thereupon censured for his action. The Town Clerk pointed out that, if the chief officer had taken a minute or two to ring the Chairman and advise him of the request, the difficulty would have been completely avoided. In this example the Chairman was personally inconvenienced by the officer's action. A more difficult problem arises where an individual councillor feels that his right to be consulted has been infringed. It is essential then that the Chairman enjoys the confidence of his committee members and that he is able to stand behind the officer who has consulted him and received his confirmation. Often questions may arise on the most insignificant matters, like approval of a seven pound expenditure for an officer to attend a conference. Simply because an item appears insignificant does not mean it will not be given a great deal of attention and importance by some councillor. The ability to foresee what kind of items will be subject to the kind of scrutiny as well as the Chairman's ability to speak with the assurance of his committee's support are thus quite important. At the same time a Town Clerk must guard against the tendency to create urgency where there is none, to leave to the last minute a decision which could have just as easily been taken by the committee a month before. All the so-called 'urgent' problems do not arise as quickly as some Town Clerks attempt to have councillors believe.[1]

The Chairman is usually the best person upon whom the Town Clerk can sound out his new ideas. This is true, first because he is the member of the committee whom the Town

---

[1] For an excellent discussion of this point see Wheare, op. cit., pp. 186–7.

Clerk sees most frequently, and secondly, because generally the Chairman is the most influential man of the committee. Consequently if the Town Clerk is able to convince the Chairman of the wisdom of a new idea, the proposal will generally be accepted by the committee and the council. The other side is that the Chairman, certainly better than any member of a committee, is able to give intelligent lay criticism of a new idea and to suggest the various political and practical difficulties which officers have a tendency to ignore, or at least to minimize.

To make the best of these contacts it is essential that the Town Clerk and the Chairman have the utmost respect for each other's ability and integrity, that each may take the other into his confidence with the complete understanding that the confidence will not be violated. Dr K. C. Wheare has outlined the dangers of the Town Clerk or any officer who, impatient to get things settled, exercises his gift for ventriloquism; of the Chairman who, anxious to lead, surrenders to the officer; of the officer who, allying with the Chairman, captures him so that they move against the foe, the committee, together.[1] There can be little doubt that not only are Town Clerks capable of these things, but they do them. Although Town Clerks have a sincere appreciation for the respective functions of the officer and councillor in local government, they must couple this respect for function with a respect for the functionaries, or it is doubtful whether the system will work as it is expected. Writers[2] and Town Clerks alike speak of the decline in the quality of councillors in recent years. Perhaps they are right, although one cannot help but feel that there are a variety of criteria with which one might assess the quality of councillors and that it may not be that the quality has changed so much as the criteria which should be applied have changed. Even so, inferior quality or no, the Town Clerk must guard against allowing this feeling or the feeling of impatience or his enthusiasm to get things he wants accomplished to alter unconsciously his respect for the function of the lay mind in local government.

[1] Wheare, op. cit., pp. 181–4.
[2] E. L. Hasluck, *Local Government in England* (Cambridge, 1948, 2nd ed.), p. 334.

THE TOWN CLERK AND THE COUNCILLORS[1]

Again, the essential element in this relationship is mutual confidence that each will perform his respective task well. It must be built upon a basic foundation of understanding, an understanding of the contribution which each—the Town Clerk and the councillor—is expected, and able, to make to the smooth operation of the local government machine. It is aided immeasurably, as just noted, by a reasonable amount of mutual respect. It can survive, nonetheless, so long as there is a reasonable amount of mutual toleration.

From the Town Clerk's side this confidence in the councillors in some measure grows in the system of things. First of all the young entrant to the Town Clerk's department, either the junior clerk or the Assistant Solicitor, who aspires to be a Town Clerk some day, either knows, or if he plans to realize his aspirations, will soon learn, a good deal about the theory of local administration, the place of the officer, the place of the councillors, the rights and duties of each. As he progresses up the ladder this theoretical understanding will no doubt be tempered by his day-to-day experience, and his individual contact with various councillors. Depending on his experiences, his confidence in them may grow or diminish. But lingering always is the feeling that councillors as a group are entitled to his confidence, and that while some may be unworthy of it, they cannot all be so. Moreover, to work well with the councillors, he knows that they must have confidence in him, and that one way to ensure this is to show that he has confidence in them.

What does the Town Clerk do to show this? Most important, he demonstrates a willingness to help and advise any councillor at any time. The Town Clerk of a northern borough makes a practice of talking with councillors when they come to sign their acceptance of office. He tells them that the door of his

---

[1] These are the ordinary councillors, not those who are Mayors or Chairmen or leaders or whips. These councillors attend three or four committees per month, read most of the literature the Town Clerk sends to them, and occasionally give a good speech in council meeting. If they attack their work with slightly more zeal and acumen than is usual, they may become chairmen or leaders or whips, but for the moment, they are simply ordinary councillors.

office is always open for them and he urges them to call freely upon him when they have a problem or need advice. In this respect the local government officer is very different from the civil servant. No civil servant would entertain a Member of Parliament's request for advice or information. The Member would have to go through the Minister either by personal contact, correspondence or parliamentary question. For the civil servant the first and only allegiance is to his Minister. A Town Clerk conversely must advise every councillor who wants advice, must secure information for every councillor who wants information, regardless of the councillor's politics, purpose or prudence.

But what about the councillor who wants to put forward a proposal with which the Town Clerk does not agree or one which considered from all angles simply does not have any merit? As far as agreement goes, the Town Clerk need not agree at all; his duty, however, is still clear. He must produce the information the councillor wants and help in the way the councillor wants help. The bad proposal is slightly different. Here it is not a question of disagreement between Town Clerk and councillor, but one of disagreement between the councillor and general opinion or a question of the lack of intrinsic merit. As one Town Clerk explained, he would feel duty-bound to give the councillor all the information and technical advice he wanted, but would also advise him concerning the impracticability of his proposal or the possibility that he would make a fool of himself. Another Town Clerk emphasized that he would never allow the councillor to leave his office with an intimation that the proposal was nonsense or something similar. If the Town Clerk acted in this way one time, the next time the councillor had an idea he either would not bring it up or not consult the Town Clerk and neither alternative would be very good for a smooth working local government. As a result if the proposal were completely without merit, the Town Clerk would explain the defects, and if the councillor persisted over these objections, the Town Clerk would advise him to go ahead, but also to be ready to meet these same objections when the Town Clerk raised them in committee. If there seemed to be slight merit in the proposal, the Town Clerk would try to help the councillor eliminate the defects. As both Town Clerks intimated, it is important that the councillor not be cut off abruptly, but that instead he should be led patiently to the understanding that his idea, although at first glance quite plausible, has a number of defects for which there are no remedies.

The Town Clerk should be willing to let the councillors have the limelight. Take as an example one authority trying to settle a problem jointly with another authority. In all probability the two Clerks will get together and discuss the possible lines of agreement. Then a deputation from each side will meet, both sides briefed by their respective Clerks, and thresh the problem over. The councillors in the end make the decision, but the Town Clerk has the assurance that the agreement will be reached along the lines dictated by reasoned analysis.

There are other minor ways of building confidence. A Town Clerk can defer to the councillors. He can address them as 'Sir'. He can grant their little desires. One Town Clerk tells about the councillor who informed him that his correspondence to that councillor had been bearing the wrong title, and how a note from the Town Clerk to his secretary correcting this quickly improved the rapport between the Town Clerk and this councillor. It is often these seemingly insignificant things which count most in the overall analysis.

The Town Clerk can also do much to foster respect for himself among the councillors, respect which goes beyond the usual respect of ability. One Town Clerk claimed that he insisted on being called 'Mr Town Clerk' in all his dealings with councillors. This was so even though in private life he was on closest terms with some of them. He felt that nothing could destroy one councillor's confidence in him quicker than the feeling that some other councillor had more influence, or was on better terms, with the Town Clerk. Another Town Clerk of a similar sized borough took quite the opposite view. He stressed the importance of the personal touch with the councillors and of being on Christian name terms with them. It is apparent that different Town Clerks with different personalities will find different approaches to reach the same objective. But whatever the approach, it is essential that the Town Clerk not take sides, not show favouritism, and deal fairly and forthrightly with all councillors.

It is a cardinal principle of councillor-officer relationships that individually the councillors have no power to order officials to do anything, no power to examine an official carrying out his executive duties. Standing Orders which often direct that a member may 'for the purposes of his duty as such member, but not otherwise, inspect any document which has been considered by a committee or by the council' serve to illustrate this principle.[1] Despite rules like this, Town Clerks from time to time find themselves burdened with awkward councillors. Awkward councillors manifest themselves in a number of ways. They may spend a great deal of time at the Town Hall desiring to look at this document or those records. Or they may submit questions or requests for information calculated to call forth a large amount of official energy. Or they may like to send notes calling attention to numerous minor failings by the officers in the execution of policy. What can a Town Clerk do to improve the relations which have in these instances obviously deteriorated? The direct method is often the best. The Town Clerk asks the particular councillor to come in and chat with him. In this way they can air their differences, break down whatever barriers seem to be blocking a more sensible relationship and reach a better understanding. Sometimes this fails; then more devious methods must be employed. As an example there is the Town Clerk who went to the party leader and suggested that his tormentor be given a committee chairmanship in an attempt to increase the councillor's responsibilities and direct his attentions to more productive work. The party leader obliged, and the appointment did precisely what the Town Clerk hoped it would.

In spite of the fact that Town Clerks encourage individuals to call from time to time, the councillor's visit to the Town Clerk's office is not very frequent, and probably becomes less frequent as the authority becomes larger partly, one would think, because of the increased pressure of business on the Town Clerk. When they do call, it is rarely to discuss a major issue of policy; their concern is for the small matters—the street which has not been repaired, the need for a new sink in a council house— matters which either affect them or their friends personally. And one would have a difficult time advocating in the era of

[1] Cf., Model Standing Orders, op. cit., no. 29.

harmonizing technology and democracy that this is other than it should be. Occasionally a councillor approaches the Town Clerk, often at the close of the meeting, and suggests a new idea or raises a question, concerning a matter which the Town Clerk may want to give some thought to before commenting. The Town Clerk may then invite the councillor to come to his office on, say, Saturday morning to talk it over. But it would be an unusual week if more than one councillor did this. More useful to the Town Clerk than the contact in his office are the contacts before and after committee meetings. The Town Clerk who arrives at the meeting a few minutes early or lingers a few minutes afterwards has the opportunity to meet informally a number of councillors, get their views and learn of their difficulties. Of course this opportunity dwindles as the Town Clerk reduces the number of committees he personally attends. All in all these contacts, though not frequent and often spasmodic, are valuable to the Town Clerk. He is thereby kept informed of the general trends of thought, and he can enlist support for his own pet ideas.

THE TOWN CLERK AND PARTY LEADERS[1]

In a party sense, the Town Clerk is not a political animal. This means that he stands outside the political arena, or better perhaps, that he sits as a dispassionate, but extremely interested, spectator inside the arena, but off the field of combat. His advice is expected to be free from political bias, whatever that means. In practice it implies that he observes the rules of fair play, that he treats the party groups as separate but equal, that he does not place his influence consistently behind the policies of one group in preference to the others, that he avoids giving advice on issues that are certain to arouse party passions. He cannot ignore that parties exist. Unlike many civil servants who do their day-to-day work somewhat removed from the political process and party conflicts, the Town Clerk is very close to the

---

[1] Not all councils are politically divided; and even those where some political division is recognized are not in reality party councils—that is, those which have two or three well organized party groups, have leaders and whips, and have an effective opposition party. The attention in this section is directed upon the party councils, although some of what is said is quite relevant to those places where party organization is loose and sometimes blurred.

party struggle; in the council it is obvious, in committee it is less obvious but often still is there.

One would think that his proximity coupled with passionate party politics might make the Town Clerk's task quite unenviable. In some instances it does. But in the majority of cases there are several saving graces which assist him. First of all, his training in law and in administration, the aura in which he works his way up the ladder, conditions him to approach problems as technical rather than political. He becomes accustomed to leaving untouched policies of a political nature. Secondly, much of what could divide parties violently at the local level has already been decided in Westminster or Whitehall. The opportunity for local parties to find outlets for their political zeal are severely limited. Thus although the party undercurrent is there to be coped with, the issues that arouse heated party passion are not numerous and are usually easily recognizable. And thirdly, there are the party leaders, individuals with whom the Town Clerk can consult.[1]

Town Clerks do meet with the party leaders on their councils and they do so frequently. The Town Clerk of a large borough said that he had almost continuous contact with them since both had offices in the council house and were in the habit of spending a considerable amount of time in these offices. He added that they were particularly useful as sounding boards for whatever new ideas came to his mind. The Town Clerk of another large borough mentioned that he had a somewhat closer relationship with the majority leader, for when anything new emerged he would notify the majority leader immediately; the minority leader, on the other hand, would have to come and ask for information when he wanted it. It should be noted that this was not so much a matter of favouritism as a matter of accepted practice, that the majority was a slim one and had changed hands once during the past five years, and that the minority had expressed their approval of the system, expecting quite naturally that they would get the same treatment when they came into the majority. In a small borough the Town Clerk said he would consult with both leaders on all major

[1] Some Town Clerks maintain that they do not officially recognize the party leaders or that they recognize them as Leader of the Majority and Leader of the Opposition.

issues; but on minor issues which were certain to be decided on a party basis, he would only consult the majority leader.

Some Town Clerks on the other hand move with less assurance among the parties and party leaders. They prefer to meet the leaders together to avoid even the possibility of the appearance of favouritism, and if it is a political compromise they seek, they would normally ask the Mayor to call the leaders together. This situation may be dictated by the particular political complexion of the council, but it is not ideal. Meetings of this kind tend to become appeals for conciliation or appeals for joint action rather than a give and take of advice and opinion. In describing his experience one Town Clerk said he had found that the advice tendered by a party leader in the presence of his opponent was often very different from the advice tendered when the party leader and the Town Clerk were alone; consequently, he preferred to consult the leaders separately and then balance their separate advice himself. If practicable this would seem to be the more satisfactory approach.

What is the value of parties and party leaders to a Town Clerk? According to J. E. MacColl, the task of the Town Clerk or any chief officer is easier:

> . . . (he) knows where he is. If he has a bright idea it is much easier for him to estimate his chances of getting it adopted. If there is a proposal floating around which he thinks unwise he knows exactly where to go to have it deflated. . . . It is easier for him to grasp the intentions of a party which has published an election address and makes some effort to achieve consistency by discussion than it is for him to assess the relative influence in the council of a number of independents operating in unstable combinations.[1]

The point is certainly valid, and there are Town Clerks who agree.

But there is another side of the story. Some Town Clerks find party government, if not more difficult, certainly disheartening. As one Town Clerk explained, it often happened that he would work hard to get a committee to accept a new idea, and then,

[1] J. E. MacColl, 'The Party System in English Local Government', 27 *Public Administration* 69 (1949), p. 72.

when the majority party considered the proposal in caucus, they would vote it down. This was more disheartening when he realized that some caucuses were attended by non-councillors who were less moved by arguments attributed to an officer and more prone to resort to party dogma in making their decision. Another Town Clerk contrasted the situation which prevailed when his council was fully independent and the one which prevails now with well-organized parties and emphasized his feelings of helplessness at times because so many decisions are taken without consulting him.

One might plausibly argue that in the latter instances the Town Clerk has not taken it upon himself to establish close relationships with the party leaders, to acquire their confidence and trust; or that the Town Clerk is still trying to operate through an old constitutional framework of committees and personal power which has been superseded by a new framework of party power. In many places this is no doubt true. Nevertheless one has the feeling that all the fault does not lie with the Town Clerks, that the tradition of neutrality of Town Clerks has been interpreted by some party leaders as meaning the Town Clerk need not be consulted. In this connection it would be noted that some Town Clerks felt that it was much easier to deal with the Labour Party leader than the Conservative. In their opinion the Labour leader was more open to suggestion, readier to take and follow advice. The Conservative leader conversely seemed to have the answer for every problem, and usually was not interested in the Town Clerk's advice. There certainly must be Town Clerks whose feelings are precisely opposite to these about the two parties, but these, nonetheless, seem to indicate that as experts are inclined to exaggerate the compass of their expertise, so it seems party leaders may tend to exaggerate the extent to which party politics are involved in a decision to be taken at the local level.

The problems brought on by the institution of well-organized parties at the local level, solved by some Town Clerks through the force of their personalities and the confidence of their party leaders, have been awkwardly side-stepped by other Town Clerks. Such side-stepping can only work against successful administration and workable government.

CHAPTER VI

THE TOWN CLERK
AND HIS DEPARTMENT

THE Town Clerk's department is organized to carry out the various functions for which the Town Clerk is responsible. Just as the Town Clerk is responsible for these functions so he is responsible for the work of his departmental staff. Consequently, although the Town Clerk may and should delegate a great number of his duties to members of his staff, he cannot delegate his responsibility for their mistakes. Any criticism of the work of his staff by the council must be directed to the Town Clerk, not a particular member of the staff. Concerning the work of his department, therefore, the Town Clerk is the supreme authority; to him must go the credit for its successes and the blame for its errors.

This principle undergoes, however, some curious alterations in practice. One might expect that if a Town Clerk, or any chief officer, assumes full responsibility, the chief officer should also have the full power to select new members for his staff. This, however, is not always the case. In some authorities interviews for the Deputy Town Clerk, Assistant Solicitors and Senior Committee Clerks are conducted jointly by the Town Clerk and an interviewing committee or sub-committee. Although the Town Clerk's views are often persuasive, and most councillors recognize that for office efficiency alone the Town Clerk must be satisfied with the new appointee, the decision rests with the committee. A more sensible arrangement, consistent with the idea of chief officer responsibility, would allow the council or a committee to establish the posts but permit the chief officers to fill them.

As with any office staff the Town Clerk must establish clear lines of delegation, must establish efficient channels of communication and must establish pleasant working conditions and promote high morale. Or to put it another way, the Town Clerk must see that everyone knows what his job is, that he is kept informed of what is going on and that everybody, if not happy, is at least contented. There is nothing special about this. It is an essential prerequisite to efficiency in any business, small or large, and in this respect local administration can claim no distinctiveness. And it is as equally true of a Town Clerk's staff that numbers two as it is of one that numbers over a hundred. It is only that in the latter case ensuring these conditions is infinitely more difficult.

The Town Clerks' departments vary in size considerably. The major reason for these variations is the size of the authority. A few examples will suffice: in one borough of slightly over 15,000 population, the department totals six; in one of almost 70,000 there are thirty-two; in one of about 272,000 there are about seventy; and in a large one of about 315,000, there are an even one hundred. But size is not the only factor. In county boroughs certain duties such as electoral registration and registration of births, deaths and marriages swell the size of the Town Clerk's department. In addition the department is often a catch-all for various functions which a local authority decides to perform but for which it does not wish to establish a new and separate department: sections like Public Relations, Road Safety and Civil Defence. And there are duties which, for reasons of co-ordination or of the personal inclinations of the Town Clerk or of simply tradition, come within the work of the department. Establishment[1] and Local Taxation[2] are examples of this category. Doubtless a more detailed survey would produce many more varied and in some instances quite unusual functions which are performed by the Town Clerk's department and which increase its size and add to the Town Clerk's responsibility.

THE DEPUTY TOWN CLERK

By statutory provision the Deputy Town Clerk is permitted to

[1] One Town Clerk described his predecessor as someone who was not willing to add to his responsibilities; thus when the council decided to add an Establishment Officer to his staff, the Town Clerk recommended he be placed under the Treasurer. The present Town Clerk is now endeavouring to transfer the Establishment Officer to his own department. It is quite conceivable that the extent of the Town Clerk's dominion depends largely upon his own wishes and desires.

[2] Local Taxation is the collection of road taxes, motor licence fees and the like. It is customary for this function to be placed under either the Town Clerk or the Treasurer or, less frequently, the Chief Constable.

act as Town Clerk should that office become vacant or the holder unable to act.[1] The Deputy Town Clerk is an important person in the Town Clerk's machinery, not so much because the statute inserts him into vacancies, but because he is second-in-command in the department.

The precise nature of this position varies from town to town. In some places the Town Clerk and his Deputy work almost parallel; they divide the committee work and legal work evenly, the Town Clerk, however, taking the more important committees and less routine legal matters. In others, the Deputy Town Clerk is made supervisor of the legal section, thus relieving the Town Clerk of all but the most important legal problems. To a certain extent the size of the authority enters here also; as the authority becomes larger and the Town Clerk's overall duties more onerous, the tendency is to draw the Deputy more parallel to the Town Clerk, but on a slightly lower plane and to place a Chief Assistant Solicitor in charge of the legal section.[2] Placing the Deputy in charge of the legal section has the advantage of freeing the Town Clerk for the administrative and co-ordinating work required of him. But since the position of Deputy Town Clerk is looked upon as the final stage in the training of potential Town Clerks, it does have the disadvantage of preventing the Deputy from acquiring wide administrative experience.

It is evident the Deputy Town Clerk, working parallel to the Town Clerk, can operate in several ways: first, he can keep himself ready to act on behalf of his chief during his chief's absence; second, he can relieve his chief by taking responsibility for action up to a certain limit on all matters handled at top level; or third, he can accept whole responsibility for action in defined fields of activity, not exclusively or even necessarily legal activity. Obviously, a Deputy can do all three of these things since they are not mutually exclusive. If one were to express a preference, it would seem advisable that the second be emphasized more than the other two, for by accepting the responsibilities for actions up to a certain limit, the Deputy

---

[1] Local Government Act, 1933, s. 115.

[2] In some small authorities, there is no Deputy Town Clerk as such, although there may be an Assistant Town Clerk or Assistant Solicitor who fulfils most of his functions.

becomes acquainted with the full range of the department's activities and with the methods of hierarchical office organization, both of which are invaluable assets should he some day become a Town Clerk. If any of these functions should be regarded as less important, it should be the first. A Deputy Town Clerk should not be expected to step into the Town Clerk's place and be able to answer all questions just as his chief would. It is certainly a waste of good talent for him to try to keep abreast of all that is going on in the authority, to duplicate, as it were, the job of his chief. He should, it is true, be able to act in the Town Clerk's absence; but this need not entail having all the answers; knowing where to find them is certainly sufficient.

Needless to say the Town Clerks generally stay in close contact with their Deputies. Many of a Town Clerk's ideas emanate from joint consultations with his Deputy, and many others are modified and improved with his help. Because of his intimate association with the background and facts of a particular issue, the Deputy may often prove to be a Town Clerk's most useful sounding board.

THE WORK OF THE DEPARTMENT

The work of the department centres on two basic functions:[1] meshing committees and council action,[2] and dispatching legal work and advice. But there are others, as was intimated above. There are co-ordinating functions such as establishment work and organization and methods studies; there are various statutory functions such as tending to the local land charges and electoral registration, and there are miscellaneous functions like public relations and the general office work. How these functions are performed and more particularly who performs them are the problems to which the discussion now turns.

Committees and Council
The participants in this function are the Town Clerk, his

[1] It is intended here to discuss the work in terms of functions themselves rather than the persons performing these functions. It is apparent that in a smaller authority, especially, various persons may work on several functions; thus a Solicitor may do both committee and legal work.

[2] Some prefer to call this the 'administrative' function.

Deputy, an Assistant Solicitor or more, the Chief Committee Clerk and his subordinates, the Committee Clerks. The work involved is the preparation of agendas, reports, minutes and meetings; in general, it is the mechanical part of the Town Clerk's relations with the councillors.

The work normally begins in the Town Clerk's office first thing in the morning as the day's post is read and sorted. The Town Clerk of a middle-sized borough makes a practice of arriving in his office at eight o'clock so that he can begin with his staff in going through the post. This meeting will be attended in the smaller borough by the Town Clerk, his Deputy or Assistant and the Committee Clerk or Clerks. In the larger boroughs, to this group may be added several Assistant Solicitors and a few more Committee Clerks, although in some places only the Chief Committee Clerk attends for that side of the staff. The Town Clerk in the small towns opens and reads the entire post, usually about ten to thirty items, and notes specific directions on each piece. As the size of the post increases, it is general practice for the Town Clerk's secretary to sort out the routine matters before he sees the post; even so, he may still see as many as sixty letters in a half-hour session. It has been estimated that about 40 per cent of the correspondence a Town Clerk receives concerns legal matters.[1] The legal letters are normally given to Assistant Solicitors to deal with, the remainder are given to the Committee Clerks who see that they reach the proper committee tray or folder. Where an immediate reply to a letter is necessary, the Town Clerk may keep the letter until he himself dictates the reply or he may ask the appropriate Committee Clerk to draft the reply along lines he suggests. Most Town Clerks emphasize that this morning meeting is very valuable, not only for the purposes of keeping the department in smooth running order, but also for keeping the Town Clerk informed on the overall work of the authority and particularly on those parts of the administrative machine which have faltered sufficiently to prompt a complaint to the Town Clerk.

The next step is the drafting of the committee agenda or in

---

[1] B. Bain, 'The Town Clerk of Norwich', 86 *Journal of Society of Town Clerks* 67 (February, 1951).

some instances the Town Clerk's report. Generally the committees are divided among the Committee Clerks. If there is a
Chief Committee Clerk, he normally takes the most important
committees—Finance and Planning, for example—and supervises the other Committee Clerks concerning the remainder.
The Committee Clerk drafts an agenda, according to the
format used by the authority, from the items in the committee
tray or folder: that is, correspondence, memoranda from the
Town Clerk, memoranda from other departments, and so on.
In drafting he is usually in close contact with the Solicitor who
handles the legal and more important administrative work of
the committee. In addition, he also contacts the other departments which normally have business for the committee, to see if
there are additional items to come from those sources.

The Town Clerks of the smaller authorities generally go
over each draft agenda carefully, adding items which have
been omitted, dropping items which are not ready for decision,
supplying additional information which the councillors will
need and revising the method of presentation where they feel
it is necessary. In the middle-sized and large authorities the
Town Clerks generally only revise the draft agenda of those
committees they attend in person, the Deputy Town Clerk or
Assistant Solicitor revising the draft agendas of the committees
they personally attend. In the very large authority the Town
Clerk may not even see an agenda until it has been finalized,
and then it is usually only the agenda of a committee he
regularly attends. But generally speaking, Town Clerks take
some part in the drafting of agendas, and even those they do
not assist in drafting, they will see in their final form so as
to keep in touch with the work of all the committees and to
remind them of meetings they especially want to attend because
some important matter is to be taken up.

Of course, much depends upon the Town Clerk's personal
inclinations. One Town Clerk of a middle-sized borough feels
it is his personal responsibility to see that documents sent to
councillors are well drafted; he, therefore, pays close attention
to all agendas and reports prepared within his department.
Another officer feels that it is somewhat demoralizing to a
Committee Clerk to have his work continually returned,
covered with blue marks, arrows and scratches, and as a result

he is rather hesitant about making changes unless they are absolutely essential. The agenda or report having reached its final draft, the Committee Clerk sees that it is duplicated. He also collects the reports of other departments and then sends all of the documents to the committee members along with the summons to the meeting.

At the committee meeting, most Town Clerks have at least two representatives, either themselves or another senior representative (usually a Solicitor), and a Committee Clerk. The Solicitor sits beside the Chairman, advises him, and occasionally introduces items; the Committee Clerk on the other hand records the attendance, notes the proceedings and decisions, and serves up the necessary documents to the Solicitor as he requires them. In some of the large authorities, a Committee Clerk may handle a meeting completely on his own, both advising the Chairman and committee and recording the procedure. And it has been suggested after a detailed study that the employment of higher quality Committee Clerks would make this practice more possible and would free the Solicitors for the legal work for which they are trained.

After the meeting the Committee Clerk drafts the minutes of the committee, and if the report system is employed, the committee reports to the council. Much as with the draft agendas, the Town Clerk goes over the draft minutes and reports, making additions or corrections as he deems necessary. He probably gives more attention to these drafts than he did to the draft agendas since this is the work of the department which the public and the press regularly see as the council agenda. Also when a minute is likely to be used in court as evidence, especially one providing that some legal action be taken, the Town Clerk sees that it is drafted in the accepted legal form. When an item of major importance is concerned, the Committee Clerk may draft the item in consultation with officers from other departments: as one example, a rent rebate scheme report drafted with the help of the Housing Manager and an Accountant. In any case, the chief officers of the departments concerned with the committee's work see the draft and have an opportunity to make corrections. And in some towns the Chairman of the committee sees the minutes or reports in the final draft before they are sent to be printed or duplicated.

These minutes or reports then become agenda for the council meeting and are sent to each member with the statutory summons at least three days before the meeting.

At the council meeting one Committee Clerk, usually seated at a table in the centre of the council chamber, notes the proceedings; another may time councillor speeches (that is, where there are time limits during debate); still another may carry notes and papers back and forth; all contributing to the smooth running of the meeting. After the meeting the Chief Committee Clerk usually drafts the minutes which the Town Clerk revises. The Committee Clerks see that the chief officers concerned with the work and decisions of their committees are informed of the council's decisions either by circulating the full committee and council minutes for the month or by sending out individual memoranda. And during the month the Committee Clerks may check with the various chief officers to see how work on certain projects is progressing, and especially to see if reports and work promised for the next committee meeting are being attended to.

It is apparent that a Town Clerk must have competent senior representatives on the committee work. They must be able to give clear and intelligent advice to the chairmen and the committees. They must know what information the committees should have at their disposal in order to reach thoughtful decisions. Above all, they must know when to call on the Town Clerk for his opinion or to request his appearance at the committee meeting. It is equally apparent that able and efficient Committee Clerks are an essential part of the system. The good Committee Clerk will draft agendas, minutes and reports in a clear, well-written, grammatically correct style. He will lighten the senior representative's burden by anticipating what information will be required by the committee. He will deal tactfully with the other departments, thus promoting good inter-departmental relations and ensuring co-ordination. He will be dependable and will follow the tight time schedule dictated by the fast-moving committee cycle. As Herbert Morrison has said:

There is an important officer attached to Committees called the Committee Clerk. . . . These men are of high standing, and they have substantial salaries. They are the eyes and ears of the chief officers concerned.[1]

Legal Function

The work involved in this function is concerned with 'legal processes'. In the large authorities this work is carried on by a self-contained, or nearly so, legal section. In the middle-sized and small authorities it is conducted mainly by the Solicitors on the staff along with their committee work. It is therefore misleading to compare the sizes of the legal staff of the various authorities. Nevertheless a few examples should be cited, simply to indicate proportions. In the borough of 275,000, where the legal section is nearly self-contained, there are a Principal Assistant Solicitor, two Assistant Solicitors and six law clerks, plus four clerks. In the borough of 300,000, where the section is not self-contained, there are the Deputy Town Clerk, two Assistant Solicitors and two law clerks. The legal section in the borough of 70,000 is the same size. The small authorities usually have only one (the Town Clerk) or two (the Town Clerk and his Deputy or Assistant) qualified solicitors plus a clerk who is able to handle routine legal work. Some legal sections are assisted by the Articled Clerks of the Town Clerk.

The predominant part of this work involves the preparation of contracts and agreements and the conveyancing of land. Every project put to tender requires the preparation of a contract; as in the normal course of business, this is usually a fairly routine matter, but occasionally there is a contract that requires some skilful drafting. Likewise almost every new house or road or school constructed by the corporation requires the exercise of the authority's powers of compulsory purchase and the conveyance of land. Next the section is concerned with the management of estates, the legal questions arising from tenancy agreements, the preparation of notices to quit and the recovery of possession. Proceedings under Public Health Acts, Housing

[1] H. Morrison, 'How the L.C.C. Does Its Work', 14 *Public Administration*, London 17 (1936), p. 26. The qualifications for a Committee Clerk are usually that he be able to type and take shorthand. Frequently he will take an examination for a secretarial qualification. His salary may rise as high as £1,000, and a Chief Committee Clerk may have an even higher salary. For an interesting but vastly exaggerated account of a Committee Clerk's duties and qualifications see R. S. B. Knowles, 'Back-room Boys of Local Government', 57 *Municipal Journal* 677 (1949).

Acts, Town Planning Acts, Local Acts and Byelaws made in conjunction with the Medical Officer of Health, the Public Health Inspectors or the Borough Surveyor consume a large amount of time and necessitate adequate preparation.[1] And litigation on behalf of the corporation and the briefing of counsel also forms part of the section's work.

It is not unusual in the smaller boroughs for the section to prosecute for the police in the magistrates' courts. There are certain dangers in this, where the Town Clerk is also Clerk of the Peace, in that the Prosecuting Solicitor may become the instructing solicitor in a case before Quarter Sessions where his chief, the Town Clerk, is clerk of the court.[2] This situation is similar enough to the pre-1835 practices in local courts to cause some concern. Needless to say, the Town Clerk should take steps to avoid the appearance that justice is not being done.

Very similar to litigation in the ordinary courts is the conduct of local public inquiries which normally arise in connection with planning proposals, although the central departments may hold them for a number of reasons. Generally these inquiries are reasonably informal; the strict rules of evidence are not religiously followed, and procedure tends to be somewhat lax. Nonetheless the preparation of an adequate case with the help of the Planning Department and the competent presentation of it before the Central Government Inspector is essential. In addition the section studies new parliamentary legislation to determine its effect upon the authority, completes the background work for any Private Bills which are planned for introduction in Parliament and periodically reviews the Byelaws and Standing Orders to determine whether they are sufficient to meet the needs for which they are designed.

The part the Town Clerk himself plays in this work varies a great deal. Where the Town Clerk is the only lawyer on the staff, he conducts a considerable amount of the work. Where the Town Clerk is not a lawyer, the burden falls upon the solicitor on the staff, if there is one, or on a private solicitor in the town. But as the size of the town increases, the Town Clerk's concern

[1] Society of Clerks of Urban District Councils, op. cit., p. 67.
[2] (Anonymous), 'Appointment of Prosecuting Solicitor', 116 *Justice of the Peace*, 131 (1952).

with detailed legal work lessens. The Town Clerk of a middle-sized London suburb estimated that his work is 20 per cent legal and 80 per cent administrative. And the Town Clerk of a similar-sized borough in the Midlands says that he is so rusty on his legal knowledge that he is very cautious about tendering legal advice without first consulting one of his assistant solicitors.

In spite of this, even the Town Clerks of the very large authorities cannot avoid doing some legal work. It is not the drafting of contracts or preparations for conveyance which concern them, but the resolution of conflicting legal opinions within the staff, the drafting of clauses for Private Bills, the suggestion of a clause for the Government's new Local Government Bill, or the conduct of major local inquiries. The Town Clerk of a very large borough in the West claims that whenever two solicitors cannot agree on the particular legal course he has them come into his office and present their respective cases, and he then decides what to do. Another Town Clerk, concerned with the application of a Local Government Bill to non-county boroughs, had his Chief Assistant Solicitor go over the entire Bill carefully and select the important clauses. Then in conference together the Town Clerk and the Chief Assistant Solicitor fashioned a few amendments which were then forwarded to the Association of Municipal Corporations and the Borough Member of Parliament. When a local inquiry involves the re-planning of the town centre, or an inner relief road, or a boundary extension, it is reasonably certain that the Town Clerk will be the advocate. These, of course, are but a few examples of instances when the Town Clerk steps in. At the same time most Town Clerks are content to allow their Deputy or Chief Assistant Solicitor to carry on most of the work of the section without interference from above, particularly where the Town Clerk has the confidence that his Assistant Solicitors will refer any difficult matters upwards.

Establishment and Organization and Methods
That a local authority, whose staff is of such size that a committee can no longer attend to the co-ordination of establishment work, should have a single person entrusted with the executive side of the work seems generally to be agreed. It is the duty of this person to act as adviser to the Establishment

Committee on all matters affecting wages and salaries and working conditions, to administer all schemes and agreements regulating remuneration and conditions of service and to co-operate with the departmental heads in this connection, and to keep under continuous review the numbers, grading and service conditions to ensure uniform standards throughout the authority's service.[1] One of the essential elements in his work, therefore, is staff co-ordination, ensuring that the same standards and rates of pay for the same work are obtained in the Treasurer's department as in the Architect's department and in fact in all departments. In addition his work is the initial step towards providing inter-departmental exchange of staff and it contributes to reducing the independence of the various departments.

As would be expected in view of the co-ordinative nature of this function, the person entrusted with it is almost without exception found in either the Town Clerk's department or the Borough Treasurer's department, the major co-ordinating departments of the administrative machine. Except in the very large authorities the chief officer of the department is usually made, at least nominally, the Establishment Officer.[2] As far as the Town Clerk's department is concerned, in at least one large city, the Town Clerk is the Establishment Officer, but on his staff is a Deputy Establishment Officer who carries out the detailed work on a full-time basis; in three other good-sized cities the detailed work is attended to by the Chief Clerk on a part-time basis.

The detailed work involves keeping abreast of all newly-negotiated national agreements for wages, salaries and conditions of service, securing the information necessary to grade new posts, supervising the employment of subordinate staff and in-grade advancements, overseeing applications for leave of absence, sickness benefits, superannuation and an infinite number of other details concerned with staffing a going business. It involves frequent consultations with the heads of employing departments if uniformity is to be attained. And it requires tact, discretion and a good knowledge of the law

[1] Royal Institute of Public Administration (Study Group; T. C. Jones, Chmn.) *The Elements of Local Government Establishment Work* (London, 1951), p. 110.
[2] Ibid., p. 109.

relating to employment, of local government legislation, of trade union law and practice, and of national insurance law.[1]

Whether the establishment function should reside in the Town Clerk's or the Treasurer's department is a question which seems to be settled in theory, if not in practice. The weight of considered opinion favours the Town Clerk's department.[2] The reasons for this are sound: since the Town Clerk is responsible for co-ordinating the whole of the work of the council, he should be responsible for staff co-ordination; since the Establishment Officer must deal with the heads of other departments, he should either be a chief officer or have the full support and backing of a chief officer; and although financial economy in staff is desirable, it should not be the only objective in establishment policy. In short the progressiveness and imagination needed in establishment policy is more likely to be provided by the Town Clerk than by a Treasurer.

Closely related to establishment work are organization and methods studies, for the size and duties of staff depend to some extent upon the office procedures and systems employed. Similarly, organization and methods work can contribute greatly to co-ordinating the administrative machine. Although these assets are recognized, organization and methods studies have not made much headway in local government. The Coventry Council invited H.M. Treasury (O. and M. Division) survey team to study completely the Corporation's administrative set-up. The group produced thirty-two reports and innumerable recommendations, not the least important of which was one advising the hiring of a full-time Methods Officer to work under the Town Clerk. Most of the metropolitan boroughs have combined to establish a Standing Joint (O. and

[1] Royal Institute of Public Administration (Study Group; T. C. Jones, Chmn.) op. cit., p. 111. Moreover H.M. Treasury (O. & M. Division) recommended that the establishment function be closely linked with the provision of certain common office services, such as provision of accommodation, office equipment, communication, enquiry bureaux, typing services, office keeping, printing and stationery, and receipt and dispatch of mail. The emphasis of the recommendation from the Establishment Officer's point of view was upon planning these services rather than upon controlling their execution. 'Coventry Organization and Methods', 32 *Public Administration*, London 52 (1954).

[2] Royal Institute of Public Administration, Ibid., pp. 112–14; 'Coventry Organization and Methods', Ibid.

M.) Committee which conducts periodic studies of similar operations in its member boroughs. An O. and M. unit has also been formed by the Oxford and Reading City Councils and the Berkshire County Council to conduct studies for those authorities. But these are on the whole isolated instances; few authorities have subjected themselves to a sweeping organization and methods study, and even fewer have placed a single person in charge of the continuous review of procedures, forms and systems in an effort to achieve simplification and economy. Nonetheless in the large authority in particular, there will be an ever pressing need for such a person as local administration becomes more complex, and for the reasons advanced in regard to the Establishment Officer, this methods officer should also be placed under the Town Clerk's direction.

Statutory Duties

By statute all Town Clerks are charged with the custody of charters, deeds and records and with the registration of local land charges. Moreover many Town Clerks either by statute, appointment or delegation are required to supervise the registration of elections, and the Town Clerks of county boroughs by statute supervise some aspects of the registration of births, deaths and marriages. Although these are normally carried on within the Town Clerk's department, the Town Clerk's concern with them is exceedingly limited.

The custody of charters, deeds and records can be viewed from two angles, historical and current. The current records present little problem for the Town Clerk; most of them are maintained by the Committee Clerks in their section or the General Clerk in the central filing section. Historical documents present a different problem. In some small authorities the Town Clerk himself sees that they are properly maintained, or if the borough has a Librarian, he is often given the responsibility of ensuring their safety and preservation. In a middle-sized authority the Town Clerk may delegate this task to a member of his own staff, perhaps an Assistant Solicitor who is especially interested in borough records and history. In a large authority, there may be an Archives section of the Town Clerk's department. This section would preserve departmental records when they cease to be current, other local records of historic and civic interest and ancient records of all kinds. It also would assist the staff of the department by carrying out research on current and historical problems and arrange special exhibitions for the public. In one authority, such a section is staffed by the City Archivist and two clerks.

The registration of local land charges and the registration of electors is carried out by one or more clerks on the Town Clerk's general staff. For the land charges, the persons responsible register the charges, make searches in the Register upon the request of the public, and answer inquiries concerning other restrictions upon property and land. The mastery of the system is not a difficult task and one needs no broad legal knowledge to become competent. Electoral registration is a larger task. It requires the organization of a personal canvass which must be thorough and accurate. For this reason these duties are usually given to an experienced clerk in the Town Clerk's department. In one authority the Chief Committee Clerk instructs the canvassers, who are hired temporarily, before the yearly survey; but the remainder of the work, however, is performed by the Registration Clerk. In another the work is done by a Senior Clerk and three assistants with the help of about fifty temporary canvassers. An Administrative Assistant assisted by two clerks organizes and operates the system in the largest of these three examples.

Under the Local Government Act, 1929, the Town Clerk must ensure the good conduct of the registration officers in the registration of births, deaths and marriages, fix their office hours and distribute registration duties among some of the officers. This means that technically the registration staff is part of the Town Clerk's department. In fact it is usually separate physically and to a large extent separate organizationally. The Superintendent Registrar administers the staff's operations, and his contact with the Town Clerk is quite infrequent. One Town Clerk estimated that he saw his Superintendent Registrar about four times a year.

Miscellaneous Functions

In addition to those functions described above, the Town Clerk's department often has several sections which perform a variety of functions. The Town Clerk's department is in this respect a kind of catch-all department, for its overall purpose has no defined limits. The Finance department handles financial matters; the Engineer's department handles engineering matters; the Architect's department, architectural matters; the Planning department, planning matters; and so on, each being a reasonably well-defined area of operation. The work of the Town Clerk's department, on the other hand, is not so easily defined. As a result when a new function is taken on by the council and it does not seem to merit departmental status or seem to fit with the work of the existing departments, it is usually accommodated in the Town Clerk's department. The ensuing brief account of some of these activities is certainly no attempt to provide an exhaustive list of operations performed by Town Clerks' departments; rather it is an account of some of the more common activities and of a few of the unusual ones which have come to the writer's notice.

Most Town Clerks' departments in authorities of middle-size and larger have a General Section. This section is entrusted with registries of various kinds—contracts, mortgages and council property, for example—receipt and dispatch of correspondence, maintenance of the petty cash account, maintenance of an inquiry office, and occasionally the organization of public functions on the Town Clerk's behalf. In the small office, work may be done by one or two clerks who also handle other work as well. In the larger authority, a Chief Clerk may be put at the head of a staff of reasonable size. The Chief Clerk may also double as Chief Committee Clerk, although in the very large authorities the two positions are separate. As Chief Clerk he is also responsible for maintaining discipline and overseeing staff problems among all but the professional members of the department.

Civil Defence is another function frequently found in Town Clerks' departments. Under the Civil Defence Act, 1948, many councils were given certain Civil Defence powers and as a result Civil Defence Committees were established to co-ordinate the work under these powers.[1] On the officer side, the responsibility for the administration of the powers has been placed upon a Civil Defence Controller (Designate) or a Civil Defence Officer,

---

[1] P. G. Richards, *Delegation in Local Government* (London, 1956), p. 119.

who is or may be the Town Clerk.[1] Where this is the case the Town Clerks are personally responsible to the authority for the recruitment and training of their Divisions in peace time, and should their appointment be confirmed in event of war, for leading the Division in these circumstances. The precise part the Town Clerk takes as Controller (Designate) or Civil Defence Officer depends largely on his personal view and the time he has to spare. Nonetheless, he usually has a Civil Defence Assistant and a number of instructors and clerical staff to perform the detailed work for him.[2]

Except where it is a department of its own or where, since this is quite frequent, no provision is made for it, Public Relations usually forms part of the work of the Town Clerk's department. The work of this section varies from place to place, but generally speaking it is responsible for keeping the public informed of the work of the council, for bringing to the notice of the council any manifestations of public opinion of importance in municipal affairs, for publicizing the amenities of the town and for answering *ad hoc* inquiries for information on many subjects.[3] In carrying out this function the section, which may be headed by a Public Relations Officer assisted by a small staff, releases information to the press, radio and other agencies, organizes press conferences, prepares various publications like the borough guidebook, a business directory and a civic newspaper, and operates an Information Bureau. In the smaller authority where the need for a special section for public relations is not great, many of these activities, the preparation of publications in particular, are carried on by members of the Town Clerk's staff or by the Town Clerk himself.[4]

Other functions under the heading of miscellany, as noted above, are numerous. In at least two large places, the Town Clerk's department has a Road Safety section, which aims to

[1] According to *Municipal Yearbook, 1958*, 65 Town Clerks are either Civil Defence Controllers (Designate) or Civil Defence Officers.

[2] During World War II about 120 Town and County Council Clerks performed in a similar capacity as A.R.P. Controllers. For an account of their duties, see T. H. O'Brien, *Civil Defence* (H.M.S.O., 1955), pp. 314–15.

[3] The forerunners of Public Relations sections were the Development Boards which were co-operative ventures of the Chamber of Trade and the council established to induce industry to settle in the town.

[4] For a good example see *Guildford and Its Government* (1957) by H. C. Weller, Town Clerk of Guildford.

keep the problem of road safety continually in the public mind, and in another a Planning and Redevelopment section, which co-ordinates the vast central redevelopment schemes undertaken by the council. In a few places the Local Taxation section for the collection of motor licence fees and similar fees is part of the Town Clerk's department. In a number of small boroughs, the Housing Manager is on the Town Clerk's staff. And it is said that some Town Clerks' departments handle the administration of cemeteries.[1]

There is one duty, however, which the Town Clerk usually cannot delegate to his staff. That is the sealing of documents. The Standing Orders invariably require that this be done in the presence of the Mayor and the Town Clerk, or their respective Deputies, who shall subscribe their names after the sealing.[2] This process is usually a regular weekly ritual which the Mayor and the Town Clerk attend to personally.

[1] L. C. Hill, 'Problems of Training for the Public Service-Local Government', 16 *Public Administration*, London 276 (1938), p. 282.
[2] See Model Standing Orders, op. cit., pp. 25, 26.

CHAPTER VII

THE TOWN CLERK AS A CO-ORDINATOR: FOR THE COUNCIL AND AMONG THE DEPARTMENTS

ORDERLY and organized operation does not come naturally to governments, big or small, or, for that matter, to any organization. Someone must have the power to pull the strings together, to tie some knots, and to cut others. Someone must see that papers and ideas are so channelled that everyone who counts sees them and takes a crack at them. Someone must make sure that when there is a job taking two, or three, or ten to do it, the right two, or three, or ten are there and doing it. In short, someone must co-ordinate.

In local government, the committee system provides the infusion of democratic control into administration. It provides a means of popular expression concerning the details of broad policy. It provides a very strong safeguard against bureaucracy and technocracy. At the same time certain advantages of a more cohesive system are sacrificed, and prominent among these is the ease of creating a well co-ordinated system of administration. Wide delegation of a council's powers to committees stresses each committee's independence and creates the tendency for councillors to view a service as the charge of a committee rather than of the council.[1] The result is many loose-ended strings, each tied to a pet project or idea.

But even though co-ordination is as necessary as taxes in running a local government, just what co-ordination is is often difficult to nail down. In fact, the word itself, 'co-ordination', is elusive; it stands for many ideas and just as many human actions. So much so, that its use is often misleading, its particular reference often misunderstood and misconstrued. Some elementary definitions or labels are thus advisable.

[1] This is a view which when evidenced in the actions of councillors, some people call the 'committee mind', that is, the tendency to regard oneself as a member of the Housing Committee and the Health Committee and the Planning Committee, rather than of a council which controls all committees.

First, there are various levels of co-ordination, and this is where much of the confusion enters. A Town Clerk is co-ordinating the work of a council when he arranges, for an item involving the work of two committees, that both committees have the opportunity to consider the item. A Town Clerk is also co-ordinating the work of a council by advising on the growth of the borough or its planning or the development of a new service which encompasses the work of several committees and departments. It is obvious that Town Clerks who do the first but not the second are doing only part of what there is to be done, even though they are 'co-ordinating' the work of the council.

H. R. Page, the present City Treasurer of Manchester, in a detailed analysis of the need for and methods of co-ordination, divided the methods into two groups: co-ordination of organization and co-ordination of development.[1] This is as convenient a division as any, for it serves to point out the distinction between co-ordination to secure the smooth flow of business, the efficient running of the administrative machine, and co-ordination to secure a balanced and integrated policy for the corporation as a whole. Of course any such distinction has its rough edges, for efficient machinery is one means towards the end of integrated policy. But at the same time, a local authority may have a smoothly operating administrative machine and very little overall policy direction. Things may get done, but no one co-ordinates the thinking about how things should be changed or what things should have priority. Thus, rough as the edges may be, the labels—organization and development—will be useful in separating the various activities of the co-ordinator.

Secondly, co-ordination in local government has two aspects. There is the co-ordination of the councillor side of operations—the committees and the council. There is also the co-ordination of the officer side of operations—the chief officers and the departments. These are not wholly separate; in fact, from one point of view, they are not separate at all, but instead very closely inter-related. Combining the efforts of two committees, it would be said, does very little good if the policy which is co-ordinated is not executed in a co-ordinated way. Similarly,

[1] H. R. Page, *Co-ordination and Planning in the Local Authority* (Manchester, 1936).

achieving the co-ordination of major policy involves initially the co-ordination of the advice coming from the chief officers. Nevertheless, although in looking at the work of the corporation one readily acknowledges this inter-relation, as far as the Town Clerk's work is concerned, he is on the councillor side dealing with people and a set of relationships different from those with whom and with which he is dealing on the officer side. It is this separation which is recognized here; and the remainder of the chapter will be divided in two sections, dealing first with the councillor side and then with the officer side of co-ordination.

But first one question must be disposed of: why should the Town Clerk be the co-ordinator? The work of most departments, and thus of chief officers, is organized parallel to one or two committees, but there are two departments which serve all committees and all the other departments, that is, the Town Clerk's department and the Treasurer's (or Finance) department. It would, therefore, seem reasonable to assume that either the Town Clerk or the Treasurer should become the co-ordinator. In fact, by force of tradition and of considered opinion over the past thirty-five years, the Town Clerk has been so designated. There are several reasons which are usually given for this preference: the Town Clerk is the centre of the committee preparation and activity which is an integral part of an authority's machinery; the Town Clerk is the chief means of contact with the world outside the authority; and the Treasurer's characteristic concern with the financial aspects of any matter is too narrow a viewpoint for an effective co-ordinator. Let it be emphasized, however, that although traditionally the Town Clerk has been thought to bear the major responsibility for co-ordination, this does not mean in fact that any one Town Clerk automatically bears this responsibility to the full or that other chief officers like the Treasurer do not foster co-ordination where a Town Clerk ignores this task or fails to perform it with sufficient imagination and skill. 'What should be' may not be 'what is'.

CO-ORDINATION OF THE COUNCIL'S WORK

The Town Clerk has by virtue of his position various means or methods at his disposal for securing co-ordination of a council's work. Whether any one Town Clerk makes use of these methods depends on what his councillors and fellow chief officers expect of him, what his predecessors have done, and what he himself wants to do. How often or how much any one Town Clerk or Town Clerks in general use these available means it is difficult to say. In any real sense, these are not activities which readily admit to quantification. Most Town Clerks use some of the methods with reasonable success; that at least can be safely ventured. Further, few Town Clerks use all the methods with complete success, and likewise few resort to none of the methods and thus fail to perform any co-ordinative function whatsoever. More precise estimates of numbers would be difficult or impossible to produce and misleading if they were produced.

Town Clerks, generally speaking, also tend to be more active in the co-ordination of organization than in the co-ordination of development. Even the relatively weak Town Clerk regards an efficiently run committee system as his responsibility. But he and many of his more forceful brethren are equally reluctant to venture into the policy co-ordination field. The consequence is, of course, that policy co-ordination is left to someone else, perhaps a strong councillor, a party leader, an inner group or, as is not unlikely, to no one. But to appreciate this fully, one must examine the methods by which Town Clerks can, and many do, co-ordinate the work of their councils.

Co-ordination of Organization
The Town Clerk's part in organizational co-ordination extends broadly to five activities: the preparation of Standing Orders and committee instructions, the formation of committees, the execution of Standing Orders and committee instructions, the recommendations for inter-committee consultations, and the preparation of reports on inter-committee or inter-department co-operative ventures.

Standing Orders and committee instructions form the major portion of a local authority's written constitution, other than the statutes. If co-ordination is to be achieved, therefore, a well-drafted constitution may be said to be an important first step, for in this way a balanced organization and defined procedures may be established. Advice on Standing Orders and committee instructions and the drafting of new sections and amendments to existing sections, in most authorities, are functions of the Town Clerk. His influence in these matters is thus considerable; his ability to foster co-ordination in this way is substantial. A few examples will demonstrate this. When Parliament places a new function within the orbit of local authority powers, some administrative arrangements must inevitably be made in order to exercise the power. A new committee may have to be established, or new powers may be added to an existing committee or several committees. It is essential that a response to the need for co-ordination be evidenced in the final decision. The Town Clerk's advice in this respect is usually paramount.

The size of committees is an important factor in achieving organizational balance. If some committees are a great deal larger than others it is reasonable to expect that these larger ones will have a better opportunity of asserting their policy in council.[1] The Town Clerk may therefore advise that all committees should be limited to a specific number of members, and conversely that certain important committees have a larger than average membership.

Committee instructions are the means by which powers are delegated to the various committees and each committee's scope of operation is defined. As an initial step the careful drafting of these instructions by the Town Clerk is a means of ensuring harmonious relations between committees. But even the most carefully drawn instructions cannot prevent some conflicts over jurisdiction between committees. Consequently the foresighted Town Clerk will see that the instructions contain some procedure for resolving these disputes. In order that the proper cross-references of various matters are made between committees, that is, that as concerns certain matters, one committee must consult another before any action may be taken, it may be advisable that the Standing Orders or committee instructions lay down rules of procedure for these matters.[2] Similarly most Standing Orders establish very rigid procedural rules for the consideration of financial proposals, supplementary

---

[1] H. R. Page, *Co-ordination and Planning in the Local Authority.* p. 4.

[2] Ibid., pp. 69–71. Mr Page cites several examples from the Standing Orders of the London County Council.

estimates and the tendering for contracts, all of which are directed towards achieving uniformity and co-ordination.

These are but a few examples of the ways in which the Standing Orders and committee instructions influence the co-ordination of a council's work. In his capacity to advise upon the preparation of these orders and instructions, the Town Clerk has a very powerful tool for setting the basic pattern for committee co-ordination.

A system of interlocking membership (that is, a system whereby councillors serve on committees with related responsibilities) enhances the possibility of co-ordination in terms of basic principles, and a well-organized committee cycle is a great aid to the smooth flow of committee business. On both of these matters a Town Clerk may have some influence. Although the Standing Orders of some councils call upon the Town Clerk to distribute voting papers for committee membership and to tabulate the results, his influence on this basis is strictly limited. This is purely a clerical duty which grows out of his position as clerk to the various committees and the council. But his influence flowing from his relations with the majority party leader or with the formal or informal Nominations or Selections Committee may be quite formidable. Thus the Town Clerk may be able to ensure some interlocking membership, and in some places he may even be adroit enough to have an extensive system instituted.[1] The situation concerning the committee cycle is somewhat similar. In order to dispatch business efficiently the cycle should be organized so that committees which deal with items initially meet early in the monthly cycle, and the committees which give secondary consideration meet later. The most obvious examples are the Finance and Establishment Committees. Since they, to a large extent, act upon the recommendations of the other committees, it is advisable that they meet late in the cycle. There are, no doubt, other less general examples involving two or three committees where the proper ordering will facilitate the smooth flow of business. An alert Town Clerk is conscious of these possibilities and suggests departures from the existing practice when they seem advisable.

[1] In Birmingham a system, evolved by the Chief Clerk in the Town Clerk's department from his own experience, was instituted. Ibid., p. 195n.

The careful preparation of Standing Orders and committee instructions is of little value unless they are properly followed by the committees in their work. The task of ensuring this observance also falls chiefly upon the Town Clerk.[1] From the point of view of co-ordination it is particularly important that items are efficiently cross-referenced between committees. This means that some system must be arranged whereby items considered by one committee and referred to another committee find their way on to the second committee's agenda. The Town Clerk's central position in respect of the preparation of agendas makes him the logical person to perform this function and makes the job of performing it relatively easy. In the smaller authority all the committee clerks are in one office so that it is simply a matter of passing along the information by word of mouth or by a note in the proper committee folder or tray. In the larger authority where the committee clerk sections are separated, a system of inter-section memoranda or extracts is generally used. Again, however, the responsibility for seeing that the memoranda or extracts are prepared and circulated falls upon the various committee clerks.

Where two committees are in conflict over the proper line of action to be taken on a certain matter, it is usually the Town Clerk's duty to try to induce a certain measure of compromise. He may advise sending a deputation from the one committee to the other, or a joint meeting of the two committees, or a joint *ad hoc* sub-committee, or he may simply request that the two Chairmen come to his office and work out some solution. As often as not, the Town Clerk's advice must be in a contrary direction, for as Dr K. C. Wheare has pointed out, he 'may find that consultation, joint discussion and co-ordination committees develop so much that they become an end in themselves'.[2] What, if used properly, can be an aid to efficient administration may become a means of delay and frustration. Thus the Town Clerk's job is also to see that joint consultations are held only when there is a genuine need for co-operation.

Lastly, the Town Clerk may organize the materials for reports on various co-operative ventures within the authority's

[1] See, *supra*, p. 105.
[2] Wheare, op. cit., p. 198.

administrative framework, such as central purchasing, central workshops and the co-ordinated use of corporation vehicles. He may collect facts and figures from the various departments, inquire of practices in other authorities of a similar size, and then produce a report to the appropriate committee upon the possible establishment of a new system or the reorgnization of an existing one. In authorities which have their own organization and methods team, the basic groundwork is a matter for their attention; in other smaller or less progressive authorities, this task is usually given to the Deputy Town Clerk or another member of the Town Clerk's staff.

These are all ways in which a Town Clerk may—and many do—act to provide a smooth flow of business within the committee structure and a balanced administrative structure which is able to handle business efficiently.

Co-ordination of Development or Policy
As was pointed out earlier, co-ordination should extend beyond the provision of a good structure. Committee policy should also be co-ordinated. The prerequisite to this co-ordinated policy is inevitably a body of co-ordinated policy advice from the officers. To a large extent, so far as this advice is forthcoming, the Town Clerk takes the lead in organizing it. At the very least he takes part in its organization. Generally speaking, these are matters which are dealt with at officer level. But as with all policy, and particularly that involving large co-ordinated schemes, this advice must be presented to a committee or the council. It is the Town Clerk's part in this presentation to which attention is now briefly turned.

Informally the Town Clerk may consult, advise and thereby co-ordinate or spawn consistent lines of thinking when he meets and chats with the various Chairmen. Likewise his presence at committee meetings gives him the opportunity to encourage co-ordinated policy and action. The frequency and influence of these meetings and appearances have already been discussed; thus it suffices here to note that within the smaller authorities they may be frequent and quite useful in bringing about co-ordination. But in the larger, and probably the majority of, authorities, the chief officer most closely connected with a particular committee spends more time than the Town Clerk consulting, advising and influencing the Chairman of that committee; and often that committee and no other. Similarly it is the Deputy Town Clerk or an Assistant Solicitor who represents the Town Clerk's department at the committee meetings. And although they can present the Town Clerk's viewpoint on any matter, only he can present it with the influence and persuasiveness which belongs to him personally. Consequently the opportunity to co-ordinate in this fashion is not used by Town Clerks in large authorities as much as other methods are.

What are these other methods? In one form, policy is co-ordinated by means of joint sub-committees formed to deal with specific problems which come within the scope of several committees. The most obvious current example is slum clearance. The first step in a slum clearance project is the determination by the Health Committee that certain houses are unfit for human habitation. Next, new places for the people living in these houses must be found. This normally involves the Housing Committee. Then the Works Committee may provide for demolition, the Planning Committee for redevelopment, the Highways Committee for new streets and street lighting, the Education Committee for new schools. Once a project is approved, it is essential that all these moves are well-timed, that each action is followed quickly by the next. It is useful, therefore, to bring all these committees together by means of representation upon one committee. At the same time the advice of the various departments must be sifted and the work scheduled according to their various capacities. All Town Clerks take some part in these proceedings because a project of this nature is fraught with legal implications—the interpretation of acts, the enforcement of bye-laws, the compulsory purchase of land, the preparation of building contracts. Beyond this, the average Town Clerk takes the lead in these situations. He makes certain that all affected departments and committees are brought together and have the opportunity to express their viewpoint on the project. If some phase or consideration is omitted the Town Clerk takes the blame for it. And the strong Town Clerk generally takes it upon himself to direct the entire project. In unusual circumstances, he may even establish a Planning and Redevelopment Section within his own department to provide for the direction and control of these kinds of projects.

A more continuing need is the policy co-ordination of various functions which affect all committees of the corporation. This is done by what are called the horizontal committees, such as Finance and Establishment, and a committee which plays a similar role but in a somewhat different fashion, the Planning Committee.

The Finance Committee reviews the estimates of the other committees for the annual budget and the requests for supplementary estimates throughout the year. It keeps a watchful eye upon the finances of the corporation as a whole and presumably balances the various demands made upon the revenues of the corporation. Because of this function it is normally the most important or second most important committee of an authority. Town Clerks almost invariably attend the Finance Committee personally.[1] This enables them to see that the general policy of development for the corporation is not unduly modified by over-zealous desires for economy.

The normal Establishment Committee considers all proposals for new posts within the departments and for regrading of existing posts, as well as handling the many other problems of staffing and organization. In this way it has the final say on the structure of the executive side of the corporation and is able to provide uniformity concerning salaries, wages and conditions of service throughout the corporation. Where the Town Clerk is Establishment Officer for the authority, he is the committee's principal adviser concerning the methods of obtaining this uniformity, and hence, co-ordination. In other places where the Treasurer or a separate Establishment Officer handles this function, the Town Clerk's part is less prominent. Nonetheless he usually has a representative at the committee who can offer his point of view if not his influence.

The Planning Committee is not a reviewing committee as the Finance and Establishment Committees are—rather its job, so far as functional co-ordination is concerned, is to provide a development plan for the authority and ensure its implementation. This development plan shows proposed land uses and

[1] See, *supra*, p. 85.

the proposed stages of any projected development.[1] One of the committee's aims is therefore to provide a co-ordinated system of land use within the borough. In this way planning touches the work of many other committees; Housing, Parks, Highways, Education, to name but a few of the more obvious. As with slum clearance, which itself forms a part of a Planning Committee's concern, the Town Clerk cannot avoid being intimately involved with planning, if only because he is responsible for the legal work of the corporation. But because of the general implications of land use upon the overall policy of the corporation, a Town Clerk's concern for planning may extend beyond the legal problems which arise. A strong Town Clerk, therefore, gives enough attention to planning to see that the technical concerns of the planners do not subvert the general policy of the corporation.

Most important, of course, is co-ordination for the overall policy of the corporation. This has been described as the anticipation of the needs of the borough and the decision as to whether these needs are catered for in the expressed policies of the various departments.[2] In a sense it is the co-ordination of foresight. It is seeing that the projected development of each service corresponds with that of the others. Moreover, it is seeing that the corporation has a consistent and balanced line of proposed development. In the smaller authorities this oversight can be provided by the council itself, for the scope of services is not great, nor are the ramifications of any general policy very complex. As authorities become larger the councils tend to become deliberative bodies and are less able to formulate consistent policy. The tendency is to establish some kind of committee to advise the council on matters of general policy. In at least one middle-sized authority this function is combined with finance and is performed by a Finance and General Purposes Committee. In the larger authorities a separate committee is, more than likely, established; for example, in Coventry the Policy Advisory Committee is charged with the duty (among other things)

to consider generally the future development of existing services

[1] Hart, op. cit., p. 517.
[2] Page, op. cit., p. 264.

or the introduction of new services, and (as may seem desirable in the Committee's judgment) either to advise the Council thereon, or to bring such matters to the notice of the appropriate controlling Committees for their examination

and in Manchester, the General and Parliamentary Committee is required to report to the Council

upon questions of policy in connection with
1. New projects of a substantial character not previously approved in principle by the Council.
2. Proposed extension of a service already in operation or programme of development where, in either case, the proposals are of a substantial character.
3. Periodic forecasts of expenditure.
4. Matters referred to them by the Finance Committee.

The Town Clerk is normally the principal adviser to these committees and usually attends their meetings personally. According to the Town Clerk of the above mentioned middle-sized authority, although the work of the Finance and General Purposes Committee is largely financial, he nevertheless takes a great deal of business to it in its capacity as a General Purposes Committee exercising co-ordinating functions. In Manchester, the General and Parliamentary Committee is one of the very few which the Town Clerk himself regularly attends. He has in his department a General and Parliamentary Officer who prepares the reports to the Committee and who is in regular contact with him. Consequently the opportunity is there for many Town Clerks to assume the leadership in guiding their authorities to consistent overall policies. Whether full advantage is taken of this opportunity one has some very grave doubts.[1]

[1] A random sample of six reports of one of these committees showed that the committee considered what might be called 'issues of overall policy' in only three instances: these issues were (1) overspill, (2) a priority scheme for projects involving capital expenditure, (3) the promotion of a local Bill in Parliament. The committee also considered a joint report of the Town Clerk and City Treasurer on the White Paper on Local Government Finance, which is related to overall policy, though certainly not within the authority's complete control. Otherwise the committee concerned itself with such items as representatives on A.M.C. committees, applications for grants from a variety of sources, subscriptions to various societies and reports on Parliamentary legislation, all within the scope of its instructions, to be certain, but equally as certain, not within the province of overall policy. This

In some authorities this deficiency may be partially compensated by strong parties. The strong party is not in itself the whole solution. The party must have vigorous leadership, leadership which attacks the pressing problems of the town with a thoughtful and consistent programme. The leaders must have ideas and be prepared to carry them into effect. At the same time the majority party must have a workable majority so that barring a major blunder it will have time to prove the worth and success of its policies. The slim majority of four or less is not enough, for then the major concern is not the success of the programme, but the size of the rate. With yearly elections, the party with a slim majority which causes any appreciable increase in the rates will more than likely find itself in the minority after the next May. As a result a workable majority as well as vigorous leadership is a necessary element if there is to be any effective contribution to overall policy by the local party groups.

In other authorities where parties are not strong, where no person steps forth to assume the role of council leader, the need for an overall policy, so far as it is present, goes unattended. The co-ordination of details, the smooth flow of business, even the co-ordination of some special large projects, are provided by the Town Clerk. But the consistent overall policy, the integrated programme for borough or city improvement, is not there. Of course the services expand a little, but by and large the work of the council drifts along the same path from year to year unless for some reason the central government steps in to alter it. This is the pattern of English local government; strong and vigorous leadership is not common, nor is it generally expected, from Town Clerks or, for that matter, from anyone else.

CO-ORDINATION OF THE DEPARTMENTS

The Town Clerk and the Other Chief Officers
The Town Clerk's position in relation to the other chief officers

confused mingling of minor duties with matters of overall policy is a common practice among those local authorities which have established committees for overall policy oversight.

is a curious one. He is neither equal with them nor superior to them. Or perhaps, it might be better said, he is both equal to them and superior; or maybe, at times equal and at times superior. In practice his position is a mixture of these possibilities.

The Town Clerk, as has been described above, is the council's legal adviser. This means he is also the legal adviser to the other departments, just as the Treasurer is financial adviser to the other departments, and the Architect places his architectural knowledge and talents at their disposal. In the larger boroughs, the Town Clerk, of course, has a legal staff which handles the corporation's legal matters and tenders advice to the other departments when they request it. In the very large authority the routine requests are routed directly to the Legal Section. The more difficult problems, however, would be sent to the Town Clerk himself who would then decide how and by whom they should be handled. In the middle-sized authorities a similar practice prevails, but undoubtedly the scope of what is 'routine' is somewhat more limited. In the smaller authority, however, where the Town Clerk deals with almost all of the actual legal work himself, the contacts quite naturally are directly with him. Thus in these matters a Town Clerk is very much a Technical Officer supplying technical advice to the other departments. And in so doing he is brought in contact with every department of the corporation at one time or another.

If the sizes of the legal staffs in the Town Clerks' departments are any indication, this work certainly constitutes the basis for a substantial proportion of the contacts between the Town Clerk's and the other departments of the council. And undoubtedly this work forms an important part of any Town Clerk's responsibilities. But in terms of the overall administrative machinery, its importance, if not its magnitude, is overshadowed by another function which has come to be regarded the responsibility of the Town Clerk: the function of departmental co-ordination.

Departmental co-ordination involves co-ordinating both the execution of a council decision and the officer advice to a committee or the council. The former might be labelled co-ordination of organization; the latter, co-ordination of development. But here the distinction is even fuzzier than it was when applied to the council's work. Execution may involve more than seeing that the right person does the right thing at the right time. It may involve some choices concerning how the thing shall be done, who among several possible 'right' persons or groups shall do it, and when it shall be undertaken, all of which may have significance concerning costs and concerning the general development of an authority's services. Thus whether an activity is tagged organizational or developmental is not very important. What is important is how Town Clerks operate with and among the other chief officers, what methods they use to bring the officers together, and how effective these methods are.

But before exploring the methods it would be useful to review the development of the Town Clerk as a departmental co-ordinator to determine what has been expected of Town Clerks in the past and what will be expected in the future.

In the Ministry of Health Annual Report for 1923–24, it was observed (at page 62) that:

It is manifest that a Town Clerk or any other officer could not properly dictate to other persons in the employment of the Local Authority, the Medical Officer of Health or the Engineer, for instance, what they should do in the details of technical matter within their particular purview. Nor could any Local Authority impose on any one of their officers duties in conflict with those conferred on any other officers by statute or by central regulations.

The proposal to make some one officer definitely responsible for the general supervision of the whole of the business of the Local Authority, and their chief adviser on all matters of policy is, however, a different question.

The Report went on to speculate:

There appears to be room for consideration whether, while maintaining to the full the traditions of local government service and, especially, of democratic control, the time has not come for some further development of the administrative arrangements of the Local Authorities, and for having one chief official who, whatever his title, shall be in a position of definite responsibility for the general official organization.

It may be premature to express any decided opinion on this

possible development, but the question clearly merits attention. Two conditions would always have to be fulfilled:

(1) the unquestioned control of the elected body.

(2) no derogation from the responsibility of the present principal officers.

The value of any such chief official as has been suggested would depend very largely on his exercising general control, on his not attempting to do the detailed work of officers expressly appointed because of their specialized qualifications, and on his working in full harmony with them.

This Report established what has come to be recognized as the broad theoretical basis for the relationship. But quite obviously if some working system is to be achieved a more definite agreement on the important concepts is necessary. For instance, what is meant by 'general supervision of the whole of the business of the Local Authority' or 'definite responsibility for the general official organization' when one notes also that there is to be 'no derogation from the responsibility of the present principal officers', nor dictation concerning the 'details of technical matters within their particular purview', nor an imposition upon the Town Clerk of 'duties in conflict with those conferred on any other officers by statute or by central regulations'? Interpreted quite literally, the Ministry seemed to have had in mind the assumption by the Town Clerk of a new service in local government, the service of co-ordination, which could be performed without altering the existing administrative structure.

The Royal Commission on Local Government, at page 137 of its final report in 1929, carried the point further. In considering the position of the Town Clerk as departmental co-ordinator, the Commission concluded that,

... The Clerk need not, and should not, interfere with the technical staff on technical questions; and in particular the responsibility of the Chief Financial Officer for financial administration should be clearly recognized; further, technical officers should not be debarred from direct access to the Committees of the Council. The questions on such points become largely academic, once the principles are established that the Clerk must be kept informed of the activities of the various departments, and of the reports which the chief officers thereof make to the Council or Committees; that the Clerk is responsible for seeing that proper co-operation exists between the various departments, and for advising the Council thereon; and that the Clerk is the channel through which the authority conducts official correspondence.

The Commission were thus of the opinion that the Town Clerk should have a right to be informed of what was happening in each department and that where he saw the need for some co-operation, he should take measures necessary to ensure it. Nonetheless the Technical Officers should still have direct access to their committees and have the right to report to the council. The extent of the Town Clerk's power to interfere with the technical departments should be: (1) to require information, (2) to see the officers' reports to the council and the committees, and (3) to secure co-operation where a matter of general policy is concerned.

The evidence given before the Commission is instructive in this regard. The late Sir Arthur Robinson, Permanent Secretary at the Ministry of Health, saw the situation in this way:

> There was (he said) a sphere for the professional officer which was a distinctly professional sphere, in which the Clerk as the general administrator would not interfere, but where a professional sphere impinges on the general sphere of policy of the council, then the Clerk comes in.[1]

As a Town Clerk of a large southern borough recently said, he would never intervene with the Engineer's selection of the kind of bridge to be built, but he would be directly concerned with a proposal by the Engineer to widen a street in the Town Centre, the distinction being that in the former the entire decision depended upon the Engineer's technical knowledge of bridge-building, whereas in the latter, although resting to some extent upon the Engineer's knowledge of road needs and construction, the decision also involved many considerations outside the Engineer's professional sphere. The basic reason for insisting upon this departmental independence was advanced to the Commission by Mr J. Ernest Jarratt, then Town Clerk of Southport and representative of the Society of Town Clerks:

[1] Royal Commission on Local Government Minutes of Evidence, XIV, Q's 40, 372–89.

The inconveniences, of course, are that when you are appointing the head of another department, if you make him feel that the good work of his department is to depend on his own organization, you may get some results; but if you interfere with the administration of his staff by making him subordinate to some other officer, you have lessened his sense of responsibility. The general experience locally is that we get better administration by looking to the separate head of a department for work within his own department and superimposing upon that the responsibility of the Town Clerk to co-ordinate the whole thing, with assistance from the council and committees. And in consultation with the heads of the departments.[1]

The principle here is quite clear: placing responsibility on a chief officer for his department leads to a higher quality officer and a more efficient department. But likewise this departmental efficiency may be offset by an overall inefficiency caused by a lack of co-ordination.

The problem can thus be narrowed. Like so many problems of government, it is an attempt to find the proper dividing place, the delicate balance, between the control necessary to achieve adequate co-ordination and the freedom necessary to ensure responsibility and efficiency. The key to this is the matter of subordination. Given the structure and the traditions of local administration, one must accept that complete subordination of the chief officers to the Town Clerk is not very feasible. But neither the structure nor the traditions rule out the possibility of a partial subordination, that is, in respect to certain activities in local administration which have an overall influence or of certain procedures which contribute to overall efficiency.

One important factor in this relationship is, therefore, the recognition by the chief officers of their partial subordination to the Town Clerk. The seeds for this recognition have existed at least since the Royal Commission. The evidence given before the Commission by the various associations of chief officers indicated a grudging willingness, but willingness nonetheless, to give this recognition.[2] It was the Conditions of Service, negotiated separately for Town Clerks (and District Clerks) in 1949 and for the chief officers in 1950, which formalized this

[1] Ibid., Vol. XIII, Q's 38, 191–2.
[2] Ibid., Final Report, 1929, pp. 132–3.

process of recognition and helped to crystallize this viewpoint. The first section of the Conditions negotiated for the Town Clerks reads:

> The Clerk shall be the chief executive and administrative officer of the council. He shall be responsible for co-ordinating the whole of the work of the council.[1]

That this caused some concern among the other chief officers is evidenced first of all by an article which appeared in the *Municipal Journal* not long after these recommendations were published. Written by a Treasurer and supposedly addressed to the problem whether the Clerk or the Treasurer should be the chief executive officer, it was in fact an impassioned criticism of Section One of the Town Clerk's Conditions, and at the same time an admission that the Clerk is the chief administrative officer.[2] Secondly, it is evidenced by the first section which the other chief officers negotiated a year later for their own Conditions:

> A chief officer shall be the executive and administrative head of the department of which he is the chief officer. He shall be responsible therefor to the council through the appropriate committees.[3]

In terms of any definition of the position of the co-ordinator and his relations with the other departments, this attack and counter-attack settled nothing. There is less in these two general statements than what the Ministry of Health had suggested over twenty years previous. But the Ministry was indicating what could be—the Conditions, generally accepted by all authorities, indicate what now is. More important, they provided something in writing, something generally agreed to, which can be, and is, pointed to by Town Clerks and accepted by most chief officers, to the effect that the Town Clerk is the chief administrative officer, the departmental co-ordinator. It was therefore a major step in general recognition by the chief

[1] Recommendations of the Joint Negotiating Committee for Town Clerks and District Council Clerks, September 8, 1949, Second Schedule, para. 1.

[2] (Anonymous) 'Clerk or Treasurer', 58 *Municipal Journal* 1743 (1950).

[3] Recommendations of the Joint Negotiating Committee Chief Officers of Local Authorities, September 12, 1950, Second Schedule, para. 1.

officers of their partial subordination to the Town Clerk and a basic step upon which a more defined relationship could be built.

An attempt at such definition was made in respect of Coventry by the Treasury Organization and Methods Division in 1953. In its Final Report the Division concluded:

> ... it is of fundamental importance to consider allocating the duties to a post of Town Clerk very different in conception from one which has come to be regarded by tradition as carrying primary responsibility for the Corporation's legal and secretarial work, with the nominal and largely undefined role of 'Chief Administrative Officer' tacked on, as it were, by an afterthought.[1]

To remedy this the Division suggested that certain duties should be assigned to the Town Clerk, under the control of the Establishments and General Administration Committee:

1. To take a continuing interest in the effectiveness and economy of all administrative arrangements throughout the corporation;

2. To ensure that administrative activities with which two or more departments are concerned are effectively co-ordinated;

3. To act as Establishment Officer and to arrange for the provision of common office services where it is more economical to provide them on a centralized basis;

4. To furnish an O. and M. service for all departments;

5. To maintain a broad view of the balance and effectiveness of arrangements made to carry out the policy laid down by the council, and to bring to the notice of departments (and, if necessary, committees) the need for any change.[2]

'These duties are wholly administrative and constitute those of a Chief Administrative Officer in the full sense of the term,' the Division asserted.

As Chief Administrative Officer or departmental co-ordinator therefore, the Town Clerk should, according to the Report, be

[1] Coventry and Organization and Methods, op. cit., p. 89.
[2] Ibid., pp. 83-4.

superior to the chief officers in certain areas of operation which affect all departments. The foremost of these is the area of establishment. By this was meant establishment work in the broad sense, that is, recruitment, training, promotion, inter-departmental transfer, grading and a continual review of the existing arrangements. To permit the initiative to come from the Town Clerk in these matters, he should also be in charge of organization and methods work within the administration with the power to examine the procedures, systems and forms used by the various departments. And similarly he should be able to arrange for the provision of common office services, such as receipt and dispatch of mail, office furniture and equipment, telephone installations and other means of communication between buildings, inquiry bureaux and typing services including training of typists and a central copy-typing pool. Establishment, organization and methods, and common services are the three areas in which the chief officers should be subordinate to the Town Clerk. Beyond this there are to be occasions when the Town Clerk has a right to enter the scene. Principally this is when two or more departments are involved in a single activity; then the Town Clerk should have a duty to see that the departments co-operate with each other. In addition the fundamental aim of the Town Clerk in this work should be economy in administrative arrangements and balance in the execution of policy. Where in his opinion these aims are not being realized, he should call the department's attention to the need for a change. Moreover in all this work, the Town Clerk should be accountable to a special co-ordinating committee, the Establishment and General Administration Committee.

This consideration of the development of the Town Clerk as Chief Administrative Officer stemmed from an inquiry into what is expected of a Town Clerk as departmental co-ordinator. A very good answer is given in the Coventry Report, but it represents a present ideal rather than a present reality. Some Town Clerks in their actions come closer to the Report's implicit definition of a co-ordinator than others, but the actions of none fit it completely. Nonetheless almost all Town Clerks have frequent contact with the chief officers and provide some departmental co-ordination. It is the circumstances of this contact and these methods of co-ordination to which attention is now turned.

Methods of Co-ordination

Before launching directly into these various methods of co-ordination it is well to consider who these chief officers are. By Section 106 of the Local Government Act, 1933, boroughs must appoint, in addition to the Town Clerk, a Borough Treasurer, a Borough Surveyor, a Medical Officer of Health and a Public Health Inspector. If it is a county borough, it must also appoint a Chief Education Officer, a Children's Officer and a Chief Constable. These chief officials form the hard-core of those with whom the Town Clerk frequently deals. In the larger authority there are many more than are required by statute—an Architect, a Planning Officer, a Water Engineer, a Housing Manager and a Parks Superintendent are but a few examples. Each chief officer is at the head of his own department and, as outlined above, reports in most cases to one particular committee. It is self-evident that as the number of departments and chief officers increases, the difficulties of the Town Clerk in bringing about departmental co-ordination increase as well. The Town Clerk who can bring together four or five other officers and survey the work of the entire corporation is perforce in a much stronger position than the Town Clerk who must bring together twenty or more officers to accomplish the same thing; not only from the point of view of the increased scope of the corporation's services, but also from the point of view of having more people with whom to deal.

But there are other factors as well. Some chief officers and departments regularly provide advice throughout the corporation on some particular function. The most notable example is, of course, the Treasurer; but others are the Establishment Officer, and to a lesser extent the Surveyor and the Architect. Other chief officers and departments form entities almost wholly separate from the rest of the corporation, the outstanding example being the Chief Education Officer, but in the large towns the trading undertakings, usually Waterworks and Transport, may be in this category. They may provide their own committee clerk and their own accountant and in this way virtually resist all contact with the rest of the corporation.

Because both of these situations can produce perplexing problems for a Town Clerk, it is well to examine the two major examples in some further detail.

The Treasurer. The Treasurer has a great influence upon one of the most important policy questions in local government, the size of the rate. It is in most places completely the Treasurer's task to prepare the annual budget. This means that he first contacts the spending departments and gets their preliminary estimates. On the basis of these, he estimates the size of the rate if all this expenditure were to be approved. The Finance Committee then sifts through the various preliminary estimates and usually recommends which items it feels might be reduced. It is then the Treasurer's job, usually with the assistance of the Finance Committee Chairman, to negotiate with the other Chairmen and chief officers in an attempt to have the estimates reduced. Finally the Finance Committee approves the estimates and transmits them to the council, and the Treasurer writes the budget speech for the Finance Chairman. The Treasurer is therefore in a pivotal position in the rate-making process. He participates in all negotiations right from the beginning and has the job of writing the general summary at the end. He is not, however, in a dictatorial position, for the spending departments must be heard, and moreover many of the items included in a budget are fixed charges which go on from year to year—interest, debt charges, salaries, maintenance of plant and equipment, or charges for expenditures which have already been approved by the council during the previous year. Nonetheless, although the Treasurer is not in complete control, his influence can be very great. Moreover during the year all supplementary estimates must be approved by the Finance Committee, and the Treasurer's advice on these matters is probably more influential than that of any other officer, including the Town Clerk. Where the Chairman of the Finance Committee is one of the leading members of the council, as is very frequently the case, the influence of the Treasurer may often spread beyond the confines of the Finance Committee.

The Treasurer also has other duties, some of which bring him in contact with the other departments: the collection and disbursement of the Borough Fund, the direction of the accountancy and internal audit systems, the tendering of advice on the procurement of loans and the financing of capital projects. He must see, as well, that the financial systems of the corporation ensure the proper handling of all moneys.

Since the Treasurer plays a leading part in rate-making and in the consideration of supplementary estimates, and since he has close contact with almost every department and usually sends a representative to each committee to advise on financial matters, the question arises as to precisely what relationship there is between financial policy and general policy. Can the two be separated, a Finance Committee setting the one, and a General Purposes or Policy Committee setting the other? Some people seem to feel that this is possible. G. E. Martin, at the time Borough Treasurer of Poplar, strongly advised that the Finance Committee should be an independent committee chosen from the point of view of financial ability and capacity.[1] The present City Treasurer of a large southern city expressed the view that the Finance Committee attempts, though not successfully, to deal with finance policy only. But the weight of practical evidence is to the contrary. Certainly financial policy, if by that term is meant the policy as to size of the rate and the policy as to the amount of indebtedness, is intimately related to general considerations of policy, the overall development of the corporation's services. For example one of the major considerations in the review of rents by a Housing Committee will be whether an increase in the rate contribution to the Housing Revenue Account is involved. Such an increase would require Finance Committee approval. In one of the largest cities the Finance Committee not long ago voted to reduce overall capital expenditure by almost 40 per cent. It is difficult to imagine any one decision taken by any one committee which would have as great an effect on general policy as this one. It must, therefore, be recognized that financial and general policy are closely intertwined. In fact, financial policy, particularly in times of tight money and limited resources, is probably the major element in overall policy.

But it is only one element. Once the rate is set, decisions about how the revenues shall be distributed and which services

[1] G. E. Martin, 'The Technique of Financial Administration of a Local Authority', 11 *Public Administration*, London 389 (1933), pp. 397–8.

receive priority remain. This distribution comprises the central element of any general policy. It is this distribution with which the Town Clerk, if he is to be the general adviser to the council, should be more concerned than the Treasurer. And it is this distribution which in most authorities is left almost entirely to the Finance Committee and the Treasurer's department with only the most perfunctory attention given by the council.

If the Town Clerk is to co-ordinate not only the departmental administration but also policy advice to the council, it would seem that he must develop the very closest working arrangements with the Treasurer, an arrangement built upon mutual confidence, sincere desire for co-operation and a recognition by the Treasurer of the limitations of financially-oriented policy and of the Town Clerk's broader duties in relation to general policy and co-ordination. In the main this kind of relationship exists between Town Clerks and Treasurers. The Treasurers are generally quite willing to admit that the Town Clerk is the chief administrative officer and is responsible for general policy co-ordination.[1] But occasionally there is one, like the Treasurer of a middle-sized county borough, who appears to take a somewhat different view. In a paper he prepared for the Student Society of the Institute of Municipal Treasurers and Accountants, he declared,

> Policy is a matter for the council but nevertheless it is essential that the policy-maker should have independent views on it, both by the Clerk and by the Treasurer.[2]

This is a sound doctrine so far as financial considerations can be divorced entirely from general policy considerations. But insofar as the two are difficult to disentangle, the task of the Town Clerk to co-ordinate council action will be more complicated the more the Treasurer regards himself as completely independent of the Town Clerk.

The Chief Education Officer. The Chief Education Officer of a county borough presents a somewhat different problem. Education is the largest single service provided by the county

---

[1] See (Anonymous), 'Clerk or Treasurer—Which Should be Chief Executive Officer?' 58 *Municipal Journal* 1743 (1950).

[2] G. C. Jones, 'The Independence of the Treasurer of Public Funds', lecture (first delivered in London, October 7, 1955).

boroughs and makes the greatest demands upon rate revenue. It is also the most independent of the council. Most Education Committees provide their own committee clerks from the Education department.[1] As a result the Town Clerk's normal method of keeping touch with the work of a committee is not available to him. This can make co-ordination in respect of education a difficult task for the Town Clerk. The Town Clerk does, however, provide legal advice to the committee much as the Architect provides architectural advice, the Treasurer, financial advice and the Engineer, engineering advice. Because designing new schools and financing building programmes are more important than the legal work that is apt to arise, the Education department probably works in closer association with the Architect and the Treasurer than the Town Clerk. Some Town Clerks see the Chief Education Officer very infrequently and their advice on matters concerning the Education Committee is seldom required. This is certainly a pattern not conducive to the exercise of departmental co-ordination by the Town Clerk.

Even though the Treasurer, the Chief Education Officer and to some extent the other chief officers act independently of the Town Clerk and each other, most Town Clerks, should they so wish, can foster some departmental co-ordination, even though in many instances it is only on a limited scale. It is the methods which Town Clerks employ in these efforts to which the last part of this chapter is devoted.

To co-ordinate the work of the departments effectively, the Town Clerk must first of all know what work is being conducted by the various departments. He must keep himself informed of the progress in every section of the corporation. To do this he has several means at his disposal. For instance, since he is the authority's major channel of contact with the outside world and vice versa, he has an excellent opportunity to keep abreast of recent developments by checking the incoming post each day. Moreover, if there is a local newspaper, he will usually read it carefully in order to ascertain any drift in public feeling. What he usually looks for are complaints. If there are no complaints about a matter, it is probably running smoothly.

[1] Of the eighty-three county boroughs, sixty-four Education Committees were clerked by members of the Education department in 1958.

Many Town Clerks also see the draft committee agendas and draft committee minutes or reports and the reports of other chief officers to their respective committees. Of course, the Town Clerk cannot require that another chief officer send his reports to him in draft, and no doubt there are some chief officers who insist on the independence of their reports and their right of direct access to committees to the point of not consulting the Town Clerk about them. Nonetheless where all officer reports are collected by the Committee Clerk for circulation with the agenda, the Town Clerk has at least advance information of them. Moreover even where this is not the practice, when a new programme or a major proposal is contemplated by a chief officer, it is not uncommon for him to send a draft copy to the Town Clerk, usually to find out whether some aspect of the problem affecting another part of the corporation has been ignored. Thus, to give one instance, a Chief Constable drawing up a report on car parks and the traffic problems of the town sent a copy to the Town Clerk. The Town Clerk, finding that it contained a number of proposals for one-way streets and that the Transport Manager had not been consulted, advised the Chief Constable to take the matter up with that chief officer before the report was finalized. At least one Town Clerk receives an annual progress report from each department and such special reports that he from time to time requests. In the case of a new service instituted under the Medical Officer of Health, the Town Clerk asked that officer for a report on the progress and success of the service after it had been operating for six months. This the Medical Officer did and was able to demonstrate sufficient progress to satisfy the Town Clerk. The Town Clerk then showed the report to the Chairman of the committee but advised that no action be taken until the service had had a full year's trial. This Town Clerk was in a much stronger position than most of his colleagues in other towns; nonetheless it would seem that most Town Clerks have ample means at their disposal for discovering what is going on in the various departments if they choose to exercise them.

But this knowledge is only a necessary prerequisite to bringing about some co-ordination. It is not co-ordination itself. A Town Clerk must act upon this knowledge so that the chief officers do not work at cross-purposes with each other, so that the departments do not duplicate each other's work, and so that no department which should be consulted is ignored. The Town Clerk also has at his disposal various means to accomplish these tasks.

First of all, the Town Clerk is in charge of drafting committee minutes; although it is normal for these to be seen by the other officers concerned with the work of the committee, the responsibility for their final form rests with the Town Clerk. If an item arises in the business of a committee about which there might be a dispute concerning which department should execute the committee's decision, the Town Clerk may settle the dispute before it begins by judiciously drafting the committee minutes. Similarly because it is common for the Committee Clerk to circulate the minutes or memoranda on decisions of the council and committee, it is relatively easy for a note to be included suggesting that on certain items consultations between particular officials or departments should take place.

The Town Clerk receives a great deal of correspondence from the general public, and this helps to keep him aware of happenings within the corporation. It also provides him with a good opportunity to bring the departments together on certain projects or to register his advice on certain matters which come within the scope of another department. As the Town Clerk goes over the post, he directs each piece to the proper department or committee and also directs that copies be made for other chief officers who are likely to be interested. In so doing, he is given the chance to add his own comments or to suggest that the officer concerned check with him before taking any action. Likewise as the person in whose name all letters involving policy matters are sent, the Town Clerk has the opportunity to see these letters before they are posted. In fact, however, the average Town Clerk sees only the most important ones. He relies on his staff and on the other chief officers to see that whatever opinions he wishes expressed are embodied in the replies.

The bulk of the Town Clerk's contact with the other departments is probably by telephone calls and letter. Most noteworthy in this regard is the increase of formality of interdepartmental communications as the size of the authorities increases. In the small authority, if the Town Clerk wants to advise another officer or wants some information he simply picks up his telephone and has a word or two with the officer and that is all there is to it. In the larger authority there is a tendency to put everything in writing. As an example a City Treasurer described a consultation by telephone which he had had with the City Architect. It concerned the grading of certain posts within the Architect's department. When they had reached a decision on the matter, the Treasurer said, 'I'll send you a letter to that effect.' The Treasurer explained that he always did this after telephone conversations so that all decisions would be recorded somewhere; that otherwise one of the officers might in the future disavow the decision reached.

Inter-departmental letters or memoranda also tend to be quite formal in the larger authorities. In one large city, for instance, the full business form is used—'Dear Sir', 'Yours faithfully', and the full address—just as if the letter was being sent to a local business firm or a government department. A similar practice was used in a smaller borough until recently. It was advanced at a chief officers' meeting that much time might be saved by an inter-departmental memo form with routing directions simply printed on the form. This gained little favour among the chief officers, and in the end it was agreed to shorten the addresses to merely, 'Town Clerk, ————', and to drop the 'Yours faithfully'. Although this formality may be a very insignificant matter in terms of time and convenience, it does evidence the very common tendency, particularly in the larger authorities, of departments to isolate themselves and to resist any effort to lessen independence.

Although the majority of contacts which the Town Clerk has with the other departments are by telephone and letter, the most important means of contact is personal consultation. The personal consultation generally speaking takes place at three levels: meetings of the Town Clerk and one other chief officer; meetings of the Town Clerk and a small group of chief officers; a general meeting of all chief officers. (The use of the term 'chief officers' in this context is not, strictly speaking, accurate. Although much of a Town Clerk's contact would be with the chief officers themselves, he also meets not infrequently with deputies and assistants in other departments when the officers are dealing with the particular matter under consideration. Likewise, the Town Clerk may be represented by his Deputy or assistants in some consultations. In the normal way much of this depends on the size of the authority.)

At the first level almost anything might be involved. The Town Clerk may go over the background of a planning case with the Planning Officer before a local public inquiry is held. Or the Town Clerk and the Treasurer may get together over the new awards by the National Joint Council or some problems which have arisen in connection with rating valuations. Or the Town Clerk may see the Engineer about a delay in a street reconstruction project. The last is a good example of how the Town Clerk acts on a complaint from the public. In one borough the Highway Committee had two years previously approved the reconstruction of a certain street. The Borough Engineer had not moved swiftly on the project and as a result, the residents began complaining to the Town Clerk. The Town Clerk then called in the Highway Committee Chairman and the Engineer and secured an agreement to push the project through quickly.

The second level is what might be called the project or scheme level. A new housing estate is planned or slum clearance project proposed or perhaps something even simpler, the assumption of an ambulance service by the authority. The problem in most of these cases is, first of all, who is going to take responsibility for what and, secondly, when are they going to do it. The best solution is to call all the interested parties together and distribute the assignments and work out a time schedule. Usually, though not always, the impetus for these meetings comes from the Town Clerk. Likewise usually, though not always, the Town Clerk attends any meeting of this kind. According to one Treasurer, if there is an important matter to be discussed, the Town Clerk is certain to be present; another Treasurer, however, intimated that unless the Town Clerk's department were directly concerned, that is, the problem involved some legal matters, the Town Clerk would probably not take part.

It is well accepted, nevertheless, that if the Town Clerk does attend, he presides. And he does just that—he does not order or direct the other chief officers to do this or that. The Town Clerk of a northern county borough was quick to assert this point as he explained the procedure on slum clearance. The chief officers would come together to work out a schedule. The Town Clerk would ask: 'Mr Public Health Inspector, when will you have your survey completed?', and 'Mr Engineer, when can you have the roads and sewers in?', and 'Mr Architect, when can you have the new buildings up?', and to himself, 'when can I have the land acquired?'. The answers are given and a schedule is planned on the basis of them. The Town Clerk makes no attempt to lay out a precise schedule or force a time limit on any officer.

Although in all authorities the Town Clerk and the chief officers meet at the first and second levels, this is not true at the third level. In some boroughs, the chief officers have a monthly business meeting; in others, they have a luncheon together which is very largely social, and in many they never meet as a group. Among those places where there are regular business meetings, the nature of these meetings tends to vary somewhat. In a middle-sized Midlands borough, the major item discussed is establishment matters, but in addition agreement on general policy, the settlement of officer conflicts and the prevention of duplication and overlapping between departments, all receive attention. In a large city, the major focus is upon planning and development, although again the meeting is also a time for airing differences and settling officer attitudes on general policy. In another large city, in addition to the discussions on general policy, problems of organizational efficiency, such as central purchasing, are tackled. In all these meetings the Town Clerk is the presiding officer and in most cases is the one to whom everyone looks for leadership.

Town Clerks generally feel that officers should not 'wash their dirty linen' before the councillors, if at all avoidable, and certainly not before the public. Thus it is highly desirable that the conflicting opinions of two or more officers be somehow resolved in private. The need is for an arbitrator and the need is usually supplied by the Town Clerk. In one county borough, for example, there was a dispute not long ago between the Chief Constable and the Children's Officer. The dispute arose when some of the children under the Children's Officer's care began some petty pilfering in a local large store. The Children's

Officer became aware of the incidents and thereupon went to the store and paid for the stolen articles, but he did not notify the Chief Constable of the incidents. The Chief Constable claimed that he should have been notified; the Children's Officer argued that he was *in loco parentis* to the children and therefore had no duty to report them. As a result the Town Clerk called them together to see if some compromise could be effected.

Disputes between officers are not common, for, as one Town Clerk explained, the officers are not children, they all realize that a job has to be done, and they do their best to get on with it. Where disputes do occur they as often as not arise from the personal animosities of the two officers rather than any great disagreement on principles. In any group of people there may be an awkward one or two. Even if the Town Clerk is unable to bring the officers to terms, he can see that both points of view are fully and fairly set before the committee so that the committee can resolve the dispute.

A more difficult issue arises when the Town Clerk disagrees with another chief officer on a matter which the Town Clerk thinks involves general policy. There is no officer who can arbitrate for the arbitrator so that, unless the Town Clerk can win his point with the officer, the power of decision must be turned over to the committee most directly concerned. In such case, the odds are weighted heavily against the Town Clerk. One of the tendencies in local government, stemming from the committee system, is what is sometimes called the 'committee mind' of councillors. This attitude when it appears in committee is one of determination to resist outside interference with the administration of the particular service, of willingness to rally in support of the committee's officer in any disagreement with another officer. Therefore unless the Town Clerk is willing to bring his disagreement before the public in council meeting, or is able to refer the dispute to one of the co-ordinating committees, his chances of succeeding are not always bright. The knowledge that he will have to combat this 'committee mind' can deter a Town Clerk from raising objections to another officer's policy, objections he knows he has no chance of following through.

It is in this connection that the implementation of the

Coventry Report, which recommended the enhancement of the Town Clerk as chief administrative officer and the establishment of a new committee designed to foster administrative co-ordination with the Town Clerk as its adviser, is of great interest. The Coventry Policy Advisory Committee accepted the major recommendations of H.M. Treasury (O. and M.) Division with reference to the Town Clerk as chief administrative officer which, so far as general administration was concerned, gave the Town Clerk the power to interfere with the work of the other departments to bring about co-ordination of council activities or to improve the level of administrative efficiency. The recommendations made it perfectly clear that the proposals were not intended to relieve the departments of their primary responsibility for their own domestic administrative efficiency and, if for no other reason, the Town Clerk has been slow to intervene. Like the large majority of Town Clerks he never requires the chief officers to file with him written reports upon the progress of their individual matters. He does, however, call informal conferences of the other officers to consider specific problems. When this occurs, they meet in the Town Clerk's office and discuss the problem, each putting his own points of view. In the end the Town Clerk summarizes the various positions and offers a solution, one that is nearly always a compromise. In this instance the position of the Town Clerk contrasts sharply with that of an American City Manager or a German Oberstadtdirektor because when the Town Clerk suggests a solution or, in fact, as he sometimes does, strongly insists upon a certain course of action, he has no guarantee that when the officers return to their own departments his recommendations will be put into effect, even though the officers have all agreed with the recommendations at the meeting. The City Manager and the Oberstadtdirektor, on the other hand, have means for ensuring that once the solution has been agreed upon, it will be put into effect.

But the Town Clerk can refer these matters to the Establishment and General Administration Committee for confirmation. It is the existence of this committee as much as a new formal definition of the Town Clerk's responsibilities which has put teeth into the Coventry Report recommendations on the Town Clerk. For example, a factory owner having complained to the

Town Clerk privately about the back-up of the sewage system after a few very moderate storms (on one occasion it had cost the company several hundred pounds to clean up the debris) informed him that if something was not done to remedy the situation, the company would have to institute a suit the next time the back-up occurred. The Town Clerk felt that a complete review of the sewage system was probably needed, and he therefore sent one of his Administrative Assistants to talk with the Engineer about a survey. The Engineer complained that his staff was inadequate to undertake such a project. The Town Clerk responded by assigning his Methods Officer to determine what additional staff the Engineer would need to carry out the survey. The Town Clerk brought this recommendation before the Establishment and General Administration Committee, they approved, the additional staff was employed and the survey began. In this instance the Town Clerk's advice was acceptable to the Engineer, but there may be times when to bring a matter such as this before the Establishment and General Administration Committee is to run the risk of airing a disagreement before the public in council, since the council would be forced to choose between the recommendations of the co-ordinating committee and the executing committee.

Should an issue of this kind reach the council, party politics would be injected into the picture, adding further complications. The decision of whether to support the co-ordinating or the executing committee would be taken and decided at the majority party caucus. The party, like the council, may be composed of 'committee mind' people, who are determined not only to protect their own committees from outside interference, but also to protect any committee so threatened. Whereas this attitude is less easy to express in council because it places the councillor in the awkward position of opposing publicly increased efficiency in government, behind the caucus doors this problem does not arise since the public is excluded. In this way the collective support of the party group might work to defeat the co-ordinating committee. In Coventry, however, this pitfall has generally been avoided. There are perhaps two reasons for this: the Chairman of the Establishment and General Administration Committee has tended to be a strong man, capable of putting effectively in party caucus the case for his committee; and the Labour party group, the majority party, made such political capital of the Report when it was implemented that they are now careful to avoid the charge being made that they are destroying their own work.

By way of a brief summary it seems that generally the Town Clerk in his capacity as departmental co-ordinator has a somewhat limited scope of action. He is, to be sure, the principal or senior official of the municipality. This means, first of all, that at any meeting of officers which he attends, he presides; secondly, that when two (or more) officers cannot resolve any differences which have arisen between them, they look to the Town Clerk for arbitration; and finally, that when a chief officer comes up with a new idea or programme for his department, he usually consults with the Town Clerk in order to determine how other departments would be affected.

In addition the Town Clerk usually takes the lead in organizing consultations on any large projects involving several departments and general meetings of chief officers, although to a certain extent his participation in these consultations arises from the fact that few large projects in local government do not in some way have legal implications. But it would be unfair to say that only when legal problems are involved does the Town Clerk appear. Whether the Town Clerk tends to dominate these consultations and meetings depends upon his strength of personality *vis-a-vis* the other officers. One may safely venture that any Town Clerk has a short lead over the other officers in this respect, in that he is the one to whom most officers look for leadership. If he is well disposed to lead, he will find that most officers will follow his lead. But at the same time tact pervades his actions, and he generally shies away from overtly forcing his wishes or ideas upon the other officers.

Even though the Town Clerk has a short lead, if he fails to show any initiative, the administrative centre may shift to the Treasurer or, particularly in the small authorities, to the Engineer. This is especially true where either the Treasurer or another officer has served the council longer than the Town Clerk. Thus a more thorough knowledge of local history (recent history, that is) and local conditions may often erase the Town Clerk's short lead.

In his capacity as Clerk to the committees and as Establishment Officer, even in the limited sense, he is able to foster a certain amount of administrative harmony, particularly as it concerns various procedures for handling routine matters, and uniformity in the grading of posts and the implementation of conditions of service. But this is co-ordination on a very limited scale.

One of the problems in local government is that of single inefficient departments. The senior official of the department may be getting on in years and losing interest, or he may just be incompetent. As a result the standard of service begins to falter. The difficulty for the Town Clerk is that problems such as these are not strictly matters of co-ordination since only one department is involved. However, it often happens that the department is not upholding its commitments with other departments and thereby may be indirectly affecting the efficiency of these other departments. What can the Town Clerk do? Some Town Clerks wait until there is a complaint from some quarter and then get together with the department head to see if the trouble can be eliminated. But this is an essentially negative approach, for the Town Clerk only acts when things have come to such an impasse that someone lodges a complaint. Moreover this approach is at best spasmodic; it rarely goes to the source of the trouble and it only solves one particular problem at one particular moment. Therefore, unless the Town Clerk has a Methods Officer or an organization and methods team at his disposal, there is very little he can do about an inefficient department. And even where there is such an officer or team, the Town Clerk, because of the traditions of independent departments and committees, needs to proceed carefully, and many times the trouble may not be of a kind that can be solved by the devices of O. and M.

As far as developing a body of consistent officer advice on general policy the Town Clerk is largely powerless. Only the rare and very strong Town Clerk would venture to suggest to one officer that his department should cut back its services while another department should be expanded, that certain services should grow in the future while others should be curtailed, that the officers should support a consonant policy of development for the borough and corporation as a whole.

In general, however, Town Clerks operate successfully

within these limitations. All the officers as a rule co-operate with each other, mainly, one would suppose, because they realize that only through co-operation will they get their own job completed and because they recognize the limitations which are placed on them by the system in which they work. Consequently the administrative machinery moves along with minor troubles easily remedied, with major breakdowns almost non-existent, and without any real overall direction.

CHAPTER VIII

THE TOWN CLERK
AND THE OUTSIDE WORLD

BOROUGH councils are placed in the midst of what seems to be a vast network of relationships. Government departments issue circulars to them, approve some of their proposals, grant them loan sanctions. For the non-county boroughs, a county council is the nerve centre for many important services within the borough boundaries. And above all the ratepayers, those who govern and are governed, are consulted by the borough council in its collective capacity and by councillors in their individual capacities. It is evident that for many of these relationships a council, whether composed of sixteen members or 160, is not able *en masse* to represent itself. It must have a spokesman who will present its views to this world outside, a negotiator who will transact its business with these outside bodies, an advocate who will contend for its opinions when they are challenged. On many occasions the Town Clerk fulfils these functions, and in doing so he is brought in contact with the Members of Parliament, government departments, other governmental bodies and the public. But in almost all of these matters he is carrying out the explicit or implicit policy of his council.

According to his Conditions of Service, the Town Clerk has certain specific responsibilities in these contacts with the world outside the authority. He is expected to conduct the official, but not technical, correspondence of the council with government departments and public boards and keep the other chief officers informed of such correspondence. No major negotiations relating to council duties or functions are to be conducted without his knowledge of them. He is responsible for conducting all important inquiries and for overseeing public notices and council advertisements.[1] These, of course, are neither the limits

[1] Recommendations of the Joint Negotiating Committee for Town Clerks and District Council Clerks, Schedule II, paras. 10, 12, 13, 14.

of a Town Clerk's normal duties in these matters, nor the extent of the council's contacts.

The Town Clerk is not the only person who represents his authority to the outside world. The Mayor invariably bears weighty duties in this respect. The Chairmen of committees sometimes speak on their committee's behalf to the government departments, county councils and the public. But the major portion of the day-to-day business with outside bodies is handled by the Town Clerk. Some of this business is, of course, conducted by the other chief officers. The responsibility for technical matters within their own particular professional spheres falls upon them. Moreover in the larger authorities, and especially in the county boroughs where the authority administers the total range of local services, the amount of contact which these other departmental heads have with outside bodies can be great. In these circumstances, the Treasurer not infrequently takes up the financial business for the council; the Chief Education Officer, matters pertaining to education; and the other officers, items coming within their departments' jurisdictions. But where the general policy of the council is, or is likely to be, involved, the Town Clerk is expected to be the spokesman or negotiator or advocate for the council.

Although the Town Clerk in most of these dealings works under well-defined instructions from his council, he also, like the spokesman for any group, bears considerable responsibility for their success. If he is a skilful negotiator, an able advocate, a convincing spokesman, the council may often succeed where it otherwise would have failed. Moreover, because the Town Clerk is the council's major spokesman it is he to whom the councillors look for advice when important negotiations are being planned or when a council action is being challenged by some outside group.[1] At the same time the council are the directors, and although they seek his advice and often follow it, the final decision of what to do, of what move to make next, is theirs. Likewise, if the council bears certain advantages in negotiations, the Town Clerk bears them also. If the council works under certain limitations, the Town Clerk also works under them. Consequently, to describe the Town Clerk in his role as spokesman is to describe a council's relations with the

[1] See, *supra*, p. 105.

outside world coloured sometimes very heavily, sometimes hardly at all, by the Town Clerk's personal ability.

There is, however, another side of the Town Clerk's relations outside the authority. He is invariably a professional man, often a university graduate, and more than likely a well-known citizen of his community. Town Clerks are from time to time given the honorary freedom of their boroughs. A few appear on the Honours Lists each year. In instances such as these it appears that they have served not only their councils but also their communities as well. Consequently, it is more or less normal for a Town Clerk to take some part in the social life of his community. But here again, because he works for the borough council he also observes the accepted mode of conduct, which is quite stringent in the case of senior local government officials.

This introduction has skimmed lightly across the surface of this phase of a Town Clerk's work. It is, therefore, well that some of the Town Clerk's more important duties as council spokesman as well as the forces which operate to mould Town Clerks in this position be examined in somewhat more detail.

THE MEMBERS OF PARLIAMENT

The extent of a Town Clerk's relations with the M.P. for his area depends almost entirely upon political factors external to the Town Clerk himself. In short it depends upon the political complexion of the council and upon the corresponding party affiliation of the M.P. In general there tends to be a closer relationship when the council majority and the M.P. are of the same party.[1] And it may be that the relationship is even closer when the M.P. is a member of the Parliamentary Opposition since he is then quite happy to make a nuisance of himself to the Government and the individual Ministers. In addition those boroughs which form complete Parliamentary constituencies are in a better position than those which form only part of a Parliamentary constituency. Therefore, the most desirable situation for establishing a close relationship with the M.P. at

[1] See H. V. Wiseman, 'The Leeds Private Bill, 1956', 35 *Public Administration*, 25 (1957).

the present time, under a Conservative Government, seems to be the one in which the borough has 'its own' M.P., who is a Labour Member and who is complemented by a Labour majority on the borough council.

Broadly speaking there are two areas in which this relationship operates: current legislation and Ministry difficulties. As far as legislation is concerned, the Town Clerk may communicate with the M.P. on a Bill which affects the local government in some way. Sometimes this is done at the suggestion of the Association of Municipal Corporations and invariably with the council's backing. A good example is the recent case of a large non-county borough in regard to the Local Government Bill in 1958. The council members were quite anxious that the Bill include a clause which made it explicit that their borough would be considered for county borough status. Consequently in addition to working through the Association of Municipal Corporations, the Town Clerk secured the support of the borough Member, and he kept the council in touch with the developments on the Bill and advised the Town Clerk as to the opportune times for the introduction of certain amendments which the Town Clerk had drafted. In this instance, at least, the Town Clerk and the M.P. were working very closely together.

Occasionally, but not very frequently, a local authority may promote a Private Bill, and, because the Town Clerk is his corporation's legal adviser, he is normally prominent in the preparation of these Bills. The procedure followed to secure Parliamentary approval of new local power is rather complicated. It is sufficient to point out here that for the most part the Town Clerk is involved at every stage.[1] The tendency may be for the Town Clerk of a smaller borough to leave much of the actual work to the borough's Parliamentary agents.[2] But in the larger authorities where the Town Clerks are more experienced and generally more able, the Town Clerk no doubt plays a more active part in drafting the clauses and seeing the Bill through Parliament. In either instance, however, the Town Clerk is certainly his council's principal negotiator with the

[1] See generally, Wiseman, op. cit.
[2] Parliamentary agents are a special breed of London solicitors who handle the legal mechanics of Private Bill promotion. They are lawyers and not lobbyists.

Parliamentary agents or with anyone else whom he may think should be interested in the Bill.

Concerning Ministry difficulties the approaches are slightly more subtle. Councils may enlist the help of their M.P. to promote some specific local cause, but the target in these instances is not Parliament, but one of the government departments. For example, the Town Clerk of a small southern borough who advanced a scheme, which his council accepted, for the sale of council houses, encountered some tardiness in the Ministry action for approval. He thereupon contacted the local M.P. who had a word with the Minister and a few days later the approval came through. In instances such as this it is possible that working through an M.P. of the majority party is advantageous.[1] On the other hand, one Town Clerk claims that the mere threat of a Parliamentary Question by the borough's Opposition M.P. is enough to make the Ministry wheels grind.

Of course there are certain difficulties in approaching the Ministries through the M.P. as the Town Clerk of a large borough aptly pointed out. Successful local authority-central government relations must have as their basis co-operation between Ministry and local officials. If a Town Clerk makes a habit of calling forth his M.P. on every little problem, it is reasonably certain that the Ministry officials are not going to be as co-operative as they otherwise might be, nor the M.P. as willing to assist as he might normally be. Thus most Town Clerks find it advisable to hold the M.P. in reserve for the most important snags and to handle the little ones which turn up now and then by direct contact with the Ministry officials.

Generally most of a Town Clerk's contact with the M.P. is by correspondence. The relations often operate in both directions, in that the M.P. often writes to the Town Clerk requesting local information on a problem one of his constituents has raised. And although the larger boroughs are

[1] The Town Clerk of a small borough recalled the occasion when a vitally needed loan sanction had not been granted. The Town Clerk wrote to the M.P. saying that the borough was having a little trouble and that it would be much appreciated if the M.P. would come down for tea some afternoon. The M.P. accepted, and the Town Clerk had the opportunity to outline the whole problem. The result of all this was a letter from the M.P. to the Minister, in what the Town Clerk described as 'typical old boy fashion'—My dear ——, I hear that things are moving very slowly on such and such. Couldn't something be done to ginger up the machinery'—and approval of the loan sanction a few days later.

perhaps more successful, it seems to be accepted generally that the M.P. will normally, if called upon, put in the appropriate word for the borough when the Town Clerk requests it.

As far as the Town Clerk is concerned, his relationship with the M.P., on the whole, depends upon how well disposed the council is to seeking their Member's help and upon the intricacies of party loyalty. These things would almost invariably transcend in importance any kind of personal relationship which might exist between the Town Clerk and the M.P.

THE MINISTRIES

In the main there are five Ministries which regularly concern themselves with local government services: the Ministry of Housing and Local Government; the Home Office; the Ministry of Health; the Ministry of Education; and the Ministry of Transport. In addition, most Ministries have some contact with local authorities in the performance of their functions.[1]

From the local authority side, county boroughs as all-purpose authorities have dealings with all these Ministries. Non-county boroughs, on the other hand, deal almost entirely with the Ministry of Housing and Local Government. This situation in turn has some effect upon the position of the Town Clerk. In the non-county boroughs where the contacts are concentrated upon one Ministry, the Town Clerk, except in those cases where a Technical Officer, like the Surveyor, corresponds with his technical counterpart in the Ministry, is the accepted channel for these contacts. In the county boroughs this is not necessarily true, although the Town Clerk is still the major channel in respect of business with the Ministry of Housing and Local Government and the Home Office.[2] According to an official of the Ministry of Housing and Local Government, almost all contact on general policy with the local authorities is

[1] W. J. M. Mackenzie and J. W. Grove, *Central Administration in Britain* (London, 1957), p. 406.

[2] Sir Austin Strutt, 'The Home Office and the Town Clerk', 95 *Journal of the Society of Town Clerks* 72 (1955). The Home Office supervises a number of local level functions which fall within the Town Clerk's particular scope: Civil Defence, electoral procedures, byelaws. It is also concerned with the Fire Service, Children's Welfare, and the Police which necessitates contact with other local government officials.

through the Town Clerk or Clerk. Occasionally a Technical Officer corresponds directly with the Ministry; but normally when this occurs, the Ministry directs the answer to the Town Clerk, enclosing a copy for the Technical Officer as well. The Chief Education Officer is probably the major channel in respect of the Ministry of Education and the Engineer in respect of the Ministry of Transport. Likewise in the larger borough the scope of 'technical matters' is doubtless somewhat larger than the same scope in the smaller boroughs. As a result what comprises technical correspondence conducted by a chief officer himself in a larger borough would in a smaller place be considered in many instances a matter of general policy on which it would be the Town Clerk's duty to approach the Ministry. Thus the increased size and the status of a borough can work against a Town Clerk's handling completely the relations of his authority with the Ministries.

These relations are conducted in two ways: by correspondence and by personal contact—that is, telephone conversations, personal meetings and deputations. Of these, correspondence is the more formal, more frequent and more routine. It is the more formal because opinions are committed to paper and become matters of record. It is the more frequent because dictating a letter is at once cheaper and often less time-consuming than a trip to London or a telephone call to the Ministry. And it is the more routine because it is both more formal and more frequent. It is not possible to categorize the subject matter of this correspondence; it traverses the whole range of subjects with which Ministries and local authorities are jointly concerned—from precisely-drafted circulars and complicated loan applications to the simplest requests for information or advice.

In the overall picture personal contact is not very frequent and is certainly reserved for the most important or most urgent matters. Its most marked characteristic is an air of informality, which is sought by both sides. Sir Austin Strutt, commenting upon the relations between the Home Office and the Town Clerk, told the Town Clerks:

Today Under Secretaries and Assistant Secretaries in the office are more than signatures on letters to you: we meet you, we do much more of our business around the table to our mutual advantage; . . . nowadays the Town Clerk . . . comes and talks [his problem] over as one administrator to another, and more often than not (and I like to think in pretty well every case) we are able to agree a line as to the course of action to be taken.[1]

In a similar manner, Sir Thomas Sheepshanks, at that time (1952) Permanent Secretary of the Ministry of Housing and Local Government, urged the Town Clerks to visit Whitehall more often, to see him and his senior colleagues. He spoke strongly in favour of

> an hour's gossip with a Town Clerk about anything and everything, [that] even though nothing specific seems to emerge, can scatter several seeds—and the ground is not really stony.[2]

A Town Clerk of a smaller borough near London emphasizes the importance of getting on familiar terms with a person in the Ministry. Once this kind of relationship is established, he feels that the Town Clerk is able to ascertain the 'Minister's feelings' very informally on a variety of pressing problems. Over the years some Town Clerks build up these personal relationships, so that in time they come to know a considerable number of people in the various Ministries and are able to approach them on a personal basis.

Whether a Town Clerk develops this kind of personal relationship depends on himself to some extent and upon his council, for a great number of them do not go out of their way to have any personal contact with the Ministries. There are several reasons for this. Some Town Clerks and their councils resent the imposition of central controls at the local level and therefore attempt to avoid any more contact than is absolutely essential.[3] Conversely, other Town Clerks accept that, given the present situation, central control is inevitable and that consequently the best way to advance the interests of their authorities is to establish good relations with the Ministries.

---

[1] Sir Austin Strutt, op. cit., p. 72.

[2] Sir Thomas Sheepshanks, 'Changes in the relations between the Ministry and Local Government during the past thirty years'. A paper delivered to the Annual Conference of the Society of Town Clerks (June 16 and 17, 1952; reported in 116 *Justice of the Peace* 456 (1952).

[3] A Town Clerk over ten years ago was so strongly opposed to central controls that he resigned from local government. 113 *Justice of the Peace* 120 (1949).

But although these principles may motivate some, there are more practical reasons why some Town Clerks do not have much personal contact with Whitehall. Many think the occasion or necessity for a trip never arises. As one Town Clerk explained, so long as a council's applications are properly prepared and are in good order, there is usually no need to supplement them with the personal efforts of the Town Clerk and other officials. Certainly the smaller authorities and those somewhat distant from London would be more likely to assume this attitude than the larger and closer ones. Some Town Clerks have other reasons for going to London and can, therefore, at times combine this business and a short chat with a Ministry official on the same trip. For example, Town Clerks are prominent in the work of the Association of Municipal Corporations and its committees may require frequent trips to London.[1] Even so, this work only involves a minority of the Town Clerks. Consequently, although this personal contact with Ministry officials may assume important proportions for some Town Clerks, for most it is safe to say the trip to Whitehall is an extremely unusual occurrence.

For what reason do these Town Clerks come to the Ministries? In most cases the Town Clerk wants the Minister's reactions to a proposed project or programme which the authority is contemplating or he wants to speed up Ministry approval of a loan on a certain project. But in some instances the Town Clerk's mission is of a more unusual nature. Consider these two examples. First, in one city a 'Home Help' service was recently instituted to provide welfare assistance for the aged in their own homes. This service was something new and was not, therefore, a normal grant-aided project. The Town Clerk, nevertheless, went to the Ministry to see if he could encourage the central

---

[1] According to one Ministry official's impression, the A.M.C. is 'all Town Clerks'. Certainly this is overstated, but Town Clerks do play an important part in the Association's proceedings. There are twenty-four Town Clerks who compose the Law Committee of the A.M.C., and this committee has the power to appoint at least two and sometimes three Town Clerks to each of the other committees of the Association. Consequently, there are Town Clerks on every one of the Association's committees, and about fifty Town Clerks take an active part in this committee work each year. 29 *Municipal Review*, February Supp. (1958). For Town Clerks who are very active in this work it can consume a large amount of time. According to his deputy, the Town Clerk of one of the largest authorities spends about half his time in London and much of it tending to A.M.C. business.

government to offer some support, his feeling being that if only a 10 per cent grant was received the trip was worthwhile. Secondly, there is the method by which a borough's application to become a city is prepared, which Sir Austin Strutt described in this way:

> I encourage the Town Clerk to come up and see me and have an off-the-record talk. I help him . . . in the drafting of the petition. I'm even prepared to vet the petition for him. I persuade him to keep the matter within the narrowest possible compass, only the Mayor and the leader of the council and the leader of the opposition knowing about it. In due course he lets me have copies of the petition in the form on which we have agreed it. Then I do the necessary consultations, both inside and outside the office, equally informally; no official letters ever pass, and in due course I submit a recommendation to the Secretary of State and if his decision is favourable the Town Clerk gets a letter from me to the effect that the Secretary of State will be prepared to consider a petition on the lines of the draft; if the recommendation is unfavourable and the Secretary of State endorses it, then I say, I'm sorry but the Home Secretary would not be prepared to entertain a petition. The Town Clerk knows where he stands and what I regard as fundamentally important is this, the corporation which seeks a mark of Royal favour is not publicly rebuked.[1]

It is this preliminary and informal consultation on projects upon which both Town Clerks and the Ministry officials place a great deal of importance and faith.

The telephone is a useful means of contact with certain real advantages and some disadvantages as well. Its advantages are that it is quick, that it is cheaper than a trip to London, and that it enables the Town Clerk to get in touch with appropriate officers and to establish contact with a person in the Ministry whom he has not previously met. Its main disadvantage is that a call must be reasonably short. Moreover one cannot normally discuss all the implications of a new project with maps, drawings and tables of figures and costs over the telephone. Therefore, the telephone is generally used to clear up some particular point not covered during a personal meeting or to raise some relatively simple query that needs an immediate answer.

Occasionally a deputation forms a part of a Town Clerk's life with the Ministries, particularly the Ministry of Housing

[1] Sir Austin Strutt, op. cit., p. 75.

and Local Government. The normal deputation arises because a local authority is unhappy with a particular decision the Minister has taken. The Town Clerk, on behalf of his council or one of its committees, then requests that the Minister or one of his higher officials receive a deputation from his authority. Or possibly he would ask the M.P. to make the necessary arrangements with the Minister. If the request is granted, the council then prepares its case and organizes its forces. The deputation may include the Mayor, a few leading councillors, the required Technical Officers and the Town Clerk (or some-times his Deputy). Occasionally the M.P. also appears. In the larger authorities, however, when a relatively less important matter is taken up, the group may include only a Chairman, a few leading committee members and the officers. The burden of preparing the case normally falls upon the Technical Officers in conjunction with the Town Clerk and the Chairman of the committee most concerned. It is usually expected that the Town Clerk presents the case, but the questions are generally directed to the Technical Officers, the Chairman and the other councillors. According to one Ministry official, Town Clerks often have specialities of their own so that, whereas they might be able to argue effectively upon a housing proposal, they might also be at a loss on a sewage problem. The deputation is normally a joint effort of the officials and a few councillors.

The deputation is probably a rather useful means of approaching the Minister or one of his higher officials for the smaller authority, and it is useful from the Ministry's point of view in that it gives the people in Whitehall an opportunity to meet a few councillors and to learn about local problems as they appear to the layman. But the very large authorities have less need to assemble their heavy artillery in order to make an impression upon the Ministry, and as a consequence one suspects that the deputation is rarely used by them. This is not to say that the Ministries never come in contact with the councillors of the large authorities. Quite the contrary is true, for it is certainly not uncommon for a Town Clerk to be accompanied by one of the committee chairmen if the council plans to take up an important matter with a Ministry.[1]

[1] See also Herman Finer, *English Local Government* (London, 1950, 4th ed.), p. 241.

Up to this point the discussion has centred upon Town Clerks approaching the Ministries. But the traffic is not all one-way. There are occasions when the Ministries seek out Town Clerks for advice. The Ministry of Housing and Local Government may be interested in determining the success of a particular Act or regulation. It would then, in addition to obtaining the views of the various local authority associations, get the opinions of a few Town Clerks who can testify from personal experience with the legislation. In addition Ministers often rely upon a Town Clerk's advice when filling a vacancy in a tribunal or nominating for a commission, for it is often felt that a Town Clerk has the best knowledge of the quality and availability of public service talent in his area. Normally an inquiry of this nature is conducted by someone in the Ministry who has had personal contact with the particular Town Clerk, and in most instances the Town Clerks are co-operative, discreet and respectful of confidence.

In general, therefore, the Town Clerk has a somewhat freer hand in dealing with the Ministries than with the M.P. His contact with Ministry officials, mainly through correspondence, is practically continuous. The possibilities of direct supervision of his actions by a committee on the council are not extensive. Moreover, because he may, over a number of years, develop a close personal contact with certain Ministry officials, a Town Clerk may be a valuable asset to a council when it must negotiate with a central department. The same, of course, would be true of other local officials who carry on such negotiations for their council from time to time, in particular, the Treasurer and the Chief Education Officer. In the main, however, the success of a council's, hence a Town Clerk's, dealings with the Ministries depends upon factors external to both council and Town Clerk.

THE TOWN CLERK AND OTHER GOVERNMENTAL BODIES

Local authorities and their Town Clerks come in contact with other governmental bodies of all sizes and kinds: the County Council, the neighbouring Rural District Council, the Gas Board, the Water Board, the Burial Committees, the area

Health Committees, the Borough Quarter Sessions. And all these may claim some part of a Town Clerk's working schedule from time to time. Thus he may prepare a case for a planning inquiry with the County Planning Officer, talk with the Clerk to the Rural District about a proposed borough boundary extension, contact a Gas Board official about the plans for a new housing estate, sit as clerk to the Joint Borough and District Water Committee or accompany the Recorder to Quarter Sessions as Clerk of the Peace. It is difficult to say that any of these are more important than the others; undoubtedly the importance differs from one Town Clerk to another, from one borough to the next. But certainly for the Town Clerk of a non-county borough the county council in its various manifestations can claim a great deal of attention, and for the Town Clerk who doubles as Clerk of the Peace, the Quarter Sessions work can at times be somewhat burdensome, although an enjoyable burden nonetheless. In view of this it is these two aspects upon which this brief discussion will concentrate.

A county council has a considerable voice in the local affairs of a non-county borough. It normally precepts for a major part of the rate that is collected; and it provides for education, planning, various health services and innumerable minor services within the confines of the borough. As a result there are bound to be occasions when co-operation between the borough council and the county council is necessary. This invariably means co-operation between officers, between the Town Clerk and the Clerk of the county council. Here again successful co-operation may depend to a certain extent on informal or personal factors peculiar to the situation. The Town Clerk of a small county town explains that by an unusual coincidence the Clerk of the county council and he, who both are about the same age, took up their present appointments at the same time, and that as a consequence they have always had a very close relationship. It is also true that the relationship tends to be closer when the borough is also the county town since the opportunity for personal contact is greater than normal, and also when the borough forms one of the larger districts in the county since its activities will have a greater impact upon the county and vice versa.

But the Clerk is not the only officer with whom the Town

Clerk is in touch. Since the Town and Country Planning Act, 1947, transferred the planning powers from the county district councils to the county councils, the county councils have devised various means of injecting local opinion into the planning decisions.[1] All of these have brought the Town Clerks in close contact with the County Planning Officer or one of his assistants, an Area Planning Officer. Where the borough has its own planning committee with delegated powers or sends representatives to an area planning sub-committee, the Town Clerk is very often the clerk to the committee, and the Area Planning Officer is normally in attendance. Moreover, the two are involved in a great deal of mutual consultation. In addition Town Clerks may act as clerks to Area Health Committees, secretaries to Divisional Welfare Committees, or Sub-Divisional Controllers-designate in the county Civil Defence schemes, all of which bring them in contact with other county officials. Likewise the other senior borough officials have a certain amount of contact with their counterparts of the county councils.

Successful relations, nonetheless, are not entirely dependent upon the officers. Quite frequently there is some overlapping membership, some borough councillors who serve on the county council as well. In these instances, a certain amount of reliance may be placed upon these persons to represent the borough council's views in the county council and vice versa. Where, however, there is no overlapping membership, the major burden of the relationship undoubtedly falls upon the senior officials on both sides.

As Clerk of the Peace, the Town Clerk performs a function, the statutory origin of which in some instances dates back at least to the fourteenth century.[2] In 1958, fifty-eight Town Clerks held appointments as Clerks of the Peace, which added to their work and to their income.[3] In the main their duties are to conduct the administrative work flowing from the Borough

[1] For detailed study of the various approaches see P. G. Richards, *Delegation in Local Government* (London, 1956), chap. 6.

[2] But see, E. Jenks, *An Outline of English Local Government* (London, 1930), 7th ed., p. 133.

[3] *Municipal Yearbook, 1958*. The Town Clerk may also be appointed Registrar of the borough civil court by the corporation. This is not very significant at present since only four of these courts still receive plaints: Bristol Tolzey Court; Liverpool Court of Passage; Norwich Guildhall Court; Salford Hundred Court. 9 *Halsbury's Laws* (3rd ed.), 486n.

Quarter Sessions: arrange for notices of sittings, record proceedings and issue orders, draw and sign bills of indictment unless the prosecutor elects to secure professional advice, issue writs of subpoena to witnesses, advise the court on points of law and practice, and administer all the other details necessary to ensure the smooth running of criminal trials.[1] These involve a good deal of attention in the two or three weeks before the Sessions and, of course, the full-time attention of the Clerk of the Peace during the Sessions. Many Town Clerks enjoy this work because by and large it is interesting and because it provides an opportunity for a holiday from the Town Hall routine for a few days each quarter. The lawyer's fascination with the courtroom is not easily dimmed.

THE TOWN CLERK AND THE PUBLIC

Primarily the Town Clerk appears before the public as his council's major negotiator and major representative. It is his name which appears at the bottom of the signboard in the market and the list of byelaws in the park. It is his name which is affixed to all official letters emanating from the council to the citizen. Mr Justice Atkinson made this point clear in his decision in *West Ham v. Benabo*, when he said:

> If the notice comes from the council's recognized agent, the Town Clerk, a recipient must be bound to assume that the demand is made with authority, and that the conditions of payment have been considered by the local authority, and that he is under an obligation to obey the demand. But if it comes from anyone else there is no reason why he should be bound to make such an assumption. The demand may have been made on the writer's own initiative without any instructions from the corporation . . .[2]

Insofar as a Town Clerk's official relations with the ratepayers are concerned, it is evident that in one sense the contacts are many and varied. The Town Clerk negotiates with the officials of a local firm to prevent it from moving elsewhere;[3] he talks with a local club president about a forthcoming garden

[1] Lord Macmillan, *Local Government Law and Administration in England and Wales* (London, 1940), 14 vols., v. 9, pp. 213–20.
[2] [1934] 2 K.B. 253. See also *supra*, pp. 39–40.
[3] Bain, op. cit., p. 70.

fête; he contacts a local resident concerning action taken in respect of a disturbance; he initiates an action to recover rent arrears on a council house. In all these instances he is acting for the council on matters which very frequently bring him in contact with a local ratepayer. This is the essence of local government—the governing body and its officials are close to the people they serve, responsive to their needs, aware of their particular problems and their special circumstances.

But in another sense, that of ratepayers coming to the Town Clerk to discuss council policy or even to talk over a case of maladministration on the part of the officers, the contact is not very frequent. Sometimes the Town Clerk gets a letter of complaint, occasionally he meets a deputation, and there are some Town Clerks who try to make it a point to see local citizens personally when they come to the Town Hall. But for the most part, the local citizenry are not very interested in council policy; and when they have a personal problem, they take it to their councillor or to the Town Hall, where an effective filtering process severely limits the number who actually see the Town Clerk. Thus even in the smaller borough the amount of personal give and take between Town Clerk and the individual ratepayer is very limited.

But at the same time some Town Clerks do give some attention to the public in general, that is, to 'public relations'; and of course, in dealing with the public in general, many of the problems of individual members of the public are solved as well. It was noted previously that in a few larger boroughs there are Public Relations Sections in the Town Clerk's departments and that in the smaller boroughs a number of the public relations functions are sometimes performed by members of the Town Clerk's staff and by the Town Clerk himself.[1] Whether the Town Clerk himself takes an active part in this function depends largely upon the time he can afford to spend and upon his own personal interests, but as with any section in his department, he is responsible to the council for its work.

The Town Clerk may, however, hold press conferences, regular or otherwise; and this may be particularly true of the Town Clerks in the smaller towns. One Town Clerk holds a regular press conference after each council meeting and goes

[1] See, *supra*, p. 146.

over the agenda and minutes with the reporters. He makes a policy of telling them whatever additional information they want and then persuading them not to print those items which may be premature in nature or prejudicial to the council's best interest. On the whole he is successful and feels that relations with the press are extremely good. Another Town Clerk holds the conference before the council meeting at which time the agenda is discussed. Under this arrangement the newspapers are able to preview the coming meeting for their readers. Although relations with the press are not all that he would like, the Town Clerk is satisfied that the council's position on any matter is always given fair hearing.[1]

On the other hand, there are some Town Clerks who prefer to avoid the press conference and in fact to avoid any contact with the press whatsoever. Sometimes this feeling stems from a very strong personal distrust of the press and its motives, best exemplified by a statement made by a Town Clerk of a middle-sized northern borough:

> If one doesn't give them a statement and say, print all of this or print nothing at all, they'll take something small out of context and blow it up beyond recognition.

But in other instances the absence of contact with the press can be traced to the wishes of the council. One Town Clerk, who was in favour of a Public Relations Section and improved public relations generally, said that his council did not believe in public relations in any form, that they felt, once elected, they were free to carry on as they thought best, and that neither the press nor the public had a right to any information. As one would expect, the press in this town tended to be very critical of the council's actions.

It would seem that councils and their officials and the press will only get along agreeably if some kind of understanding is reached between the two groups so that information is passed freely but not indiscreetly to the press and that the press in return respects the confidence shown them. It would seem also

---

[1] For another account of a Town Clerk who found the press conference a valuable instrument of public relations, see A. Spoor, 'The Public's Part in Administration', 17 *Public Administration* 149 (1939).

that a regular press conference held by the Town Clerk in conjunction with a senior Chairman or leading councillor is a very useful way of establishing this understanding.

The Town Clerk, of course, meets the public in another capacity, that of well-known citizen. As a consequence of his historical origin, he is 'Town Clerk', that is Clerk of the Town, not like his counterparts in the counties and urban and rural districts who are styled 'Clerk of the Council'. There are a few Town Clerks who feel very strongly about this, who feel that their scope of duty extends beyond the work of the council. And they point to the rationale in the *De Winton* case and sometimes to the *Re Hurle-Hobbes ex parte Riley* decision as the legal basis for their duty to the ratepayers. But on the other hand, not all Town Clerks feel such a strong responsibility to the ratepayers. They express the view that their primary duty is that of Clerk to a Council and that their main allegiance is to their council. This attitude does not completely obscure the fact that the Town Clerk may, by virtue of his education, professional status, or simply his senior position in the borough's government, still be a well-known member of his community. But it does serve to emphasize the close connection between the roles of council representative and citizen and the difficulty a Town Clerk often feels he encounters in trying to find the proper balance between them.

Because of their position Town Clerks are not infrequently asked to speak to various groups within their community. Whether they accept depends almost entirely upon their personal inclinations. Some feel that speaking is part of the job of being a Town Clerk; moreover they enjoy it. Other Town Clerks either take a more restricted view of their position or do not derive much pleasure from this kind of activity; they therefore usually decline. Nonetheless all acknowledge that the opportunity to speak is there if one wishes to take it. The topics are almost without exception uncontroversial: 'Your Local Authority', or 'My Job', or 'The Borough History'. Only the rare and foolish Town Clerk would venture forth upon some aspect of his council's policy without the full approval of his council to do so.

Local organizations, clubs, societies and other groups, however, may present some problems for a Town Clerk. About

55 per cent of the Town Clerks are members of some kind of local organization within their boroughs. Some of these organizations are financed in part by the local authority, and it is the usual custom in these circumstances to make the Town Clerk the Honorary Clerk or Secretary or Solicitor of the group. Others are quite separate from the council and from local government generally: sports clubs, cultural societies and all the other kinds of organizations which are so common in modern communities. Many Town Clerks, like other individuals, follow their own inclinations and take part in the activities of these groups.

But there is also a considerable segment of the Town Clerks who do not take part in any of these activities. They advance various reasons for this non-participation; the major one is a fear of conflict of interest between the council and the organization—in the words of one Town Clerk:

> My feeling is that a Town Clerk cannot very well take an active part in a local civic organization as well as safeguard the interests of his council in possible negotiations with such associations.

Others indicate that council work and particularly evening committee meetings severely limit the opportunity to participate in organizations outside the council. Moreover, some prefer to keep themselves free to visit, assist and address any organization within their community. Politics is another deterrent. As an example, take the Town Clerk who, talking about a community where he had previously been Town Clerk, said:

> I was not a member of Rotary, although I understood the opportunity was there. Reason—a highly political council, of whom several Conservatives and no Labour men were Rotarians. Rotary itself is non-political, but membership would have induced personal friendship with the Conservatives, which could have been construed by the other side as bias. Perhaps I was over-cautious, but I had to remain carefully balanced on my politically neutral fence.

Another Town Clerk, formerly a club member, withdrew because he found the club small-minded and boring. Perhaps the soundest reason was given by the Town Clerk of a very small borough in the West; he did not belong to any organizations in his community because none existed.

The Town Clerk who declined to join Rotary for fear of appearing to have some political bias is, if not typical, at least indicative. Town Clerks run from even the semblance of connection with local party politics as they would some fearful disease. Some Town Clerks carry this attitude so far as not to vote in municipal elections. Others who do vote, do so for purely personal reasons—that is, they prefer the personality of one candidate to that of another, having in mind naturally that the winner becomes a councillor. This apoliticalness in general carries over to the national scene as well. It is interesting to note, therefore, the House of Commons Disqualification Act, 1957, included the Town Clerk and the Deputy Town Clerk among those disqualified.[1] In practice, or as a matter of custom, they have been barred from political office for a long time. And there is the exception to prove this rule—the Town Clerk of Bangor, W. E. E. Jones. Mr Jones sat in the House of Commons as the Labour representative from the Conway Division of Caernarvonshire from 1950 to 1951 and at the same time maintained his position as Town Clerk. He also stood unsuccessfully as the Labour candidate in the General Elections of 1951 and 1955.[2] But he did not stand in the 1959 General Election.

It is evident, however, that in a number of places, certainly those where the party divisions on the councils are sharply drawn and particularly the smaller boroughs, the requirement that a Town Clerk maintain political neutrality extends somewhat beyond the confines of the council chamber, committee room and the municipal offices. That this extension may cause difficulties for some Town Clerks is possible, but not extremely likely. It is a situation to which one, over the course of one's career, learns to adjust. But in the same light it is a situation which contributes to making Town Clerks as a group somewhat cautious individuals and to the lack of boldness and imagination sometimes so wanting in the holders of this ancient and honourable office.

[1] House of Commons Disqualification Act (1957), Schedule I, part 3.

[2] W. E. E. Jones, a graduate of the University of Wales and London University and an admitted solicitor, has been Town Clerk of Bangor since 1939. He won the Conway seat in 1950 by a majority of 803; lost the same seat in 1951 by 583, and in 1955 by 4,824. Although he has been a Labour candidate, his council has been composed largely of Independents with a sprinkling of Liberals and Labourites.

CHAPTER IX

SOME CONCLUDING COMMENTS

THE PRESENT

I T is common for those who describe the position of the Town Clerk to ascribe whatever power or influence he may have within the administrative structure of local government to personality, and to assert generally that the nature of the office varies considerably in somewhat similar proportions to the variations in the personalities of its holders. 'Personality' is a very convenient and useful word for describing intricate relationships in the world of politics and public administration. Anyone describing the American Presidency during the time of Franklin Roosevelt would come up with something substantially different from one describing it during the time of Dwight Eisenhower. And few would contest the proposition that the differences in the personalities of these two men contributed to any change in the office's character. But at the same time no one would attempt to describe the powers of the American President wholly, or even largely, in terms of the personality of the occupant of that office. But this is often what is done concerning the Town Clerk, and although such a description has some validity, it is certain that the term 'personality' so applied could be subjected to considerable refinement and the analysis in these terms subjected to some limitations or restrictions.

In the first instance, therefore, one may apply this personality concept in a very narrow sense. The customary approach is to draw the distinction in terms of two very wide extremes: the timid, reticent, introverted Town Clerk, who would not even try to lead, on the one hand; and the imaginative, energetic, extroverted Town Clerk, who is in the midst of everything his council is proposing to do, on the other. As one would expect, very few Town Clerks fit either one of these caricatures. Instead the vast majority fit somewhere between these personality extremes. Some Town Clerks are well versed in some particular aspect of local administration or take a particular interest in some phase of the council's operations; in these circumstances they might quite naturally voice strong opinions to the councillors and to the other chief officers and follow the work very closely. Thus at times a Town Clerk may display boldness and initiative and at other times reticence and inertia. Consequently it is the frequency with which one or the other of these traits is revealed, not the fact that they are revealed, that is important.

But there is more to this concept of personality than the simple outward display of timidity or boldness. Certainly there are more significant aspects of Town Clerks' personalities which mould the character of the office. Whether a Town Clerk thinks of himself mainly as corporation solicitor or as chief administrator, what a Town Clerk conceives is the function of a chief administrator, whether a Town Clerk enjoys legal work or has grown tired of it over the years, whether a Town Clerk is satisfied to offer advice to be taken or ignored or feels rebuffed when his advice is summarily dismissed—all these attitudes or traits vary from person to person, shape personality, and shape Town Clerks.

Beyond this there are circumstantial factors which also have some effect. Some councils traditionally expect their Town Clerk to give a strong lead in the council's work; others prefer to ensure that the reins of control and direction remain firmly in the council's hands. Moreover, there is the attitude of the councillors individually—whether they are in the habit of coming to the Town Clerk for advice or tend to look to some other officer. Doubtless the length of service a Town Clerk has had with his council enters here. If in terms of service the Town Clerk is the most senior chief official, councillors will often come to him simply because he has a good knowledge of the background of the problems now facing the authority. But if another chief officer is more senior, councillors may often prefer to consult that officer. Equally important are relations with the party leaders. If a Town Clerk has been able to establish good relations with the party leaders, has encouraged them to confer with him freely and frequently, his position may be considerably enhanced. Otherwise, the Treasurer may appear stronger by virtue of his relations with the Finance Committee Chairman who not infrequently is the leader of the majority party group. And to a large extent these relations depend upon the party leaders themselves, for they for various reasons may choose not to work closely with the Town Clerk or any other officer. All these factors, which are certainly external to the Town Clerk himself and only partially under his control, also contribute to shaping his position in any given town.

In spite of these personality and circumstantial factors, there are certain elements of the organizational and traditional position of the Town Clerk in local administration which give him some power and influence. Some of these elements apply to all Town Clerks and some apply to only a few. First, the Town Clerk is clerk to all committees except, in many cases, the Education Committee and the trading committees. In this position he can easily require that all reports to committees cross his desk before being sent to the members. He can in this way survey the current operations of his authority's administration. He can acquire a total view. Whether he acts upon it is another matter, but councillors and officers alike know that he is an authority's major spokesman to the central government and other outside groups; he is expected to conduct all major negotiations; he represents the authority to the outside world. As a result those who deal with him in this capacity look upon him as a responsible and important individual, and this attitude may have an impact upon how he is viewed from the inside as well. He is invariably regarded as the senior local official, and when officials meet, he is expected to preside and perhaps to lead. In addition he may be the chief adviser to a policy co-ordinating committee or to an administrative advisory committee and have some specific powers relating to the preparation of reports for these committees. But such a position is not common among Town Clerks. Nor is it extremely common that he should be in charge of establishment matters or organization and methods studies; but, when he is, his position is considerably stronger.

The fact that the Town Clerk is almost always a solicitor is of mixed value in this regard. Since he is a professional man who has acquired a recognized standard of training and has demonstrated a large amount of ability in doing so, he is entitled to the respect of his colleagues. But he is also classified. He, like his colleagues, is a technical officer, responsible for a technical phase of local administration. The other officers look upon him as a chief administrator to be sure, but they see him first and foremost as a lawyer, as responsible for the legal side of local administration. Moreover, the Town Clerks themselves tend to regard the office as essentially a legal position and certainly as one requiring a legal qualification. The Society of Town Clerks, with the help of the Law Society, has strongly resisted any attempts by local authorities to look outside the legal profession for their Town Clerks. Consequently he is forced into a position parallel to the other chief officers, and each officer is responsible for his own professional or technical sphere. And doubtless these technical spheres cover wider areas than those which would exist if some one executive were completely in control of the entire officer side of the administration. Because of his responsibility for legal affairs, therefore, the Town Clerk tends to become largely a technical officer responsible for one department plus an undefined amount of co-ordination.

Before concluding this brief analysis a few words of general caution should be offered. First of all, as has been pointed out consistently in what has gone before, the size of the authority has a large influence upon the position of the Town Clerk. In the small authority, where he is the only member of the staff with a legal qualification or legal experience, much of his time is consumed by legal work. Of course, if he has under him one or two experienced clerks with whom he can entrust some of the detailed legal business, he is then freer to concentrate upon matters of general administration. In the middle-size authority, he is in a much better position. He has a staff large enough to handle all the details of his departmental responsibilities. In addition, the number of departments and the size of the executive side of the administration have not passed beyond that which can be effectively surveyed by one man. In the large authority, however, the number of departments, each headed by a chief officer, works strongly against a Town Clerk who tries to maintain an efficient department and give more than a superficial and spasmodic attention to overall co-ordination and general administration. A general surveillance is not impossible but it is extremely difficult.

It also should be noted that, in discussing the Town Clerk's influence and power, in seeking to define those factors which affect his position, attention has been given only to his power, influence and position *vis-a-vis* the other chief officers, that is, his standing among those on the executive side of local administration. There can be little doubt that his standing among the officers affects his relations with the councillors and, as was indicated above, the opinions and actions of the councillors of and towards him affect his relations with the other chief officers. But a Town Clerk's relationship with the councillors is by and large not greatly different from that of the other officers. It is grounded in the theoretical division between policy and execution and influenced largely by the size of the authority and the attitudes of the councillors. Few difficulties arise in this relationship. And it is not an issue about which there is much debate.

Generally speaking, therefore, the office of Town Clerk in each of the 431 boroughs is moulded by three factors: organization or structure, circumstances, and personality in the broad sense. Where the position has been enhanced by the addition of overall co-ordinating functions, personality and circumstances play lesser roles. But this kind of enhancement is not general, so that whether a Town Clerk is influential or not influential depends greatly upon himself and the particular circumstances in which he is placed. But all three play important parts in shaping the role of a Town Clerk.

THE FUTURE—LAWYER OR CHIEF ADMINISTRATOR

For a number of years the position of the Town Clerk has been subjected to considerable debate and the established system has been strongly criticized. The Royal Commission and the Hadow Committee spent considerable time reviewing his position and his training. The Treasury (O. and M.) Division analysed in detail the position of the Town Clerk in Coventry and recommended some significant changes in his powers and duties. Writers like Professor W. A. Robson and Lord Simon have long advocated greater powers and a wider basis of recruitment for Town Clerks. Basically the controversy revolves around the question of whether a Town Clerk should be primarily a lawyer or primarily a chief administrator.

The criticism of the present system seems to take two directions. There are those who, first of all, assume that the present functions and duties of a Town Clerk are those of a chief administrator. From this it is argued that because the present Town Clerks have been legally trained, have proceeded to their present positions through the various legal appointments in a Town Clerk's department, and remain responsible for the legal work of the council in addition to the chief administrator responsibilities, local authorities are not securing the best talent available for their chief administrators. On the other hand, other critics hold that the Town Clerk, as the position is presently constituted, is not a chief administrator at all. Instead it is contended that Town Clerks are now primarily lawyers absorbed with legal problems and that what is needed in local government at the present time is a real chief administrator who will direct the executive side of local administration.

Quite obviously there is a considerable difference between the assumptions from which these criticisms are made. Precisely what a chief administrator is and what his proper duties are is not generally agreed. The critics do agree, however, that the positions of chief legal adviser and chief administrator should be separated and that a chief administrator should be appointed exclusively on the basis of his administrative ability. To implement such a departure from present practice would quite naturally raise certain problems. It is well, therefore, that these problems be examined.

Under the present system a person enters a Town Clerk's department as a junior clerk or Assistant Solicitor and moves to a town clerkship on the basis of his success on the legal side of local administration. Much of his concern at the lower levels is with detailed legal work—legal research, drafting documents, prosecuting minor offences. This is the accepted path to a town clerkship, and anyone who hopes to become a Town Clerk knows where to begin his career. In support of this system it is asserted that lawyers make the best administrators because they have learned to look at all sides of a problem. But, one might say, lawyers look at all sides of a problem only within the narrow framework of legal rules and precedents. And, it may be added, certainly Civil Service practice and experience do not bear out this assertion that lawyers make the best administrators.

Secondly, the present system may be supported by an argument like this: although an aspirant rises through what are technically called 'legal appointments', he actually acquires considerable administrative experience along the way; as an Assistant Solicitor he may handle one or two committees, help prepare the agenda, occasionally brief the Chairman; as Deputy Town Clerk he often supervises a large amount of administrative work and organizes schemes and negotiates with other officers. On the other hand, it may be contended with equal validity that junior officers in other departments, especially the Finance and Education departments, do very similar work. They attend committees, brief Chairmen, organize work within their departments and negotiate with other departments. Is this not also good training for chief administrators?

At the same time, although these arguments in support of the present system may be countered effectively, it is quite justifiable to ask what reasonable alternative there is to the present system. If the accepted system is to be discarded, a more suitable system must be substituted for it. What, then, are the other possible systems? One possibility is to organize an administrative class similar to that of the Civil Service, with entry regulated by examination and dependent upon, in most instances, a good university degree. Entrants would be assigned to purely administrative positions in the various departments and move upwards to more responsible posts, becoming the chief administrator of an authority in the end. The difficulty of introducing such a class in local government is that few authorities have a large enough organization to provide administrative work at lower levels such as would justify the employment of the type of person envisaged. Only perhaps in the ten largest authorities would there be any openings such as this, and even in these authorities the number would be extremely limited. It would be impossible to establish any orderly system with so few people; the limitations on advancement and the possibilities of stagnation would probably deter the type of entrant sought from even applying. An administrative class is somewhat impractical for a local government administration which is mainly concerned with the application of technical knowledge to current localized problems.

Another possibility, however, is that the chief administrator be drawn from among the other officers as well as from among the legally trained. This possibility has some merit, for it would widen the field from which the chief administrator might be chosen, and it would place emphasis upon administrative rather than technical ability. In a very few instances authorities, other than the small authorities, have appointed a Treasurer or an Education Officer as their Clerk. The London County Council, however, is the only authority which has made a policy of at least considering applicants other than lawyers for the position of Clerk. Although this may be done on occasion by a few authorities without altering the administrative structure, it is only natural to assume that general application of this practice would lead to enhancing the position of the chief administrator *vis-a-vis* the other officers. This would occur because positions formerly held to be equal with the Town Clerk would now only be steps on the way to becoming a Town Clerk. Moreover, viewing this in perspective, this is precisely what some of the critics of the position of Town Clerk as now constituted would like to see. And it is one of the major reasons behind their desire to separate the positions of legal adviser and chief administrator now combined in the one office.

Thus a second problem is: what is to be the position of the chief administrator in the administrative framework and what are to be his powers and function? In the present arrangement, the Town Clerk as chief administrator has somewhat limited powers. The other chief officers are on a level equal with him, at least from an organizational point of view, and have their own separate responsibilities to committees and to the council. The value of this arrangement is that it encourages persons of talent and ability to seek these positions. The disadvantage is that efficiency and sense of direction are lost through a lack of overall guidance and co-ordination. Those who feel that the Town Clerk in his present position, relying heavily upon personality and circumstances, is able to provide sufficient co-ordination, support the present pattern. Those who feel a stronger co-ordinator is needed advocate some reform in this direction. Consequently a central problem is whether the Town Clerk's position is presently strong enough to supply the needed co-ordination.

But before discussing this larger problem, it is advisable to investigate a few lesser ones. If it is proposed to alter the position of Town Clerk as chief administrator, how should it be altered, what powers should be added to it, what functions made his responsibility? In this connection analogies are usually drawn with City Managers, the Irish and American concepts of the chief administrator in local government. A brief analysis of each would, therefore, be useful.

The American City Manager, or Council-Manager, system[1] grew from a local government reform movement about forty-five years ago. In pattern its organization is similar to that of a large business corporation: a small board of directors, the elected councillors; and a general manager, appointed by the directors to direct the executive side of local operations. In theory, as in English local government, the council is responsible for policy, the Manager for execution and advice on policy. The very small size of the council (usually less than fifteen) and the absence of committees, however, mean that policy matters do not extend to matters of detail as they often do in the English system. The Manager's term of appointment is invariably at the discretion or whim of the council. Like the English local government officer, he is appointed during the pleasure of the council; unlike his English counterparts, 'during pleasure' often has a very literal meaning. He is traditionally non-political, although the Americans and the British tend to interpret 'non-political' in slightly different ways. Nonetheless the intent behind this tradition is the same as are the difficulties which arise from non-observance. The general framework in which City Managers and Town Clerks work, therefore, is greatly, but not totally, dissimilar.

The City Manager, however, is in complete control of the executive arm of local administration. All technical officers are appointed and may be dismissed by him. He may arrange the departments in the way he finds most efficient. He receives regular reports from the departments, written and oral, and takes a particular interest in the financial matters of the administration. He supervises the budget preparation and the

---

[1] There have been many variations grafted on to the basic idea of City Manager government, so this brief generalized account deserves taking with several grains of salt.

consideration of supplementary estimates. His interest is in financial policy as distinct from financial management, which he leaves to the accountant; however, the accountant is accountable to the Manager, not the council. A Manager normally takes a large interest in public relations, in publicizing the work of the council and securing support for its programmes. He often has a great amount of contact with local citizens who have problems or complaints and is generally expected to be a community leader. Often the focus of local government is upon him rather than the council.

The Irish City Manager is slightly different. His powers and duties are defined by national legislation. The council, small like its American counterpart, possesses certain reserved powers, the most important being making the rate, borrowing money, adopting permissive legislation and directing the Manager to perform specific acts. The bulk of the remainder of local powers and functions are under the direct control of the Manager. In theory the Manager is almost separate from the council. He has his functions which he can carry out without any interference from the council. He is appointed by a Local Appointments Board and may be removed only by a two-thirds vote of the council and the approval of the Minister of Local Government and Public Health. Moreover he may take part in the discussion in the council meetings; but he may not vote. His position *vis-a-vis* the council is exceptionally strong; in this respect he is closer to the French Prefect or a Continental Burgomaster than the American City Manager.

As far as administrative organization is concerned, however, his position resembles more closely that of his American counterpart. He is the undisputed head of the executive side. All reports to the council must be made through him. He takes a large part in the preparation of the annual estimates and general financial policy. But he does not have complete power over the appointment of his subordinates. The interviewing and selection of departmental chiefs is done by the Local Appointments Board in a fashion similar to that for the appointment of the City Manager himself. In theory, at least, he has not quite the powerful hold over the technical officers that the American City Manager has.

Quite expectedly the strength of both the Irish and American

City Managers flows from their complete control of the executive side of the administration, the power to distribute executive functions among the departments and to oversee the work of the entire establishment. But there are a few practices followed by City Managers which evidence this strength and which are almost completely foreign to Town Clerks. For example, they frequently have their departmental heads prepare reports for them on the progress of the work in their departments and sometimes have these reports supplemented by special meetings and consultations. They also may take it upon themselves to inquire into the efficiency of operations in the departments and make whatever alterations they deem necessary. And most important of all, they prepare the annual budget estimates and generally direct the formation of financial policy—estimates, rates and capital expenditure. They studiously keep themselves informed on the financial condition of the corporation and the major issues of financial policy.

That the City Manager system, that is, a single executive head for the entire executive side of administration, could be introduced into English local government is beyond the realm of possibility, and even desirability. City Managers entered American local government in an era when local administration was crumbling internally from graft and corruption and gross inefficiency. Generally speaking, the Irish experience was similar, except that the breakdown came after the rebellion and City Managers resulted from central government legislation rather than from local movements for reform. Consequently in both instances extreme changes to meet pressing problems, not moderate alterations to achieve a more workable system, were instituted. The problems in English local government are not equally as pressing.

Moreover one of the great virtues of English local government is the committee system which is, in turn, an outgrowth of large councils. City Managers can only function properly with small councils and without committees, at least as committees are known in England. Much of the work entrusted to the committees in England is the responsibility of the City Manager in the United States and Ireland. Whereas under the City Manager system work is channelled from the council to the Manager to the departments, in England the line runs from the council to the committees to the head of a particular depart-ment. To substitute a City Manager for committees in England would not be sound.

Nonetheless, there are practices under the City Manager system which are instructive if the chief administrator concept is to be developed seriously. Certainly the fundamental reasons for desiring a chief administrator in English local government are to achieve executive co-ordination and efficiency and to provide the council with consistent overall policy advice. The basic structural requirements are, therefore, that he be attached to no particular department and that he not be in control of all of them. He must have sufficient powers in relation to the other officers and departments to accomplish his major tasks, but not enough to make them completely subordinate to him. The question then is: what organizational structure would most nearly achieve this?

The major requirements, it would seem, are that he be responsible to the council or its committees for administrative organization and efficiency, for financial policy, and for a consistent plan of development for the local authority and the town as a whole.

This would mean, first of all, that he should be in charge of establishment matters and organization and methods surveys. He should have the power to inquire into the organizational efficiency of any department and should prepare for the council a periodic report on the executive structure of the administration with recommendations for its improvement.

In the second place he should supervise the preparation of the annual estimates and advise on supplementary estimates, capital expenditures and the procurement of loans. The details of budget preparation would, as they are now, have to be attended to by the junior accountants in the Finance depart-ment. But the negotiations with party leaders, Chairmen and department heads after the initial stage of preparation should be organized and overseen by the chief administrator. He should also draft the budget speech for the Chairman of the committee responsible for estimate preparation, either the Finance or the Policy Advisory Committee. In this way he would have the general oversight of the financial condition of authority. The Treasurer would remain responsible for overall financial management; the collection of rates; the keeping of accounts; the maintenance of an audit system. But he would also have a duty of reporting to the chief administrator periodically on general financial matters.

Thirdly, he should be responsible for taking an overall view of the development of the town—its physical development and the development of its services. He should, like the present Town Clerks, be clerk to the committees and should have under him a group of responsible committee clerks who would prepare agenda, collect reports from the other departments and attend to the many details of the committee system. All officer reports to committees should cross his desk before being sent to the members and he should have the right to comment upon any of these reports in light of general corporation policy. In this connection he should take a leading part in the preparation of the Development Plan and should be responsible for suggesting modifications and overseeing its implementation. In addition he should prepare for council consideration a consistent plan for the development of its services and for possible innovations and should generally direct this development. Moreover, like the present Town Clerk he should see that projects are properly co-ordinated, that disputes between officers are properly arbitrated, and that the council is advised on its Standing Orders and general constitution. He would not be directly responsible for advising the corporation on legal matters although anyone selected as chief administrator would be expected to have a sound general knowledge of local government law. He would, of course, be his council's major negotiator with the outside world and would be expected to ensure good relations with the public.

The heads of the departments should, as they do at present, attend the committees concerned with the work of their departments and advise the Chairmen and members. However the chief administrator or one of his representatives should also attend and be free to offer advice on any matter. It would be expected that releasing the chief administrator from specific departmental duties would enable him to attend more committees personally.

The major difficulty in continuing the committee system much as it is now is that the chief administrator if he wishes to exercise his powers will be confronted by the 'committee mind' attitude and the tendency to support the committee and the department head at the expense of the dictates of general policy. It would certainly help for the chief administrator to have a Policy Advisory Committee and an Administration Committee to which he could refer matters of policy and overall administration. It might also help for the chief administrator to have the duty to report regularly and directly to the council on the progress of the executive machinery as a whole and on policy issues of great importance. But in the end the success of the chief administrator in overcoming the difficulty will depend upon the stature of his position, upon the administrative ability of the occupant of the office, and upon the willingness of the councillors to trust the judgment of the chief administrator on issues of policy and general administration. The wider area of recruitment and the increased powers should make these conditions more likely than they now are in respect of the Town Clerk.

The question remains, however, as to whether there is a need for such a chief administrator in English local government. The case, it would seem, is reasonably strong in the instance of the large boroughs, those with a population of 150,000 and above. In authorities of this size co-ordination is no longer a duty which can be loosely attached to the chief legal officer and the clerk of the committees. The number of departments and committees defy co-ordination of the half-hearted kind. Moreover in many of these places the councils need thoughtful advice on overall policy if they are to solve many of the long-range and far-reaching problems that face them. There is a need in many of these places, especially those without strong and energetic party leadership, for someone at the centre of things with enterprise, initiative and vitality, and with the power to channel these qualities in the right direction. Outside the London area there are twenty-four boroughs with populations over 150,000. In general, it would be a considerable improvement if these authorities appointed a chief administrator from those of high administrative ability in any profession and entrusted him with sufficient power over the executive side of operations to effect the co-ordination and efficiency needed.

But what should be done in the smaller authorities? Those in the 75,000 to 150,000 range might well adopt the chief administrator, although in this class, certainly the lower part of it, the need for a full-time co-ordinator is not as great. In the vast majority of towns, those under 75,000, the resources and, because almost all are non-county boroughs with limited powers, the scope of operations would not justify a chief administrator who does not have departmental responsibilities as well. In these instances the best system is probably the one which now, in theory at least, exists: a lawyer Town Clerk with limited duties as chief administrator. Perhaps his duties might be enhanced: establishment matters brought within his purview if they are not already there; a committee to which he might take general policy and administrative organizational matters established and established for that purpose only. But generally as now his ultimate success would depend upon his own ability, initiative, personality and the general circumstances surrounding him.

One of the problems which would face these authorities is the procurement of Town Clerks with the requisite talents. There have been serious deficiencies in the system which have deprived local authorities of sufficient high quality entrants to their legal departments. This has been particularly true of the university graduates, many of whom, deterred by high premiums for articles and low wages, or no wages at all, for three years, have chosen the Civil Service, the public corporations or industry where they begin at a good salary and where they have prospects of rising to high administrative posts without the need of an additional qualification.[1] If local authorities are to secure the legal talent they require and if the small authorities are to be

---

[1] For a more complete development of this problem see, B. Keith-Lucas, 'The Training of Town Clerks', 31 *Public Administration* 13 (1953). But note that since this article was written the situation has been improving. The Oxford University Appointments Committee reports that a growing number of authorities (at Oxford: five in 1957, fifteen in 1961) are actively seeking graduates and offering attractive terms, including no premium for articles and a salary between £645–£815 per year. This salary is better than most arrangements for private articles (no premium and salary of £250–£400) and competitive with the Civil Service and private industry. Concurrent with the greater interest shown by the local authorities, the number of graduates entering local government service has been rising. The Committee credits the Society of Town Clerks with doing much to force a break away from the traditional system.

assured of good administrative ability among their Town Clerks, they cannot afford to permit this source of talent, the university graduates, to go largely untapped. One solution would be a more liberal use of young barristers in local government. Another lies in some arrangement effected between the Law Society and the local authorities whereby candidates of high quality would be employed by an authority at a competitive wage and articled to a solicitor on the staff directly upon their leaving the universities. A start has been made in this direction, but much broader local authority participation will be needed if the smaller local authorities are in the future to be able to find Town Clerks who possess the required ability and, one would hope, the initiative and the personality to be successful in their chief administrative officer roles.

It would be difficult to say that the long-run success of local government in England depends upon these alterations in the office of Town Clerk. For certainly local government is built upon stronger foundations than its internal structure: the desire of people not only to rule by ballot but to manage by wide participation in their own local affairs, and the willingness of Governments to tolerate and perhaps encourage local differences in an era of their diminishing significance. But local authorities and local government would benefit from consistent overall policies, from more cohesive executive action and from increased initiative and enterprise. Strengthening the position of the Town Clerk would constitute a significant step towards these things. It is, therefore, a step worth taking.

INDEX

* M M H *
* T T H *

GEORGE ALLEN & UNWIN LTD
London: 40 Museum Street, WC1

Auckland: 24 Wyndham Street
Bombay: 15 Graham Road, Ballard Estate, Bombay 1
Buenos Aires: Escritorio 454-459, Florida 165
Calcutta: 17 Chittaranjan Avenue, Calcutta 13
Cape Town: 109 Long Street
Hong Kong: F1/12 Mirador Mansions, Kowloon
Ibadan: P.O. Box 62
Karachi: Karachi Chambers, McLeod Road
Madras: Mohan Mansions, 38c Mount Road, Madras 6
Mexico: Villalongin 32-10, Piso, Mexico 5, D.F.
Nairobi: P.O. Box 12446
New Delhi: 13-14 Asaf Ali Road, New Delhi 1
São Paulo: Avenida 9 de Julho, 1138-Ap. 51
Singapore: 36c Prinsep Street, Singapore 7
Sydney, N.S.W.: Bradbury House, 55 York Street
Toronto: 91 Wellington Street West